D1349564

University of Aberdeen
THE MACKIE MONOGRAPHS

3

SCOTLAND
AND THE
LOW COUNTRIES
1124-1994

Edited by
GRANT G SIMPSON
Department of History
University of Aberdeen

TUCKWELL PRESS

First published in 1996 by
Tuckwell Press Ltd
The Mill House
Phantassie
East Linton
East Lothian EH40 3DG
Scotland

All rights reserved
ISBN 1 898410 75 5

British Library Cataloguing-in-Publication Data
A Catalogue record for this book is available on request from the British Library

Printed and Bound in Great Britain by
Short Run Press Ltd., Exeter, Devon

Contents

Introduction

The Mackie Symposia, supported by the funds of the late Dr J R M Mackie of Glenmillan, are intended to explore the links which Scotland has had with the rest of the world, in many ways, to many places and over many centuries. The papers published in this volume were delivered, with one exception, as contributions to the Third Mackie Symposium on 'Scotland and the Low Countries', held at the University of Aberdeen in September 1992. (The one additional item is Professor Philippe Contamine's study of 'Froissart and Scotland', which he originally read at a conference in France and which he has generously agreed to present here, in a slightly revised version, in English.)

The distance between Scotland and the Low Countries, by sea journey, is not vast. From Edinburgh, for example, the coasts of Norway and of the Netherlands are almost equidistant and, as Dr Alexander Stevenson pointed out some years ago, the sailing distance from Leith to Sluis, the dependent port of Bruges, at 385 miles, is shorter than that from Leith to London, at 415 miles. Of course, geographical proximity does not necessarily spawn close relationships. Even so, contacts between Scotland and the Low Countries go back, in documented history, at least as far as the twelfth century. In the middle ages, all of this took a variety of forms. Scotland's trade with Flanders, based upon the former's wool exports and the latter's cloth manufacturing industries, was the central element of the Scottish kingdom's interaction with the European economy. Commercial bonds encouraged closer political relations and, in the train of these developments, Netherlandish religious, cultural, and (especially after the foundation of the university of Louvain in 1425) intellectual developments began to influence Scotland. Throughout the medieval centuries links were further underpinned by Netherlandish emigration to Scotland in the twelfth and thirteenth centuries and by Scottish emigration to the Low Countries in the later medieval period. The magnitude and diversity of these disparate activities might, indeed, suggest that the Low Countries, rather than France, deserve accreditation as Scotland's 'auld ally' of the middle ages. In the early modern period the vitality of this bond was maintained, and arguably strengthened by the Protestant inclinations of Scotland and the northern Low Countries, but in many ways it waned following the Anglo-Scottish Unions of 1603 and 1707. With foreign policy increasingly determined in London, Scotland was downgraded diplomatically, losing much of its diplomatic utility to continental powers as an irritant with which to keep England in check and, at the same time, no longer itself in need of continental alliances to provide security against English incursions. Economically, meanwhile, Union made for easier Scottish access not only to English but also to the increasingly profitable colonial markets at the expense of traditional European trade routes. The growing commercial importance of Glasgow and the west coast was symbolic of Scotland turning its back on the older North Sea world, while the increasing significance of the Empire to British, Dutch and Belgian psyches encouraged political and economic rivalry between, rather than co-operation with, European powers. Cultural and intellectual connections between Scotland and the Low Countries were, of course, maintained, but it is perhaps a sign of the diminishing significance of direct contacts that contributions to this volume for the modern period have to include comparative in addition to relational studies.

Although general works on Scottish history quite frequently mention Netherlandish associations of earlier centuries, there is no single published work which covers the topic adequately. J Arnold Fleming's *Flemish Influence in Britain* (2 vols, Glasgow, 1930) contains some matters of interest, but tends to be prolix and uncritical. Particular aspects of the relationships between the two areas have, however, received rather more attention. James Ferguson's *The Scots Brigade in Holland, 1572-1782* (3 vols, Scottish History Society, 1899-1901) provides a substantial documentary collection related to military and mercenary affairs; and at much the same time as these volumes were published there was a flurry of interest in the trading contacts too. Cosmo Innes edited the *Ledger of Andrew Halyburton, 1492-1503* (Edinburgh, 1867), the ledger belonging to the Scottish conservator in the Low Countries. *The Scottish Staple at Veere* by the late John Davidson and Alexander Gray, published in 1909, has wider coverage than the title would suggest, and this was followed in 1910 by *The Scottish Staple in the Netherlands* by M P Rooseboom, a volume which included transcripts of a number of important documents relating to commercial and diplomatic matters. Most importantly of all, H J Smit carefully edited considerable quantities of source material on trade in *Bronnen tot de Geschiedenis van den Handel met Engeland, Schotland en Ierland* (4 vols, The Hague, 1928-48). With the notable exception of Dr Alexander Stevenson in his doctoral thesis 'Trade between Scotland and the Low Countries in the Later Middle Ages' (University of Aberdeen, unpublished Ph D thesis, 1982), Scottish historians have made rather less use of this work than they might have done and even fewer have explored the other extensive publications of the Rijks Geschiedkundige Publicatiën, many of which also contain a good sprinkling of Scottish references.

In general, political, intellectual and cultural links have received very patchy attention from historians though, that said, certain episodes and topics have been investigated in some depth. Count Florence V's claim to the Scottish kingship in the late thirteenth century, for example, has been the subject of a number of articles in both English and Dutch, though language barriers perhaps explain the reluctance of Scottish scholars to take full cognizance of Netherlandish scholarship. Intellectual and legal interactions have been explored by, among others, Professor Roderick Lyall for the medieval period ('Scottish students and masters at the universities of Cologne and Louvain in the fifteenth century', *Innes Review*, xxxvi (1985)) and Professor Robert Feenstra for the early modern period ('Scottish-Dutch legal relations in the seventeenth and eighteenth centuries', in T C Smout, ed., *Scotland and Europe, 1200-1850* (Edinburgh, 1986)), while Dr John Morrison (notably in a forthcoming volume entitled *Union Street and Beyond*, edited by Terry Brotherstone and D J Withrington) has undertaken extensive research on the subject of Netherlandish influences on nineteenth-century Scottish painting.

It is clear that other elements of the story, especially in the modern period, still await investigation. Three examples may be mentioned. Contacts through, and comparisons of, each country's colonial experience would undoubtedly repay closer study: it was, for example, an Aberdonian, Robert Williams, who at the end of the nineteenth century obtained concessions to develop mineral resources in Leopold II's Congo Free State. In the present century the experience of Belgian refugees in the Glasgow area during World War I have not been fully analysed in print although sources for such a topic do exist. And, more recently still, the sociology of the Dutch community settled in north-east Scotland since the start of the oil industry in the 1960s could reveal much about the economy and society of both Scotland and the Netherlands.

This monograph, however, does not aim at comprehensive investigation and given the increasingly narrow specialisms of professional historians it seems unlikely that such a volume will, or even could, be written in the foreseeable future. Instead, the aim of the present publication is to illuminate particular linkages or comparisons. Some of the contributors have chosen to revisit some reasonably familiar topics with fresh ideas, while others have opted to pursue areas which are either understudied or relatively unknown. The topics investigated deliberately cover a broad range of themes drawn from a rich and varied tale.

In organizing the original Symposium, and in the processes of editing, my colleague Dr David Ditchburn has given invaluable assistance. I am also very grateful to my friend Dr Sonja Cameron for her contributions in copy-editing, typesetting and indexing. Dr Eric Robertson's conscientious work provided the translation of Professor Contamine's paper.

Aberdeen, 1995   *Grant G Simpson*

1

TWELFTH-CENTURY FLEMISH SETTLEMENTS IN SCOTLAND

Lauran Toorians

Flemings in twelfth-century Scotland: no-one doubts their existence, and yet no-one has ever been able fully to tell their story. I do not pretend that I can fill this gap in our historical knowledge, for that could only be done with a great deal of fantasy. What I propose to do in this paper is to show how terse and fragmentary our sources are, and try to sketch something about the background against which these Flemings moved about.

First it is useful to establish some definitions. What, for instance, is a Fleming? Two definitions seem possible here, and I will use them loosely and in combination. The one: 'A Fleming is a person from the county of Flanders, or dependent on the count of Flanders'; the other: 'A Fleming is a person speaking Flemish'. Both definitions give rise to problems.

Outside the Low Countries the name Flanders in the Middle Ages was as loosely used as 'Holland' is today, and so in the British Isles the term 'Fleming' may well cover people from Artois, Cambrai, Hainault, Brabant, Zeeland and Holland as well. Language is a problematic criterion also, as in medieval times the county of Flanders was already bilingual. Furthermore, neither Flemish (or Dutch) nor French are exclusively used in Flanders, and so language can never be a criterion in itself. To complicate the linguistic matter even more, the division between Flemish and French was in medieval Flanders much more a division between social classes than between different geographical areas. The linguistic border probably ran more or less along the present south-western border of the French département du Nord (south-west of Lille to Dunkirk), enclosing the area known today as French Flanders.

In south-western Wales, where Flemings also settled in the twelfth century, available sources mention Flemish as one of the languages spoken there. And in the area around Haverfordwest, Pembrokeshire, a Flemish speech-community must have existed and perhaps even survived into the sixteenth century.[1] About Scotland no such information is available, and although Scots contains a considerable number of Dutch loan-words, none of them can be assigned to a period as early as the twelfth century.[2] Sometimes, personal names may betray a Flemish, or

---

[1]For a recent article, containing full references to earlier literature, see my 'Wizo Flandrensis and the Flemish settlement in Pembrokeshire', *Cambridge Medieval Celtic Studies*, 20 (1990), 99-118.

[2]David Murison, 'The Dutch element in the vocabulary of Scots' in A G Aitken et al., eds, *Edinburgh Studies in English and Scots* (London, 1971), 159-76.

at least a 'continental Germanic', origin, as, for example, with Willelmus Fine-mund, who was lord of Cambusnethan in Lanarkshire in the 1150s.[3] If 'Finemund' means that William was a man of refined speech he would in English have been nicknamed 'finemouth', without the -n- before the final dental consonant.

Dutch borrowings in Scottish Gaelic have never been looked for, but a colleague has pointed out to me a possible example, which might be of interest here.[4] The Gaelic word *blàr* has exactly the same meaning as in Dutch: 'having a white forehead, especially of cows and horses'. Celticists have tried to link this word in Gaelic to Old Irish *blár* and Middle Welsh *blawr*, both meaning 'grey', which is semantically not very convincing.[5] But, even if this example holds, it is only an isolated case, though it might neatly illustrate the early sixteenth-century Scots poem about 'How the first Helandman of God was maid, of ane hors turd in Argylle, as is said', in which the first thing the Highlandman wants to do is to go 'doun in the Lawland (...) and thair steill a kow'.[6]

With or without a clear definition, Flemings occur in most books on the history of Scotland. In J D Mackie's *History of Scotland* 'Flemings' occur with four references in the index, of which only one is to a passage where Flemings in Scotland are more than just mentioned. The subject is the wool trade, as an indication of the fact that a burgh was economically not a fully self-supporting entity. 'The presence of Flemings in the early burghs', Mackie writes, 'may be indicative of a trade in wool, which rose to considerable proportions in the southern lands, ... and Berwick became the great exporting centre. There the Flemings had their own house, the Red Hall, under whose burning timbers they all died during the brutal sack of the city by Edward I in 1296.'[7]

This burning of Flemish traders in their Red Hall in Berwick must have made an enormous impression on later historians, for the incident can be found in nearly every general history of Scotland. Mackie's namesake R L Mackie, for instance, recalls the incident in a rather more colourful way. After describing how Edward could enter the town without meeting any resistance, except from the Red Hall and from the castle, he writes: 'The castle surrendered before nightfall; the thirty gallant Flemings, however, defended their hall even after it had been set on

---

[3]Willelmus Finemund appears in *Liber S. Marie de Calchou*, (hereafter *Kelso Liber*), (Bannatyne Club, 1846), no. 1. See R L Graeme Ritchie, *The Normans in Scotland* (hereafter Ritchie, *Normans*), (Edinburgh, 1954), 287, and n.5; and G W S Barrow, *The Kingdom of the Scots: government, church and society from the eleventh to the fourteenth century* (hereafter Barrow, *Kingdom*), (London, 1973), 329.

[4]Dr P C H Schrijver (Leiden University), personal communication.

[5]Problematic is the fact that Modern Irish *blár* also has the secondary meaning 'blaze on animal's forehead'.

[6]Anonymous, Bannatyne MS. (1568), ff. 162b-163a. Quoted from John and Winifred Macqueen, *A Choice of Scottish Verse, 1470-1570* (London, 1972), 138.

[7]J D Mackie, *History of Scotland* (2nd edn, Harmondsworth, 1978), 59.

fire, and to a man perished in the flames'.[8] And even John Prebble, in his popular *The Lion in the North*, recalls this heroic moment in similar words.[9]

Referring to the *Chronicle of Walter of Guisborough*, Professor Duncan tells us that these Flemish traders held the Red Hall 'on condition of defending it at all times against the English king', but styles this information 'monastic gossip' and 'a most unlikely tale'.[10] More important is his remark that the Red Hall most probably had its origin in the first half of the thirteenth century. But this still does not take us back into the twelfth.

That wool from Scotland, and even more important, from England, was essential for the cloth industry in Flanders from about 1100 is common historical knowledge. Twelfth-century sources, however, are scarce and not very informative when it comes to personal doings of the people involved in this wool-trade.[11] Furthermore, though it is generally accepted that many of the burgesses populating the burghs set up by Kings David I and Malcolm IV were Flemings, hardly any of them are named as such in the surviving documents. Still, Berwick's Red Hall shows us that we might expect Flemish traders in these burghs. Indicative of their presence are remarks like that by Malcolm IV, when confirming to the canons of St Andrews the obligations and rents due to the church of the Holy Trinity. The king specified that these rents were due 'as well from Scots as from French, as well from Flemings as from English, living within or without the burgh'.[12]

When it comes to persons, our problem may be demonstrated by two examples. One is a man called Mainard, King David's own burgess in Berwick and later given by the king to Bishop Robert of St Andrews to be reeve there. Ritchie says of this Mainard that he has a French name, but that Bishop Robert described him as a Fleming.[13] The name may, however, be Germanic if it means something like 'the strong one', as in Old English *mægnen-heard*, a poetic word meaning 'strong'. Duncan, who mentions this same man also, obviously considers him *not* a Fleming.[14] Duncan contrasts this Mainard with another burgess, whom he does consider a Fleming, namely Baldwin 'the lorimer', living about 1160 in Perth.[15] In this case Ritchie also mentions this same Baldwin 'the lorimer', but without call-

---

[8]R L Mackie, *Short History of Scotland*, ed. Gordon Donaldson (Edinburgh, 1962), 58.

[9]John Prebble, *The Lion in the North: a personal view of Scotland's history* (Harmondsworth, 1973), 74.

[10]Archibald A M Duncan, *Scotland: the making of the kingdom* (hereafter Duncan, *Scotland*), (Edinburgh, 1975), 515. The reference is to the thirteenth-century *Chronicle of Walter of Guisborough*, ed. H Rothwell (Camden 3rd ser., lxxxix, 1957), 275.

[11]On Scots trade with the Low Countries in general see Alexander Stevenson, 'Trade with the South, 1070-1513', in Michael Lynch, ed., *The Scottish Medieval Town* (Edinburgh, 1988), 180-205.

[12]*Liber Cartularum Prioratus Sancti Andree in Scotia* (hereafter *St Andrews Liber*), (Bannatyne Club, 1841), 194. Quoted in Ritchie, *Normans*, 329. On the subject of early Flemish burgesses, see also below, p. 30

[13]Ritchie, *Normans*, 329. Unfortunately Ritchie does not give a source reference here.

[14]Duncan, *Scotland*, 477, also without source reference.

[15]Ibid., 476-7 (and see also 468).

ing him a Fleming.[16] I have not found any reference to a statement from the sources in which this Baldwin 'the lorimer' is actually said to be from Flanders - he merely seems to have a Christian name favoured among Flemings. Other explicitly named Flemings are Michael Fleming, who was sheriff of Edinburgh in 1190,[17] and a Jordan the Fleming who gained fame in Alnwick in 1174, and who seems to have possessed land in Crail, Fife, but of whom nothing more is known.[18]

But my theme here is 'Flemish settlement', which implies more than individual traders or craftsmen working in Scotland. In two instances the term 'settlement' seems to be applicable to groups of people who apparently originated from Flanders. The cases are already quite well known and have been described by Ritchie, Barrow and Duncan. The areas involved are Upper Clydesdale and Moray. The explicit evidence for Flemings is, again, scarce. In many instances Flemishness is supposed only, on the basis of the names of the people involved and because of the close relations binding them together.

The Flemings named as such in Upper Clydesdale are Baldwin, lord of Biggar and sheriff of Lanark (I am not even sure about this one); Lambin, whose brother is named as 'Robert, brother of Lambein Fleeming'; and Theobald the Fleming, who was granted land in Douglasdale in the 1150s. In Moray all we have is one name: Berowald the Fleming, to whom Malcolm IV gave Innes and Nether Urquhart in the sheriffdom of Elgin.

The general context of both these settlements has been given by Ritchie, Barrow and Duncan. In short there is the fact that in both areas the traditional rulers had been ousted by King David, who replaced them with newcomers who had no local ties and could be trusted as faithful followers of the crown. In Moray, the Flemish character of this settlement is hard to define. Only Berowald is stated to be a Fleming. The other settler of importance has always been taken as such, mainly on the grounds of his Flemish-sounding name: Freskin.

Berowald had earlier held land in West Lothian, where he left his name in Bo'ness (Berowalds-toun-ness).[19] He was granted a toft in the burgh of Elgin and became known among historians as the first landowner in Scotland whose feudal

---

[16]Ritchie, *Normans*, 313-14, and 313, n.3, quoting from a charter, but not giving a reference.

[17]Named in the *Acts of the Parliaments of Scotland*, ed. T Thomson and C Innes (Edinburgh, 1814-75), vii, 144. Referred to in Barrow, *Kingdom*, 301; and Duncan, *Scotland*, 386.

[18]Jordanus le flameng, alias Jordanus Flandrensis. *Kelso Liber*, no. 27, *Registrum de Dunfermelyn* (hereafter *Dunfermline Reg.*), (Bannatyne Club, 1842), 88. Referred to in G W S Barrow, *Anglo-Norman Era in Scottish History* (hereafter Barrow, *Anglo-Norman Era*), (Oxford, 1980), 376 and n.5.

[19]Duncan, *Scotland*, 138.

service was explicitly defined as including castle-ward.[20] His grandson appears in a charter from 1226 as 'Waltero filio Johannis filii Berowaldi Flandrensis',[21] and it has been suggested that Berowald himself was one of the many Flemings who fled from England in 1155.[22] This makes it impossible to know how much 'Flemishness' was left in Berowald.

Freskin is never called a Fleming in the sources. He was granted Duffus, where he built a motte, and other lands near Elgin, by King David I. Like Berowald, he held lands in West Lothian as well, in Uphall and Broxburn, south-east of Bo'ness. All we know about him is that his son William was confirmed by Malcolm IV in the lands which were given to Freskin by David I.[23] His family became very powerful in Moray, and his sons adopted the name *de Moravia*, Murray. His son Hugh was given, or perhaps only confirmed in, the territory of Sutherland by the king,[24] and his grandson, known as 'Willelmus de Moravia, miles' and 'dominus de Suthyrlandia', became, by about 1230, the first earl of Sutherland.[25] Gilbert, son of Freskin's younger son William, was archdeacon of Moray from 1203 until 1222, and bishop of Caithness from 1223 till 1245.[26]

It is impossible to be sure if any of the other settlers in Moray were Flemish and so we should be rather careful about using the term 'Flemish settlement' in this case. Important for the position of the Murrays, and their role as settlers, is the statement by Barrow that 'they were never simultaneously major vassals of the king of Scots and of a foreign king ..., and their lands in Scotland were held for knight-service, binding them in strict loyalty to the crown'.[27]

In Lanarkshire, we seem to be on firmer ground. The most important man there was Baldwin the Fleming, who was lord of Biggar and was the first known

---

[20]*Registrum Episcopatus Moraviensis* (hereafter *Moray Reg.*), (Bannatyne Club, 1837), appendix, p. 453. See Ritchie, *Normans*, 376-7, and 377, n.1; Duncan, *Scotland*, 139, 191, 477.

[21]Charter by Alexander II, mentioned in Ritchie, *Normans*, 377, n.1; printed in Duncan Forbes, *Ane Account of the Familie of Innes* (Spalding Club, 1864), 52 (with facsimile).

[22]Gervase of Canterbury, *Chronicle of the Reigns of Stephen, Henry II and Richard I* (Rolls Series, 1879-80), i, 161. Referred to in Ritchie, *Normans*, 377.

[23]For Freskin see *Origines Parochiales Scotiae* (hereafter *OPS*), (Bannatyne Club, 1851-5), ii, 626, 654, and *Moray Reg.*, pp. xii-xiii. He is discussed in Ritchie, *Normans*, 232-3; G W S Barrow, *Kingship and Unity: Scotland 1000-1306* (hereafter Barrow, *Kingship*), (London 1981), 47, and Duncan, *Scotland*, 189.

[24]Hugh Freskin appears in *Moray Reg.*, no. 1, and *Registrum Episcopatus Glasguensis* (Bannatyne and Maitland Clubs, 1843), no. 11. See Ritchie, *Normans*, 233, n.2, 375, n.1. Duncan, *Scotland*, 197, considers Hugh a grandson of Freskin.

[25]*OPS*, ii, 626, 654, *Moray Reg.*, pp. xii-xiii, no. 1, 131. Referred to in Ritchie, *Normans*, 232, n.3, 233, n.2; Duncan, *Scotland*, 384, 397; and Barrow, *Kingship*, 149.

[26]Ritchie, *Normans*, 233, n.2.

[27]Barrow, *Kingship*, 52-3.

sheriff in Lanark, first recorded in 1162.[28] If he is the same man as the 'Baldwinus flam.' who witnessed a charter of c. 1150 by Bishop Robert of St Andrews, he may have had some relationship with Freskin of Moray, as 'Hugo fil. Fresechin' and 'Jordane Heyrum' appear as other witnesses to the same charter.[29] Whether this Jordan is the same as the Jordan the Fleming whom we noted earlier cannot be shown, but other relations between the settlers in Lanarkshire and those in Moray will be seen in what follows.

In Lanarkshire, Baldwin had a stepson John, who left his name in the village of Crawfordjohn at the southern limit of this settlement.[30] Baldwin's son and heir Waltheof was taken prisoner at Alnwick in 1174.[31] In addition to holding land from the king, Baldwin also held land from fitz Alan, but had granted this fief in turn to Hugh de Pettinain, who got his surname from a village just west of Biggar and left his Christian name in the Houston in Renfrewshire which he held from Baldwin as well.[32] Botherickfield, in the same parish of Houston in Renfrewshire, is named after Hugh's son Bodric.[33] Elsewhere, Hugh was a royal tenant himself, and he also held a Stewart fief of which he granted part to his brother.[34] Furthermore, this same Hugh de Pettinain, and his son Reginald, held land in Romanno from the unnamed father of Philippe de Vermelles, whose name betrays an origin in Flanders.[35]

If we pursue this side-track for a while, it is interesting to note that Philippe de Vermelles, or perhaps his father, had been introduced into Scotland by Robert de Quincy, who was the first of this important family in Scotland and appears in the king's service before the end of the reign of Malcolm IV.[36] The origin of this family lies in Cuinchy, to the east of Béthune in French Flanders, and they may first have come to England as followers of Gunfrid of Chocques, who came with, or in the wake of, William the Conqueror.[37] This Gunfrid originated from Chocques, which is only about two miles west of Béthune. Robert's earliest lands in Scotland

---

[28]*Registrum S. Marie de Neubotle* (hereafter *Newbattle Reg.*), (Bannatyne Club, 1849), p. xxxvi; and *OPS*, i, 83. See Ritchie, *Normans*, 375, n.1; Barrow, *Kingdom*, 282, 329; Barrow, *Anglo-Norman Era*, 37-8; and Duncan, *Scotland*, 137.

[29]*Glasgow Reg.*, no. ix. Ritchie, *Normans*, 375, n.1, notes that this charter has been considered spurious and that names may have been added to it later.

[30]For this 'Villa Johannis priuigni Balduini' (c. 1159) see *OPS*, i, 161-2. References in Ritchie, *Normans*, 375, and n.2; and Barrow, *Anglo-Norman Era*, 36, 67, n.31.

[31]Barrow, *Kingdom*, 288.

[32]*OPS*, i, 83, 138. See Ritchie, *Normans*, 375; Barrow, *Kingdom*, 329; Barrow, *Anglo-Norman Era*, 38.

[33]Barrow, *Kingdom*, 329; Barrow, *Anglo-Norman Era*, 36, 38.

[34]Duncan, *Kingdom*, 140.

[35]Ritchie, *Normans*, 288.

[36]See ibid., 288, and n.4-5; Barrow, *Kingdom*, 329.

[37]A useful survey is still the article by Robert H George, 'The contribution of Flanders to the conquest of England, 1065-1086', *Revue Belge de Philologie et d'Histoire*, v (1926), 81-99. See also David C Douglas, *William the Conqueror: the Norman impact upon England* (London, 1964), 266-7.

were around Tranent in East Lothian, where other Flemings held land, and he may have been the king's justice in Fife.[38] After his arrival, Robert de Quincy brought several other Flemings to Scotland, and it is interesting to list those. Apart from Philippe de Vermelles, I have also found the following: Alan de Courrières, Hugh de Lens, Robert de Béthune, Robert de Carvin and Roger de Orchies.[39] All these names refer to places in a fairly small area between Lille and Lens in what was then the county of Flanders.

Returning to Baldwin and his successors in Clydesdale, we find Waltheof's son Robert as lord of a Richard Bard (Baard, or Baird), who, like his father Richard Bard, senior, held land of the fitz Baldwins in Strathaven. Again, this family of Bard is of uncertain, but assumed Flemish origin, and our Richard Bard, junior, appears in the sources in association with a Richard of Ghent who died in Cleveland in 1139.[40] Cleveland is known for its large proportion of Flemings among the Anglo-Norman landowners. It is apparently from there that many Flemings came to Scotland.

Another man from Cleveland, and of possible Flemish origin, was Roger Wyrfalc, and he in turn was associated with Hugh 'of Bygris', the son of Robert son of Waltheof son of Baldwin. This Roger Wyrfalc held land in Laurencekirk in the Mearns, which had formerly been held by Hugh fitz Baldwin, and he held this with the consent of Robert son of Werenbald who held Kilmaurs in Cunningham from a Morville.[41] This Robert, or his father Werenbald, was the ancestor of the Cunninghams and again a man of supposed Flemish origin. The charter in which this gift is confirmed is witnessed by a Hugh de Beumes ('de Beaumys'),[42] a name which probably refers to a modern Beaumetz, of which there are three in the modern département Pas de Calais (between Thérouanne and Hesdin, south of Arras, and near Cambrai) and one in the département Somme (near Doullens). If this Hugh was from one of these three places in Pas de Calais he might be considered a Fleming as well.

Returning from supposed to named Flemings we now turn to Robert, who left his name in Roberton in Upper Clydesdale and who appears as 'brother of Lambein Fleeming'.[43] It is after this Lambin that nearby Lamington is named. This

---

[38]*Regesta Regum Scottorum* (hereafter *RRS*), ed. G W S Barrow et al., i (1153-1165), (Edinburgh, 1960), ii (1165-1214), (Edinburgh, 1971): i, 283, n.1. See Ritchie, *Normans*, 285-6; Barrow, *Anglo-Norman Era*, 22-3; Duncan, *Scotland*, 203. Also Grant G Simpson, 'An Anglo-Scottish baron of the thirteenth century: the acts of Roger de Quincy, earl of Winchester and constable of Scotland' (Ph D, Edinburgh University, 1965).

[39]Barrow, *Anglo-Norman Era*, 23, and n.103-4, with reference to *St Andrews Liber*, 354, and an unpublished knight-service charter (c. 1170): SRO GD 241/254.

[40]Barrow, *Anglo-Norman Era*, 173-4, with reference to *Kelso Liber*, nos 181-2.

[41]Barrow, *Anglo-Norman Era*, 112 and n.130, and 198, with reference to *St Andrews Liber*, 279-80, 285-7, 334-5.

[42]*Liber S. Thome de Aberbrothoc* (hereafter *Arbroath Liber*), (Bannatyne Club, 1848-56), no. 272.

[43]*OPS*, i, 107. See Ritchie, *Normans*, 375 and n.4; Barrow, *Kingdom*, 329; Barrow, *Anglo-Norman Era*, 45, n.66.

Lambin appears in the sources also as Lambin Asa, generally taken to mean 'Lambin son of Asa'. The estate Lambin had in Lamington was a fief held from the crown direct, like most of the other 'Flemish' estates in the area. Apart from this estate, he also held Draffan and 'Dardarach', in Lesmahagow parish, in feu-ferme from Kelso Abbey.[44] In the same period, the 1150s, the abbot of Kelso gave another estate, in Poneil on the Douglas water, to another explicitly named Fleming, Theobald, and his heirs. Lambin the Fleming's son James held Loudoun as an under-fief of Richard de Moreville.[45]

There were still more men in Upper Clydesdale of supposed Flemish origin, like Wice or Wizo, and Simon Loccard. Wice left his name in Wiston and gave, during the reign of Malcolm IV, the church of his estate and its two dependent chapels to Kelso Abbey. These chapels were those of neighbouring Roberton and Crawfordjohn, two estates we have already noted.[46] Simon Loccard gave his name to Symington on the Clyde and also held land in The Lee, north-west of Lanark, in an area where names like Lokhartbank and Lockart Mill show up on the map.[47] Like other landowners in Upper Clydesdale, he also held land further west, where he left his name in yet another Symington, in Ayrshire, which he held of the Stewarts.[48] Just like Lambin, Simon Loccard had a brother who stayed in his neighbourhood, Stephen Loccard left his name in Stevenston, in Cunningham, which he held of a Morville.[49] The Loccards also held land further south, in Annandale, and probably either Simon or Stephen can be seen as the founding father of Lockerbie, Dumfriesshire.[50] It was Simon Loccard who witnessed William I's charter (1165x72) of Annandale to Robert de Brus at Lochmaben.[51] Malcolm, son of Simon Loccard, also appears as witness in an Annandale charter.[52]

Interesting, but again without proof, is the possible relation between Flanders and the family of the famous Bruces. That there were more relations between 'Flemish' Upper Clydesdale and Annandale, the power base of the Bruce family, may be gathered from the fact that a further unknown Agnes de Bruce owned a knight's fee in Thankerton about 1185. Her name survives on the map in Annieston, between Thankerton and Symington in Clydesdale.[53] Another indication

---

[44] For Lambin see *Kelso Liber*, no. 102; *St Andrews Liber*, 152; and *OPS*, i, 113. References in Ritchie, *Normans*, 375 and n.4; Barrow, *Anglo-Norman Era*, 45 and n.68.

[45] Ibid., referring to unpublished Loudoun charters, 129 and n.65. Further references are to W Fraser, *The Lennox* (1874), ii, no. 1, and *Kelso Liber*, nos 104, 114, 115, 284, 349.

[46] For Wice see *Kelso Liber*, no. 1 (1156) and *OPS*, i, 146 (and 148). Reference in Ritchie, *Normans*, 376, and n.2.

[47] 'Symonis Loccard' in *OPS*, i, 144 (and see 121, 145). References in Ritchie, *Normans*, 376, n.1; Barrow, *Anglo-Norman Era*, 46.

[48] Duncan, *Scotland*, 181.

[49] Barrow, *Anglo-Norman Era*, 46, and n.73.

[50] Ibid., 46, and n.74.

[51] *RRS*, ii, no. 80.

[52] *Calendar of Documents relating to Scotland*, ed. J Bain et al. (Edinburgh, 1881-1978), i, no. 606.

[53] *Kelso Liber*, no. 275. See Barrow, *Anglo-Norman Era*, 36-7, 111-12.

of Flemish influence in Annandale itself may be seen in the names Kirkpatrick-Fleming, just east of Annan, and Wyseby which might derive its name from another Flemish Wice or Wizo.[54]

Back to the Clyde: Thancard, also supposed to be Flemish, held an estate at Thankerton by Bothwell of an Olifard, and across the South Calder near Motherwell and in Upper Clydesdale near Lanark, of the crown direct.[55] To finish this list there was William, the first of the Douglases, for whom there are strong suggestions, but again no proof, of Flemish origin.[56] He held an estate of the crown along the Douglas Water and was a brother (or perhaps a brother-in-law) of Freskin of 'Kerdal' of whom it has been suggested that he was related to the Freskin we met in Moray.[57] This Freskin of 'Kerdal' was an uncle of the Brice ('Bricius') of Douglas who became prior of the Tironensian priory of Lesmahagow and, in 1203, bishop of Moray. In this function he introduced many of his own brothers into his diocese, where he provided them with lands.[58] Here, in Moray, they gained the riches which they later brought back to their base along the Douglas Water.

After this repetitive list of mainly possible, but unproven, Flemings, at least one thing becomes clear. The group of settlers in Upper Clydesdale formed a closely knit community consisting of people who both had numerous relationships of all sorts with one another, and who were actively involved in other areas with important settlements, as in Moray, Cunningham and Annandale. The one thing for which the sources do not even give us a single indication is who the people were whom these new landowners were ruling. Do we have here an actual settlement planted into former wasteland, or did a sitting population get new lords?

Looking at the map, I tend to opt for the former interpretation. Most of the names on the Ordnance Survey map of the area seem to stem from this period of twelfth-century settlement or later, and Celtic names are remarkably rare.[59] Even most of the burns running into the Clyde between Lanark and Crawfordjohn have names in Scots.

Furthermore, the name Coulter appears for a hamlet just south of Biggar, surrounded by names like Coulter Mains, Coulterhaugh, Culter House, and the like. Especially in Flanders, and not in other parts of the Dutch-speaking area, the word *kouter* is not only used for the iron knife-blade of the plough, but since the

[54]Ibid., 48, n.84.

[55]For Thancard see *Registrum Monasterii de Passelet* (Maitland Club, 1832), 98, 310, 412; *RRS*, i, no. 304; *RRS*, ii, no. 310; *Kelso Liber*, no. 183; *Arbroath Liber*, no. 99; and *OPS*, i, 107, 143-4. References in Ritchie, *Normans*, 375, n.5; Barrow, *Kingdom*, 289; Barrow, *Anglo-Norman Era*, 45-6, and n.70; Duncan, *Scotland*, 181.

[56]For William Douglas see Ritchie, *Normans*, 233, n.3, 289; Barrow, *Kingdom*, 329; Duncan, *Scotland*, 395-6. References are to *OPS*, i, 152, 155-6, and *Kelso Liber*, nos 189, 202.

[57]Ritchie, *Normans*, 233, n.3.

[58]Ibid., 332-3; Duncan, *Scotland*, 279.

[59]Ordnance Survey, *Landranger* 72 (Upper Clyde Valley). Scale 1:50.000 (Series M 726, Sheet 72, Edition 3-GSGS. 1987).

twelfth century also for the field system of the agrarian community. In the bordering French-speaking areas the term was *coultre, coulture*.[60] If this interpretation is correct, the relatively level Coulter in Upper Clydesdale would probably be the site of the old field system belonging to Biggar, while the hill to the north-west of the town, which is named Biggar Common, might have been the common grazing. Similarly, at the bottom of Clydesdale between Wiston and Symington we find a Feufield, and, nearer to Symington, a Broadfield.

An exercise like this on a modern map may be very fascinating, but it is also rather dangerous when we have no other sources informing us about the changes in the landscape and the use made of the land during the past seven or eight hundred years. Since I do not even know what the landscape looks like in reality today, I will not pursue this exercise here.

If this part of Clydesdale was not cleared - or flocked with sheep - before the twelfth century, then our 'Flemish' settlers must have brought with them a considerable workforce of new farmers. In Pembrokeshire, where the situation was slightly different, as the Flemish settlers there played a defensive role against the Welsh as well, it is obvious that a whole group of Flemings came into the area to replace the Welsh population. In Lanarkshire there is no possible way of knowing if or how this happened, but since most of the Flemings holding estates in Upper Clydesdale came from England, and often also held lands in Lothian, it is more likely that if they brought in a new population this consisted of farmers from these areas.

At this point it may be illuminating to take a look at the Low Countries and the processes at work there. Not so much because this will tell us anything about the Lanarkshire Flemings, for of these incoming families of *novi homines* it remains true, as the seventeenth-century historian Hume of Godscroft wrote: 'We do not know them in the fountain, but in the stream; not in the root, but in the stem; for we know not who was the first mean man that did raise himself above the vulgar.'[61] But if we still believe we are talking about Flemings in some real sense, the situation in Flanders (and the Low Countries in general) at the time these people left it, might help us to understand why they left their old homes and why they were welcomed in their new ones.

One of the general trends which made people move about in Europe was a booming population growth in the eleventh and twelfth centuries. Especially in Flanders this must have been enormous, and towns rose up in a number and density previously unsurpassed north of the Alps. This urbanisation began in the south of the county, with towns like Ypres (Ieper), Arras (Atrecht), St-Omair (St Omaars), Douai (Dowaai), Lille (Rijsel) and Tournai (Doornik). The economic base for these cities was the production of, and trade in, cloth of a high quality. A

---

[60]A Verhulst, 'Le paysage en Flandre entérieure; son évolution entre le IXe et XIIIe siècle', *Revue du Nord*, 62 (1980), 11-30.

[61]Said of the Douglases, but quoted as a general statement concerning 'many more Normans in Scotland' in Ritchie, *Normans*, 289-90.

growing population, however, also required more food, and so more land under cultivation.

This need coincided, probably more or less accidentally, with the first collective enterprises to defend the low-lying coastal areas against flooding. These works were mainly undertaken under the guidance of Benedictine and Cistercian abbeys.

In the tenth century the north-western coastal area of Flanders consisted of flat saltings. In charters we find these areas often as *mariscos*, the size of which is defined by the number of sheep which can be fed on them (sometimes specific numbers are stated for summer and winter grazing).[62] Early in the eleventh century a start must have been made on building dykes to guard these saltings against flooding. The first references to this activity are circumstantial only, and our knowledge is partly based on the occurrence of place-names containing the word 'dyke' like *Tubendic* (1025 and 1038) and *Isendycke* (1046).[63]

The part which the count of Flanders played in this activity is brought to the fore in the years between 1055 and 1067, when the archbishop of Reims praised Count Baldwin V (1035-67) for his inventiveness and zeal in cultivating lands which seemed altogether useless for agriculture.[64] It is important that these new lands are stated to have yielded harvests which were even better than those of the fertile old lands.[65] This remark may be of more importance than has so far been thought, for we should perhaps conclude from this that the coastal saltings were rapidly changed from grazing areas for sheep into arable lands.

If this was the case, then the need to feed a growing population must have clashed with the need to produce enough wool to supply the equally growing cloth-industry in the cities with enough raw material. Hence, the cultivation of new land in Flanders may have been a direct cause for the overseas wool-trade in which England and Scotland became all-important. Significantly, this trade started about 1100.

The first real polders, reclaiming land from the sea, were created in this same area at about the same time. They must have been the first of their kind in Western Europe. Shortly after 1100 we first find the name *Cadesand* (Cadzand), indicating a set of quays (*cade-*) or dykes, and in a charter dated between 1138 and 1153 the word polder (*polre*) occurs for the first time. The reference is to a Sudhpolra near present-day Nieuwpoort (West-Flanders).[66]

---

[62]Maria K E Gottschalk, *Historische geografie van westelijk Zeeuws-Vlaanderen tot de St-Elisabethsvloed van 1404* (Assen, 1955), 16. (The work cited is a dissertation, containing a summary in French; quoted hereafter as Gottschalk, *Historische geografie*.)

[63]Ibid., 20.

[64]Ibid., 21

[65]Ibid., 21, 31, with reference to F L Ganshof, *Vlaanderen onder de eerste graven* (hereafter Ganshof, *Vlaanderen*), (Antwerp, 1944), iv ('Het economisch leven').

[66]Gottschalk, *Historische geografie*, 21-2. *Cadesand* is first found in a charter, 1111x15, in the *Cartulaire de Saint-Bavon à Gand (655-1255)*, ed. C P Serrure (Ghent, 1836-40), no.

That these newly-claimed and cultivated lands were populated rapidly can be inferred from the frequency with which new parishes were created.[67] Probably most colonists came from the directly adjoining coastal area, but others may have been attracted from further away. For those the term *hospites* occurs in the sources.[68] The general impression is that the newly cultivated lands were populated with serfs, dependent on the abbey or the secular ruler supervising the cultivation. There must have been a great need for land, for it seems even to have been fairly common for freeborn men, and, significantly, women, to give themselves into serfdom to an abbey in exchange for land.[69]

Whether in the already densely populated Flanders *hospites* were actually invited from abroad is not very clear. Wherever in Europe *hospites* were received, however, they were given attractive rights, or were treated as free people.[70]

In other parts of the Low Countries, land reclamation and cultivation started at about the same period. Here we can see how, for example, in the large bogs in Holland and Utrecht the count would 'sell' a certain piece of land to an individual or a group of co-operating 'buyers'. 'Buying' and 'selling' are the terms used in the charters in which such acts were recorded, and the whole seems to have functioned mainly as the creation of a concession with its own jurisdiction. The leader of the group of buyers was often given the position of bailiff, and the buyers were free to hand out parcels of the newly created jurisdiction for cultivation to whomever they liked. Rights and duties were fixed on favourable terms to make the new area attractive for settlers.[71]

Sometimes the buyers were themselves the first cultivators, but even then the charter often left them the freedom to sub-let part of their concession to others for whom we might perhaps use the term *hospites*. More frequently, it seems that the buyers consisted of a small group of entrepreneurs (or, more rarely, a single individual) acting as middlemen for the cultivators or colonists. In such instances it

---

18. *Sudhpolra* in *Cronica et cartularium monasterii de Dunis*, ed. F vande Putte (Bruges, 1864), 433.

[67]Gottschalk, *Historische geografie*, 27-9.

[68]Ibid., 31, 35. Also Ganshof, *Vlaanderen*.

[69]Gottschalk, *Historische geografie*, 35-7. Studies referred to are those by J Calbrecht, *De oorsprong der Sinte Pietersmannen* (Louvain, 1922) and P C Boeren, *Etude sur les tributaires d'église dans le comté de Flandre du IX aus XIV siècle* (Amsterdam, 1936).

[70]Gottschalk, *Historische geografie*, 31, 35 (with reference to Ganshof, *Vlaanderen*), suggests that a large number of strangers were attracted by the land reclamations in Flanders.

[71]The standard study for this juridical context of the reclamations in Holland and Utrecht is the thesis by H van der Linden, *De cope: Bijdrage tot de rechtsgeschiedenis van de openlegging der Hollands-Utrechtse laagvlakte* (hereafter Van der Linden, *De cope*), (Assen, 1956), which also contains a summary in French. In the charters the terms *vendere* and *vendito* are used, and the Dutch word *koop* (Middle Dutch *cope*), 'purchase, buying', occurs frequently as second element in place-names originating from such transactions.

seems even to have been quite normal to 'buy' a concession first, and only to start looking for *hospites* (cultivators/colonists) afterwards.[72]

A term sometimes used in charters to designate the entrepreneur is *locator*, which might perhaps be understood as 'allocator' of the different plots in the new jurisdiction to the various colonists. Probably, in places where the cultivation was led by religious houses, as along the coasts of Flanders and the Northern Netherlands, these houses themselves acted as *locatores*, while the secular lords made use of middlemen to organise the practical realisation of extending their jurisdiction into the wilderness.

Unfortunately, none of the sources concerning all this give us any information about the *hospites*: who they were, where they came from, or how exactly they were brought together. Flemings, but in fact people from the Low Countries in general, were acting as colonists not only in the British Isles, but also in northern Germany and in northern and north-eastern France. Considerable numbers of low-born Flemings may also have been found in the wake of their nobility in the kingdom of Jerusalem, which existed from 1100 until 1118 under the two successive kings Godfrey of Bouillon and Baldwin I, who was also count of Flanders.[73] Overpopulation was the chief reason for this readiness to leave Flanders and search for new opportunities elsewhere.

If we now look at the Flemings in Scotland and south-western Wales, they seem to fit into this general picture very well, though there are some marked differences also. In Pembrokeshire they seem to have been deliberately planted to form a buffer between the Anglo-Norman invaders and the native Welsh; in Moray and Lanarkshire as new settlers without traditional ties to the region, to break the old alliances of the native population or earlier rulers and so bring the area more securely within the power of the Scottish kings. Furthermore, they seem, both in Wales and in Scotland, to have come not so much as cultivators, but more as sheep-breeders and wool-merchants, directly in the interests of the cloth-industries in Flanders.

As traders and as people with an urban experience they were of use in the new burghs as well. In Wales there are indications suggesting a real Flemish population in at least the area around Haverfordwest. In Scotland evidence for such a massive plantation is not available, but the possibility cannot be ruled out. That Flemings in expatriation kept in touch with their homeland is not at all unlikely. In 1170 Slavic invaders could plunder a Frisian settlement near Lübeck without meeting much resistance. A number of the men had left the settlement temporarily to settle matters of inheritance 'at home' in Frisia.[74]

---

[72]Van der Linden, *De cope*, 109-14.

[73]For Flemings in the Crusader States see Alan V Murray, 'The origins of the Flemish nobility of the Kingdom of Jerusalem, 1100-18', *Mediterranean Historical Review*, 4 (1989), 281-300.

[74]W Jappe Alberts and H P H Janssen, *Welvaart in wording: Sociaal-economische geschiedenis van Nederland van de vroegste tijden tot het einde van de middeleeuwen* (The Hague, 1964), 72.

What remains is the strong impression that both in Wales and in Scotland Flemish *locatores* were acting as organisers of these settlements. This of course raises the question of how these *locatores* knew there was work for them in Scotland and Wales, or how the Anglo-Norman barons and Scottish kings knew where to find the right *locatores*. In other words: how organised was this 'emigration business'? Unfortunately, this question will remain unanswered, unless new sources come to light.

2

FLORENCE V, COUNT OF HOLLAND, CLAIMANT TO THE SCOTTISH THRONE IN 1291-2: HIS PERSONAL AND POLITICAL BACKGROUND

Johanna A Kossmann-Putto

It would be carrying owls to Athens to dwell at any length on the details of Florence's involvement in the Great Cause itself. They have been the subject of thorough research by Scottish historians and all relevant documents are available in Stones and Simpson's well-known source edition. I only mention here a few facts: after the death of King Alexander III and of his heir, the Maid of Norway, a number of claimants to the throne presented themselves. Among the most tenacious was Florence, count of Holland. His great-great-grandfather had married Ada, granddaughter of King David I and sister of King Malcolm IV and King William the Lion. Florence V claimed his right to the throne in the first place as a descendant from King David, and at a later stage on the allegation that Ada's third brother, Earl David, had for himself and his descendants waived his title to the succession to the Scottish throne. This meant, Florence declared, that he had a better right to the throne than his distant cousins, Balliol, Bruce and Hastings, his most important rivals who all descended from Earl David. Although he could not, at first, show the necessary documents to prove his case, he assured the court convened in 1291 to weigh the various claims, that he would be able to provide them. King Edward I of England, as judge, allowed him ample time to produce them. And then, just before the matter was to be finalized, Florence withdrew his claim. Not because no document could be shown: two Scottish prelates had, in fact, supplied *inspeximuses* of what was said to be the authentic relevant charter. Complicated intrigues preceded his withdrawal from the competition and led to a pact with Bruce - studied by Grant G Simpson in a short but important article of 1957. But it is difficult to explain Florence's behaviour. How seriously did he aspire to the Scottish crown?

To Dutch historians, Florence's Scottish enterprise is as puzzling as it is to their Scottish colleagues. There is, to start with, a regrettable lack of documents on the Dutch side: a register in the General State Archive, composed after the death of Florence's successor in 1299, contains copies of the two *inspeximuses* which I have just mentioned, actually forgeries (or *inspeximuses* of forgeries), apparently brought back from Scotland to The Hague after the withdrawal of the claim. The story of Florence's pretensions is also mentioned in a chronicle, written by a contemporary who was well-informed on the count's activities and must have had close connections with the inner circle of his court. It is called 'Melis Stoke's rhymed chronicle'.[1] It contains a long passage on Florence's Scottish policy and suggests that at his court this policy was followed with sympathetic interest. The author was thoroughly disappointed when at the critical moment Florence gave up his claims. Treason lay behind it, he thinks, but also says that the count *sold* his rights. What, we must ask, motivated the count of Holland?

In recent years, Florence's endeavours have sometimes been explained as an expression of dynastic pride. On this view, the count owed it to himself and to the honour of his dynasty to aspire to the Scottish throne, and truly believed in his right to rule Scotland. We should not reject this idea out of hand. Florence had reason to be proud of his ancestry. The House of Holland was ancient, although not powerful. It had its roots in the ninth century. Its origins are vague, but as far as we can retrace them, its members belonged to the nobility of the Empire. All sought their brides inside the German Empire, usually in nearby Nether-Lorraine and the Nether-Rhineland. There is, however, one exception to the rule and this was to involve Florence V in the Great Cause: in 1162 Florence III married Ada, granddaughter of King David of Scotland. The marriage does not fit at all into the normal pattern of the dynasty of Holland. Dutch historians, as far as I know, have never given a second thought to this anomaly, but anomaly it is. There were, in the twelfth century, no special ties between Scotland and Holland that could possibly explain it. Florence III's foreign policy was concerned with the traditional relations and conflicts of his House with neighbouring Utrecht and Flanders, but much of his time went into the service of the emperor. Florence III was very much Frederick Barbarossa's man. Even before he had succeeded his father as count of Holland, he appeared as a witness in Barbarossa's charters; he followed the emperor on his Italian campaign in 1158 and again in the 1170s. At that time he figures prominently among the witnesses in several charters, being mentioned first in line after the ecclesiastical witnesses in most of them. In later years we find him at Barbarossa's court in the Rhineland and eventually he followed his lord on the Third Crusade. He died in the Holy Land and was buried in Antioch next to the emperor. It seems reasonable to suppose that the Scottish marriage of 1162 was arranged by the entourage of the emperor and served some interest of the German Empire rather than one of Holland. It was also, perhaps, slightly above Florence's station as a modest count: not until some years afterwards was he raised to the rank of prince of the realm, *Reichsfürst*, on a personal title. However that may be, in 1162 Florence sent the abbot of Egmond - the Benedictine monastery closely connected with his House - to Scotland and the prelate brought the bride to Holland with a large fleet (*cum magno navium apparatu, ornatu et milicia*

---

[1] It is by no means certain that Melis Stoke, a clerk in the chancery of Holland in the four-teenth century who is connected with the chronicle, was the author; he may have been a later copyist, see H C Peeters, *De Rijmkroniek van Holland, haar auteur en Melis Stoke* (Antwerp, 1966).

advectam, says an Egmond Abbey chronicle). The marriage took place at Loosduinen, one of the count's manors not far from The Hague.[2]

The next counts of Holland once more sought their brides in the Empire. Dirk VII was fully occupied with wars with his neighbours and, like his father, in imperial politics he kept on the side of the Staufen. The fact that his main opponent, the duke of Brabant, most of the time took the side of the other party, the Welfs, must have strengthened his determination to persevere in this traditional policy. Some years after his death his brother William managed to dispossess Dirk's daughter of her rights and to get himself recognized as ruler of the county. His niece had married the count of Looz, south of Maastricht, another ally of the Staufen. It is not surprising to find uncle William on the side of Brabant and the Welf party, which included King John of England. When in the course of the struggle for Holland the niece fell into William's hands, he sent her in safe custody to the English king, who held her a captive until a treaty with her husband had been concluded. But when in 1214 the Welf alliance was badly defeated at the battle of Bouvines, William - like the duke of Brabant - hastily went over to the other party. He did not, however, withdraw into the small-scale politics of the Low Countries. He had accompanied his father, Florence III, on his crusade in 1190 and seems to have kept a taste for large international enterprises. He joined the expedition that was meant to dethrone King John, his former ally, in 1216 and shortly afterwards went on a new crusade to Egypt. His second wife was a widow, the daughter of the duke of Brabant who just before the fatal battle of Bouvines had married the head of the Welf party, the unlucky Emperor Otto IV. The duke of Brabant was probably glad to be able now to remarry her off to his faithful follower, the count of Holland, but doubtless the alliance enhanced the prestige of the House of Holland.

Like father, like son. The fourth Count Florence joined a crusade in his turn, and he married Machteld of Brabant, a full sister of his father's second wife, also a widow. He died in a tournament in France in 1234, slain - according to tradition - by a rival in a love-affair. During the first half of the thirteenth century the duchy

---

[2]'Liber S. Adalberti', in O Opperman, ed., *Fontes Egmundenses* (Utrecht, 1933), 91; a less precise version in the later 'Annales Egmundenses', ibid., 168. The 'feudum ac terra quam progenitores nostri comites Hollandie a domino illustri Scotorum rege et suis progenitoribus hactenus tenuerunt' (the fief which the counts of Holland until now have held from the king of Scots), which, in 1249, William II granted to his sister Aleyd and her husband, the count of Hainault, 'in connubium conferendum' (Koch and Kruisheer, *Oorkonden Holland and Zeeland*, ii, no. 815), was apparently Ada's parental heritage or dowry. William, it seems, intended it to revert to the count of Holland after the death of the last-living. The two beneficiaries were not allowed to sell or otherwise alienate the land 'nisi manu nostra et assensu super hoc plenius requisito' (without our assent and unless through our hand). Some time after the death of Count John of Hainault (1256) (the title to) this land and fief was apparently passed on to Aleyd's sister Margaret, married to the count of Hennenberg. In the scanty Dutch documentation referring to Ada's dowry no mention is made of the name, size or location of the 'land and fief' in question and there are no indications that the beneficiaries acquired actual possession of the land.

of Brabant was predominant in the Nether-Rhine region and the counts of Holland profited from the alliance. It was thanks to the duke of Brabant (Henry II, brother-in-law of both William I and of Florence IV), that the House of Holland reached its height. When in 1247 the Emperor Frederick II Hohenstaufen had fallen in disgrace with the pope, and the papal party in the Empire no longer recognized his authority but wanted to elect somebody else in his place, the crown was offered to the duke of Brabant. But Henry II was far too prudent to accept such an unstable position and proposed his young nephew, William of Holland, as a candidate. The papal party agreed and as a result the count of Holland rose to the dignity of king of the Romans. He married the daughter of a powerful German prince, the count of Brunswick, a marriage more in agreement with his rank in the Empire than with his personal status or with that of his territory. After the death of Emperor Frederick and, some years later, of his son Conrad IV, William's position was more or less assured. But when, in 1256, he went on a campaign to suppress a rebellion in the north of his own territory, he was killed. His son and successor, Florence V, was then one and a half years old.

The dynasty of Holland, as we have seen, was not lacking in honour. That is not to say that the counts of Holland in the thirteenth century were powerful. Compared with the dukes of Brabant and the counts of Flanders, their territory was small and economically unimportant. Its history was somewhat bizarre. The first members of the House of Holland we have some information about, dating from the early tenth century, held their fiefs and *allodia* in the north of the later province of Holland: the Isle of Texel opposite the present marine base Den Helder, and a small strip of sandy lands farther down the North Sea coast. Here, shortly after 922, Dirk I set up Egmond Abbey as a religious centre for his family. His lands bordered on a large stretch of very low fenland which in the course of the century was added to the possessions of his House. In later years it was called West-Frisia. The counts soon moved southwards, acquired fiefs in the region near the mouth of the Rhine and also near the mouth of the river Maas, where they started to levy toll from passing merchants. And as early as the late tenth century they began to expand their territory by well-organized reclamation of hitherto uninhabitable marshland. But their preoccupation with the rich possibilities offered here led to the loss of control over what had once been their base.

Then, during a crisis at the end of the eleventh century, they lost practically all their possessions. These were soon reconquered, but for decades afterwards the counts of Holland had to recognize the overlordship of the bishop of Utrecht. They were then at the nadir of their power, but kept marrying ladies from the best aristocratic circles of the Empire and, when the House of Hohenstaufen had come to reign in Germany, managed to keep in favour with the new rulers. With their help the counts regained their independence from Utrecht and their status as immediate vassals of the Empire. But they did not regain a grip on West-Frisia. This region, although theoretically still part of their territory, was a constant source of unrest, in open revolt as often as an occasion presented itself. Fighting the Frisians was a task most counts of Holland undertook at some moment during their period of rule. After 1256, when West-Frisians had killed King William (and hid his body, because they were upset when they found that their victim was the king of the Romans), the West-Frisians acted as if they were completely independent: an enemy country, in the eyes of the Hollanders.

At the other side of Holland, one count, around 1200, wanting more liberty of action in the south, unwisely attacked Brabant: as a result he lost the important region of Dordrecht. It was a settlement on the river Merwede, part of the Maas delta, that was developing into a transit port of some importance. After mediation, the count of Holland got it back, but now as a fief from the duke of Brabant. In the following decades, relations with the dukes were friendly, but they were then the dominant power in the Low Countries as a whole and, consequently, in Holland as well.

The count of Holland's position in Zeeland was uncertain. He held there some isles directly from the Empire, but others in fief from the count of Flanders with whom he had to share the profits of government. King William tried to use his royal authority to change that situation but at the time of his death it was clear that he had failed. The nobility of Zeeland, moreover, were numerous, enjoyed rebelling against the authority of the count of Holland and were not averse to siding with the Flemish count when this served their purposes.

In the thirteenth century relations with the bishop of Utrecht offered no special difficulties. On the other hand some of the bishop's vassals, with lordships just over the Holland border, were gaining in strength and formed potentially dangerous enemies.

When King William died in 1256, his son Florence inherited as count of Holland not so much power but, rather, many serious problems: a territory that no longer embraced West-Frisia and of which the economically most promising parts, the region of Dordrecht and the Zeeland Isles (which at that time began to take part in the North Sea trade), were held in fief from others. He was probably brought up with pride in the exalted status of his father, and William's ignominious death was humiliating enough. It is not amazing that the struggle with the West-Frisians and the retrieval and burial of his father's remains had a strong priority in his mind, as he showed from the moment he was old enough to act independently. But the first decade after William's death was a period of guardianships. First came William's brother, Florence the Guardian, an experienced regent since he had acted in that function in the preceding years during William's absences. He concluded the treaty with Flanders over the Zeeland possessions, on not unprofitable conditions, and intervened with some success in Utrecht. After two years he died in a tournament. The guardianship was now entrusted to the boy's aunt, Aleyd of Avennes, the widow of John I of Hainault, a county situated between Brabant and France. The House of Avennes had strong anti-Flemish interests. Aleyd had the support of some influential members of the Holland nobility. Court intrigues caused her removal: a new guardian was chosen but his main achievement was the defeat of Aleyd and the allies she had found in Zeeland. New machinations followed, the original court clique removed the guardian and since

Florence conveniently had come of age by that time (majority began at the age of twelve according to the common law of Holland) the boy could assume the government himself, if only in name. The Avennes influence seems to have been restored at the same time, as was to be expected. One wonders how much the cunning and ruthlessness towards his opponents, which Florence showed in later days, owed to the atmosphere of intrigue in which he was brought up. A more positive characteristic, his talent as a shrewd but skilful diplomat, may also have been developed in those early days.

At eighteen, Florence came into action. His entourage, it seems, had not expected this. He organized his first campaign against the West-Frisians, after entrusting those parts of his territory which he held in fief from others, Zeeland and the region of Dordrecht, to his cousin Florence of Avennes, who was appointed governor for a limited number of years. But the campaign of 1272 was a sad failure: the army of the Hollanders fled in disorder, and the until then reliable population of the land around, and north of, the town of Haarlem, so-called Kennemerland, rose in a dangerous rebellion, in which one of the main vassals of the bishop of Utrecht joined. So for several years Florence then concentrated on pacifying the Kennemers and on winning a strong position in the bishopric by what must be called a shrewd but unscrupulous policy.[3] As a result, in the end the bishop was totally dependent on the count of Holland, his mightiest vassals were forced to give up important fiefs that were taken over by Florence, and had to exchange their feudal bonds with Utrecht for an overlordship of Holland. In this way the count expanded his territory and got a hold on these lords. But although he tried to tie them to his own interests, they remained his personal lethal enemies.

Long before Florence had attained his ends with regard to Utrecht, he realized that in Zeeland his cousin Avennes had won an alarmingly strong position for himself in co-operation with the local nobility. Florence therefore allied himself with the count of Flanders and tried to remove the Avennes by force from the county. After 1277 the conflict ran so high that arbitration from outside became necessary, and it is interesting to see that the king of England now stepped in, in order to reach a settlement. King Edward I had a strong interest in a balance of power between the House of Avennes and Flanders, the main market for English wool. In 1281 Edward probably decided to strengthen his position in the Low Countries by offering to the count of Holland what seems, at first sight, a most honourable agreement: the king's son and successor Alfonso was to marry Florence's only child, the baby Margaret. In fact, the arrangement was most unfavourable for the count. Margaret's dowry was to comprise half her father's territory: the king was to choose which part would be hers at the time of the wedding. Margaret was to inherit the other part at her father's death. The agreement was sealed at Westminster in 1281 and Florence must have been under considerable

---

[3]This and other unfriendly qualifications of Florence's policy in Gosses' refreshingly ironic paragraph on the count's activities, I H Gosses and N Japikse, *Staatkundige geschiedenis van Nederland* (3rd edn, The Hague, 1947), 100-7.

pressure from the king to accept it. There was one important reservation: if the count should have a son, the agreement was to be reviewed.

The contract ran counter to the constitution of the German Empire, since Holland was a fief from the Empire and could not be freely disposed of. Therefore, Florence was to seek the emperor's consent to the deal. Perhaps the English king had been impressed by Florence's diplomatic talents shown during the talks with Avennes; in any case he charged him with conducting negotiations with the emperor on his own behalf. Florence took the first steps to comply with this royal demand, but then asked the king's permission to postpone the talks so that he might be able to start on a second campaign against the West-Frisians. Although strategically this campaign was far better prepared than the first, and Florence (following his father's example) at once began to build a stronghold in the enemy country, he again failed in his effort to subdue the Frisians. But this time he was successful in one important respect: as he notified King Edward during the summer of 1282, he had been able to retrieve his father's remains, which were now to be buried in Middelburg, in Zeeland. The shame of the House of Holland had been effaced. It is certainly not accidental that during the following years Florence asked the Flemish poet Maerlant to translate Vincent de Beauvais's popular *Speculum historiale* and to incorporate the history of Holland in this new Dutch 'Historical Mirror', and ordered a separate chronicle of the dynasty, later known as Melis Stoke's rhymed chronicle, to be written. He also had his architect add a large and beautiful banqueting hall to the residence his father had built at The Hague. All these activities were certainly expressions of his restored pride in the dynasty.

During the following years, the Low Countries and the adjacent Nether-Rhineland were in uproar over what is called the War of the Limburg Succession between the duke of Brabant and the count of Guelders. Florence did not participate in it in any active way, but he profited from it. It depends on the historian's point of view whether the agreement between him and duke of Brabant is attributed to the count's, or to the duke's, successful diplomacy. But the result was that in 1283 Florence declared that he sided with the duke of Brabant - which meant protection for the duke in the north and would keep Flanders in check[4] - whereas the duke renounced his overlordship over the region of Dordrecht. The effect of that concession may have been largely theoretical, but it removed one complication that had been implicit in the marriage contract with King Edward.

The next year, King Edward was again mediating in Florence's conflicts. His envoys arranged that a controversy with the count of Guelders and a new one with the bishop of Utrecht were to be decided by the English king and some others. The same envoys were charged with a matter of more private importance: the renegotiation of the marriage contract of 1281. Earlier that year Florence had got

---

[4]J F Niermeyer, in *Algemene geschiedenis*, ii, 294, gives Florence the credit for this deal, H Pirenne, *Histoire de Belgique*, i (5th edn, Brussels, 1929), 250, credits Duke John I of Brabant; in his wake also P C Boeren, *Een Nederlandse wacht aan de Rijn, Jan de Eerste, hertog van Brabant* (Amsterdam, 1942), 146.

a son. It was now decided that this boy, Jan, who after his father's death was to succeed him as count of Holland, should marry Edward's youngest daughter, Elizabeth. The arrangements were facilitated by the sad fact that Edward's son Alfonso, Florence's prospective son-in-law, died before the new contract was concluded. The new settlement no longer implied a regular sell-out of Florence's rights and in this sense it was far less detrimental to the interests of the county than the first. Edward, however, still kept a strong hold on Florence - and on Holland - by stipulating that Elizabeth's future husband should be sent over to England before the age of seven and stay there until the marriage had been effectuated. The boy was, in fact, to be held as a hostage. It was a most humiliating condition and one we do not find in the treaty (concluded a few years before) concerning the marriage between another daughter of Edward and the son and heir of the duke of Brabant.

The negotiations, started at Haarlem in 1284, were concluded in October 1285, when Florence swore to the contract at the small town of Alkmaar. None of our sources suggest that at this last meeting the situation at the Scottish court was discussed, although the fact that King Alexander - after the death of his last son - now had no other successor but an infant granddaughter, must have been the talk of the day at Edward's court at the time. If the matter came up at Alkmaar, probably Florence's own Scottish forefathers were also mentioned during the conversation. Alkmaar was only a few miles away from Egmond Abbey, where about that time the author of the Stoke chronicle was engaged in the study of the abbey chronicle, which contained a passage on the Scottish marriage of 1162. If, indeed, this clerk who was so near to Florence's court had found the reference before the autumn of 1285, Florence certainly had been reminded of his Scottish family connections, when the envoys met him at Alkmaar. Is it unlikely that he mentioned his relationship with Earl David to the envoys and that these reported the matter to the king? Since the documents at Egmond Abbey contain no reference to any waiving of claims by Earl David, Florence cannot have thought he had a special right to Alexander's succession, should the king die without a descendant.

The next few years were uneventful, but during 1287 and 1288 Florence, by sheer luck, at last got a strong grip on West-Frisia. Heavy floods had ravaged the region and one of Florence's officers seized the opportunity of conquering the isolated villages of the fenland. Florence immediately ordered the building of more fortresses and garrisoned them. In 1289 one group of inhabitants after another came to offer their submission. But then things went wrong on the Zeeland side again. A dangerous rebellion broke out among the nobility and Flanders came to their assistance. The duke of Brabant offered to mediate between the warring parties, but could not prevent Florence's capture by the count of Flanders. Florence in the end was forced to meet the demands of his nobles and to recognize once more the count of Flanders as overlord of the greater part of Zeeland. The success in the north had humiliation in the south as its counterpart, even though Florence withdrew the concessions to the Zeeland nobles not long after he had been released.

These events just preceded what in Dutch historiography is called Florence's Scottish adventure. Edward had not interfered in the Zeeland affair, but in 1291 he sent his envoys to Holland who brought a letter for young Jan. Florence thanked Edward, told him the outcome of the war in Zeeland and promised that he would soon come over to England. It is quite possible that King Edward's envoys notified Florence that his presence was required at Norham. But since Jan by then was nearing his seventh birthday, it is evident that one reason for Florence's journey was to bring his son to King Edward's court. That means that, before, or as soon as, he arrived at Norham, where he presented his claim to the Scottish throne, he must have had an opportunity to discuss the future with King Edward, including the matter of the Scottish succession.

Florence's claim, G W S Barrow says in his biography of Robert Bruce, 'was originally purely formal, not to say frivolous'.[5] Indeed it is usually thought that the initiative for the action came from the count of Holland. Another interpretation, however, is possible. If we look at the relations between the count and the king of England, it appears that, as could be expected, the king is the dominating person, Florence the man who follows his lead. Whatever, in the course of the years, Edward decided in connection with Holland and its count was in the interests of his own policy. There is little reason to think that in the Scottish cause the roles were reversed. We should remember that, if Florence had been successful, the next heir to the Scottish throne would have been young Jan, Edward's future son-in-law, who was now totally in the king's power. There can be little doubt that Edward, who had originally planned a marriage between his own son and successor Edward and Margaret, the heiress of Scotland - a plan that failed through the girl's death - at some time considered the advantages of a malleable son-in-law on the Scottish throne. In any case, when Florence, at the second session of the court, reinforced his claim by the pretext of the lost documents that could prove his case, he cannot have done so all by himself. When he sailed from the continent he simply did not know the story that the documents were to illustrate. I am not competent in the matter of the Great Cause itself and of the forgeries that, after the 'search' ordered by Edward, turned up (and were not presented to the court at the critical session). There are, however, some points to be made from a Dutch point of view. Florence himself not only did not apparently have the forgeries at his disposal at the start of the proceedings in 1291, he did not have the means of fabricating them himself either: he lacked the necessary minimum knowledge of Scottish history and of Scottish diplomatic customs, and none of the few clerks his chancery consisted of could have been of any help. As Simpson remarked in 1957, King Edward's chancery, on the contrary, was in an excellent position to produce the forgeries,[6] and so, in a way, was Bruce.

---

[5]Barrow, *Bruce*, 43. (For this, and other abbreviated references, see Bibliographical Note, at end.)

[6]Simpson, 'Claim', 122; nevertheless the author excludes the possibility of either Edward's or Bruce's responsibility for the forgeries. M Prestwich in his biography of Edward I agrees with Barrow that Florence's pretensions seemed frivolous, *Edward I* (London,

Moreover, to quote Barrow again, 'it hardly seems likely that the count was really anxious for the Scottish throne'.[7] He may have felt attracted by the prospect of kingship - his actions, generally, were influenced by his father's example - but the drawbacks of a Scottish kingship were clear enough. Florence still had not a perfect grip on the nobles of his own territory, as the recent rebellion in Zeeland had made all too apparent. How was he to control the far mightier lords of Scotland, a country that was enormous, compared with Holland? It was not to be expected that he could maintain himself without strong military assistance from King Edward and in any case he would have to recognize the king's overlordship over Scotland. His situation in this respect would not have been different from that in which John Balliol found himself during his short reign. With regard to Florence's own county he detested the feudal ties that had bound it to Brabant until 1283, and still bound it to Flanders notwithstanding his efforts to have them severed. It is, on the other hand, unlikely that he started on the whole enterprise with the sole thought that he might turn it into financial profit - whatever the outcome in 1292. All these considerations suggest, I think, that in the matter of the Scottish succession, the count of Holland did not act on his own initiative but did what the king of England wanted him to do.

The outcome, as everybody knows, was an anti-climax. The count did not produce his forged documents which must have been in his hands, but withdrew from the contest. According to the Melis Stoke chronicle he was well paid by one party for this withdrawal and it is logical to suppose the winner, that is Balliol, to have been the person who paid.[8] The Stoke chronicle also mentions that the transaction was concluded on the advice of some bad councillor. The relevant passage suggests that at Florence's court the rumour went that the king himself was the bad adviser. And although, as Mackie remarked in the Pelican *History of Scotland*, there is no proof that Balliol owed his victory to Edward's favour,[9] the settlement certainly met with the king's approval. For some years after Florence's Scottish adventure, king and count remained on excellent terms. In 1284 Florence was the main negotiator for Edward when the latter aimed at, and concluded, a treaty with the king of the Romans.

Their relations became utterly spoiled, however, in 1295 and the reason was simple: Florence pursued a policy that was not compatible with King Edward's

---

1988), 367, and does not link the position of his son Jan with his claim; actually, he pays no attention at all to the political benefits Edward hoped to gain from his marriage arrangements in the Low Countries.

[7]Barrow, *Bruce*, 48.

[8]Jan Wagenaar, the conscientious eighteenth-century historian who wrote an authoritative 21-volume *Vaderlandsche Historie*, does not hesitate to conclude from the Stoke passage that it was Balliol who paid Florence a considerable sum (vol iii, Amsterdam, 1770, 57). Wagenaar, however, who had no knowledge of the forged documents, thought Florence's case very weak, and supposed that Florence entered the competition 'more to render a service to King Edward than because he could think himself entitled to the Scottish Crown in preference to others', ibid., 56.

[9]J D Mackie, *A History of Scotland*, (2nd edn, Harmondsworth, 1974), 66.

own purposes. The count attacked Flanders with his army at the very moment the king was building up a coalition against France and trying to bind Flanders to his cause. Edward showed his discontent by some measures that were harmful to the commercial interests of the town of Dordrecht and to the fiscal interests of the count of Holland. A shame, says the Stoke chronicle, and proof that the word of an Englishman is not to be trusted. Florence himself was furious and now stood open to suggestions that he should join the French alliance which King Edward was trying to counteract. Florence's treaty with the French king meant a full reversal of his year-long foreign policy and it was contrary to the interests of Holland and Zeeland and their developing commercial ties with England. Perhaps the idea appealed to his sense of intrigue. But a policy of playing off two parties against each other in order to reinforce his own position, which had been successful in his dealings with a weak bishop of Utrecht, could not work with the strong opponent King Edward was. Thoughts of his son Jan, a hostage at the English court, do not seem to have bothered him. In fact, Florence more or less expected Edward to annul the marriage contract and to send the boy home. But Edward did nothing of the sort. Instead, he contacted some of Florence's personal enemies amongst the count's vassals, who agreed to kidnap Florence and to bring him over to England where he was then to be forced to comply with Edward's demands.

The scheme miscarried disastrously. The conniving nobles captured Florence but were prevented from bringing him aboard a ship to England. When they tried another route, they were waylaid by people from a nearby village who intended to free the count. In a panic, the kidnappers brutally killed Florence and then took flight. Chaos must have broken out in Holland as soon as the news spread. This is shown dramatically by the preparations for Florence's burial: first his remains were transported (by boat) northward, presumably for interment in Egmond Abbey. But the mourners did not go beyond the town of Alkmaar and then (the only possible reason for this being that it was not safe to go on) they decided on a temporary burial in the parish church. Afterwards the body was taken southward. But apparently then it was thought too risky to venture on the long journey to Middelburg in order to bury Florence at his father's side, and so he was interred in the nunnery at Rijnsburg, the burial place of his wife and other female members of his House.

Several noble factions in Holland and Zeeland now initiated conflicting policies of their own. One faction urged King Edward to send young Jan (who was by then twelve years old and officially no longer a minor) over to Holland, which the king did, after a hurried-through marriage with Elizabeth at the port of departure, Ipswich. Jan was accompanied by some English councillors whose advice he had promised to follow in everything. But the murder of his father had unleashed a new series of rebellions and the boy died three years later, at the age of fifteen, before the situation had become truly stabilized. His heir was John of Avennes, count of Hainault, member of the French coalition. What Edward had hoped to gain from family ties with the count of Holland, a reliable stronghold in the Low Countries, had come to nothing.

In Dutch historiography Florence V has been in turn admired and strongly criticized.[10] The Melis Stoke chronicle, written at Florence's own request, naturally gives a very favourable impression of his actions and the author's fine account of the murder and of the feelings it aroused amongst loyal adherents - including a moving story about two dogs who refused to leave their master's bier - has done much to give Florence the status of popular hero in later centuries. Nowadays, historians mingle approval with criticism, but admiration usually prevails. Recently, non-historians have even developed a sort of Florence cult and the count rises in stature in their hands. It has become usual to describe him as a Powerful Prince, the equal of kings, very popular with every Hollander apart from his nobility. The latter notion has formed part, since the early sixteenth century, of the popular-hero tradition.

Actually, I prefer a more sceptical interpretation of the available evidence concerning Florence's position. It is certainly wrong to call him 'a powerful prince'. The count's grip on his territory was precarious during most of his active years.[11] Moreover, on too many occasions, he had to comply with King Edward's demands whether they suited his own interests or not. The notion that he was Edward's ally on an equal footing cannot be upheld: it is clear that the king used him for his own political purposes and let him fall as soon as the count acted contrary to Edward's interests. This is one of the reasons why I cannot truly believe that Florence set out on his Scottish adventure on his own initiative.

This is not to belittle Florence's evident qualities. His personal, physical courage is clear from his behaviour in wars and tournaments. He was an able politician, with a general idea about what was needed to consolidate his county and to achieve his purpose. His tenacity towards West-Frisia was successful after long years of frustration. He was not only an able strategist, he was also a ruthless schemer, who liked to play off one party against the other to his own profit, a practice that bore fruit in the chaotic conditions of Utrecht. He was not an original man: in most respects his policy was modelled on the policy of his father as count of Holland.[12] The only new element was the English alliance, an additional indication, perhaps, that this was King Edward's not Count Florence's policy.

---

[10]Hugenholtz, *Floris V* (1974), 108-14, gives a survey of the relevant historiography from Melis Stoke onwards.

[11]The count's dependence on the support of his own nobles is the theme of J M A Coenen, 'Graaf en grafelijkheid in de dertiende eeuw', in W van Anrooij and others, *Holland in wording: De ontstaansgeschiedenis van het graafschap Holland tot het begin van de vijftiende eeuw* (Hilversum, 1991), 27-56.

[12]Unlike his father, King William II (and Florence the Guardian, who was a member of the committee which brought Richard of Cornwall to the continent after his election as Roman king), Florence V did not involve himself in imperial politics. But, since the election of Rudolf of Habsburg in 1273, this abstinence is too general a phenomenon in the Low Countries to be relevant for the subject of this paper.

Bibliographical note

For Florence's participation in the Great Cause, see G W S Barrow, *Robert Bruce and the Community of the Realm of Scotland* (3rd edn, Edinburgh, 1988), 39-49; E L G Stones and Grant G Simpson, eds, *Edward I and the Throne of Scotland 1290-96* (2 vols, Oxford, 1978), i, passim; Grant G Simpson, 'The claim of Florence, count of Holland, to the Scottish throne, 1291-2', *Scottish Historical Review*, xxxvi (1957), 111-24. On all other aspects, it is necessary to turn to publications in Dutch. The *Rijmkroniek van Melis Stoke*, edited by W G Brill (Utrecht, 1855), is available in a photomechanical reprint (Utrecht, 1983). The modern edition of charters of the House of Holland, A C F Koch and J G Kruisheer, eds, *Oorkondenboek van Holland en Zeeland tot 1299* (The Hague, 1970 ff), has not yet gone beyond the year 1278; for the later years of Florence V the older editions by L Ph Ch van den Bergh and J de Frémery must be consulted. J G Kruisheer's study of the chancery of Holland, *De oorkonden en de kanselarij van de graven van Holland tot 1299* (2 vols, The Hague, 1971), ii, contains a useful list of abstracts of all charters issued by the counts of Holland. A well-documented biography of Florence V, *Floris V, graaf van Holland en Zeeland, heer van West-Friesland*, by H Obreen, dates from 1907 (Ghent). *Algemene Geschiedenis der Nederlanden*, ii (Utrecht, 1950), contains an elaborate chapter on Florence's policy by J F Niermeyer, with a very favourable view of the count. A compact and unannotated, but solid and well balanced study by a specialist on Melis Stoke, F W N Hugenholtz, *Floris V* (Hilversum, 1966, enlarged reprint 1974), is excellent on Florence's policy towards Utrecht and Flanders (I disagree, however, with the interpretation of the count's relations with England and on some minor points). Triennial symposia devoted to Florence V and the history of Holland in the late middle ages have been held since 1978; the papers, by professional historians and others, are published in the Muiderberg Symposia series (The Hague, 1979; Hilversum, 1991 ff).

3

THE FLEMISH DIMENSION OF
THE AULD ALLIANCE[1]

Alexander Stevenson

Despite the hallowed place of the Auld Alliance with France in Scottish popular tradition, its origins and early history have remained remarkably obscure. That it was cemented by a common enmity towards England is generally agreed, but as a defence against English hostilities its recorded achievements are surprisingly slight. Narrowly defined, early Franco-Scottish contacts were few. Two vital components seem to be missing: how physical contact was maintained and what ties there were in the long intervals between embassies, treaties and military expeditions.

Much as foreigners generally ignore the fact that Scotland is historically distinct from England, so too there is a tendency to forget that Flanders was for centuries part of the kingdom of France. Belgian historians have been reluctant to dwell on the former dependence of any of their territories upon France; and, on the only border area where French sovereignty has been rolled back, the French themselves are reticent. Add to that English historians' tendency to exaggerrate the independence of Flanders, by over-emphasising its ties with England, and it is not surprising that the Scots have customarily drawn a mental line approximating to the modern frontier between France and Belgium.

Actually, Flanders was part of the Frankish heartland, from which the Germanic Franks expanded to conquer what became France. The county of Flanders developed between the ninth and twelfth centuries as a northern march of the French kingdom.[2] Its counts were among the most powerful of the peers of France and several were notably active in French affairs. Thus Count Baldwin V was guardian of Philip I of France in the only royal minority of the eleventh century; and Count Philip d'Alsace was the power behind the throne in the only royal minority of the twelfth century, that of his godson Philip Augustus in 1180. Seven years earlier it was this position of influence, as the French king's foremost adviser,[3] which brought about the first Franco-Scottish alliance. Perhaps because of

---

[1]This paper is dedicated to the memory of my father, Robert Stevenson, who read much of it in draft and without whose encouragement and support my research into Scoto-Flemish contacts would not have been undertaken.

[2]Henri Pirenne, *Histoire de Belgique* (hereafter Pirenne, *Histoire*), i (5th edn, Brussels, 1929), 56-60, 103-18, 203-7, 217-9; Jean Dunbabin, *France in the Making, 843-1180* (Oxford, 1985), passim. The counts also secured territory along the east bank of the river Scheldt and reclaimed lands in the delta, which were known collectively as imperial Flanders because they lay within the borders of the Holy Roman Empire.

[3]Marcel Pacaut, *Louis VII et son royaume* (Paris, 1964), 38, 176.

a wish to find earlier origins,[4] it is an event that has received surprisingly little attention - notwithstanding William the Lion's humiliating recognition of English suzerainty to which it led (with all the bitter consequences that entailed) and the exceptionally detailed contemporary chronicle which describes the entire episode.[5]

The chronicler Jordan Fantosme implies that it was Philip d'Alsace, count of Flanders, who first persuaded Louis VII of the value of an alliance with the king of Scots against Henry II of England. The Scots were to be brought into a grand alliance, with Henry's rebellious sons, and proposals were apparently sent to Scotland by Philip in the younger Henry's name. The proposed bait was the return of Cumbria to the Scottish crown, but this proved insufficiently attractive to William and his council. Rather than fight against Henry II, Fantosme states that William first sought Northumberland from the English king in return for Scottish support. Only when that was refused did he put the same proposal to the French court, accompanied by a request for Flemish reinforcements. And, Fantosme continues, it was Philip who championed the Scots' terms, persuaded Louis to accede to them, and promised forthwith to send aid from Flanders.

Badly co-ordinated plans were made for Franco-Flemish assaults on Henry II's French territories, a Scoto-Flemish invasion of northern England, and Flemish landings in Suffolk which, it was hoped, would lead to general rebellion in England. But the war was lost on all fronts, with the rout of the Scoto-Flemish army at Alnwick and the capture of King William, in July 1174, its greatest disaster.[6]

There were widespread reports in England that the Flemings who landed in Suffolk were weavers, attracted by the lure of English wool.[7] Not only do commercial ties provide a key to Flemish interest in England, they are also the probable reason for the count of Flanders' knowledge about Scottish affairs and his interest in establishing closer relations with the Scots.[8]

By the 1170s there was a large Flemish community in Scotland and commercial ties must have been close. Flemings played a vital part in the transformation

---

[4]A late medieval legend that the Franco-Scottish alliance originated in the reign of Charlemagne probably derives from reports of Frankish contacts with the Irish (*Scotti*); and the suggestion of an earlier alliance with Louis VII is derived merely from English rumours of a Scottish embassy to France in 1168: Alan O Anderson, *Early Sources of Scottish History* (2 vols, Edinburgh, 1925), i, 251; Sir Archibald C Lawrie, *Annals of the reigns of Malcolm and William, Kings of Scotland* (Glasgow, 1910), 116-17.

[5]Jordan Fantosme, 'Chronique de la guerre entre les Anglois et les Ecossois', in *Chronicles of Stephen, Henry II, and Richard I*, ed. Richard Howlett (Rolls Series, no. 82), iii (hereafter Fantosme, 'Chronique'), 222-377.

[6]Fantosme, 'Chronique', 243-377; Austin L Poole, *From Domesday Book to Magna Carta, 1087-1216* (2nd edn, Oxford, 1955), 276-7, 333-7; Archibald A M Duncan, *Scotland, the Making of the Kingdom* (Edinburgh, 1975) (hereafter Duncan, *Kingdom*), 228-30.

[7]Fantosme, 'Chronique', 287-9; Gervase of Canterbury, *Historical Works*, ed. William Stubbs (Rolls Series, no. 73), i, 246.

[8]For an outline of Philip d'Alsace's exceptionally active commercial policies, see H van Werveke, 'The Low Countries', in *The Cambridge Economic History of Europe*, ed. Sir Michael M Postan, E Rich and Edward Miller, iii (Cambridge, 1963), 342-50.

of the Scottish economy during the twelfth century and in the foundation and early development of the Scottish burghs. There was extensive feudal settlement of Flemings throughout southern Scotland and along the Moray Firth;[9] and most of the earliest recorded residents of Scottish burghs, merchants and craftsmen, have Flemish names.[10]

Principal and earliest of these is Mainard the Fleming, whose departure from Berwick and consequent transfer of allegiance from David I to the bishop of St Andrews is recorded in a unique charter of about 1144. It describes how Mainard had come to St Andrews, with the active encouragement of David I, to build and establish the new burgh. Like the chief executive of a new town today, his tasks must have been to organise the construction of the burgh, to find craftsmen and merchants to settle there, to persuade other merchants to come there to do business, to advise the bishop and his tenants how to develop the commercial potential of their estates, and thus to promote the burgh's trade.

Apart from the opportunities afforded by a backward country, whose monarchy was actively seeking to promote economic development - the property, the trading privileges common to burgh settlers, the lack of competition - what attracted the Flemings to Scotland were its pastoral products and fisheries. Belgic and Frankish fishermen were reported to be active in the Firth of Forth during the reign of David I.[11] But the earliest direct reference to Scottish trade with Flanders is an undated charter of Philip d'Alsace, endorsed by Pope Lucius III in the early 1180s, which exempted the monks of Melrose from all tolls in Flanders, and guaranteed them protection in any dispute between English and Flemish merchants.[12] The implication is that by the 1180s trade links were well-established and that both Flemish and Anglo-Scottish merchants were involved (in twelfth-century charters the native inhabitants of south-east Scotland are invariably referred to as *Angli*). The early importance of Flemish trade with Scotland is clarified in a list, drawn up about 1200, of goods from most parts of the known world then traded in

---

[9]Geoffrey W S Barrow, *The Anglo-Norman Era in Scottish History* (Oxford, 1980), 35-60; Duncan, *Kingdom*, 137-9. Estimating the extent of Flemish settlement is complicated by the fact that Flemings were almost invariably included within the term *Franci* in twelfth-century Scottish charters: Sir Archibald C Lawrie, *Early Scottish Charters* (Glasgow, 1905) (hereafter *ESC*), passim; Geoffrey W S Barrow and others, eds, *Regesta Regum Scottorum* (Edinburgh, 1960-) (hereafter *RRS*), i-ii, passim. See also above, p. 3.

[10]Four of seven burgh residents named in charters of the reign of David I have names that are certainly Flemish, one has an Anglo-Saxon name, and two have Franco-Norman names that were also common in southern Flanders: *ESC*, nos. 169, 193, 238, 248, 268.

[11]Alexander P Forbes, ed., 'Fragment of the life of St Kentigern', in *The Historians of Scotland*, v (Edinburgh, 1874), 131.

[12]Cosmo Innes, ed., *Liber Sancte Marie de Melros* (2 vols, Bannatyne Club, 1837), i, nos. 14 and 15.

Flanders: in which Scotland is listed second, after England, supplying wool, hides, cheese and tallow.[13]

The Flemish woollen cloth industry developed rapidly during the twelfth century, to become the largest commercial enterprise in medieval Europe, transforming Flanders into the richest and most urbanised territory north of the Alps. Scattered references to wool imports from England suggest that Flemish wool supplies were insufficient to meet local demand by the early twelfth century;[14] and cloth regulations and tariffs of the thirteenth century indicate that British wool was found to be superior to that of Flanders. Thus, at Bruges, cloth regulations of 1282 decreed that cloth made from English wool was to be marked with three crosses, from Scottish wool with two crosses, from Irish wool with one cross, and from Flemish wool with a half cross; and at St Omer, in the mid-thirteenth century, duty was levied at 3s. per sack on wool from England and Scotland, but only at 2s. 6d. per sack on wool from Wales and Ireland (the wool of no other country is mentioned).[15]

In the twelfth century most of Scotland's trade was probably with southern Flanders. St Omer was Flanders' principal early entrepôt, and Arras was Flanders' principal city and financial centre.[16] Significantly, the battle-cry of William the Lion's Flemish levies was 'Arras'.[17] Only after Philip Augustus's seizure of southern Flanders did the centre of the cloth trade shift decisively northwards, although Scotland continued to trade extensively with St Omer until the fourteenth century.

Until the thirteenth century Scottish connections with France must have been much less important than with Flanders. But from the late twelfth century onwards the French crown pursued a consistent policy of reducing the power and independence of the French magnates, and the counts of Flanders were among the first to be brought to heel. What became the county of Artois was unwisely offered by the childless Philip d'Alsace as a dowry on the marriage of his niece to Philip Augustus, albeit he carefully retained a life-interest. His death in 1191 gave Philip Augustus the opportunity to occupy most of Artois, including Arras, in the name of his son Louis; and Louis seized the rest for himself, including St Omer, in 1212. Following the defeat and capture of Count Ferrand of Flanders, at the battle of Bouvines in 1214, the subjugation of Flanders was completed. Thereafter the French crown secured personal oaths of allegiance from the Flemish barons and

---

[13]L Gilliodts van Severen, ed., *Cartulaire de l'ancienne estaple de Bruges* (2 vols, Bruges, 1904-6) (hereafter Gilliodts, *Cartulaire*), i, no. 14. The only fish listed were herring from Denmark, as a minor Danish export.
[14]Terence H Lloyd, *The English Wool Trade in the Middle Ages* (Cambridge, 1977) (hereafter Lloyd, *Wool Trade*), 1-6.
[15]Georges Espinas and Henri Pirenne, eds, *Receuil de documents relatifs à l'industrie drapière en Flandre* (3 vols, Brussels, 1906-20), i, 396; iii, 367.
[16]Jan A van Houtte, *Bruges: essai d'histoire urbaine* (Brussels, 1967), 18; Pirenne, *Histoire*, i, 207-8.
[17]Fantosme, 'Chronique', 305, 353.

urban patriciate, heard Flemish cases on appeal, and increasingly intervened in Flemish affairs.[18]

Despite the disruption of the early thirteenth century, the cloth industry expanded rapidly within the reduced county of Flanders and became central to the economy of much of northern France: from Picardy, where many of the dyestuffs were produced, to the Champagne fairs, where much of the cloth was sold. And it was this growth in demand (not just for wool, but also for cowhides, sheepskins and fish), combining with the long period of peace with England, which brought about Scotland's so-called 'golden age'.[19] The importance of these links is attested by the series of marriage alliances made between the Scottish royal house and the northern French nobility during the thirteenth century: Alexander II's marriage to Marie de Coucy in 1239, the marriage of Alexander III's eldest son to Margaret of Flanders in 1282, and Alexander III's marriage to Yolande de Dreux in 1285. French influence must have been strong in thirteenth century Scotland but, as in the twelfth century, it would have been filtered mainly through Flanders.

Ironically, far from strengthening ties, the Flemish marriage alliance seriously damaged Scoto-Flemish relations because of the Scots' failure to maintain payments on a pension of £1,000 *per annum* (perhaps £1 million in modern money), settled on Prince Alexander's widow under the terms of the marriage treaty. In April 1292, while the Scots were distracted by the Great Cause, the count of Flanders ordered the seizure of all Scottish-owned goods and money in Flanders, in an attempt to recover the arrears.

Peace overtures were made by the Bruges authorities in June 1292. But it was not until July 1293, after the dispute had been submitted to the bishop of Durham for arbitration, that a provisional settlement was reached with the count of Flanders, guaranteeing reciprocal protection and freedom of trade to Scottish and Flemish merchants, except for debts relating to Margaret's pension. In November 1293 John Balliol agreed to pay the arrears in full by the following Easter and on 16 May 1294 he ordered resumption of the annuity with effect from 1 August.[20]

It is against this background that the much better known affairs concerning England need to be viewed. In parallel with these developments, the count of Flanders was secretly negotiating with Edward I of England for the marriage of his daughter Philippine to Edward of Caernarvon, later Edward II. As Anglo-French relations deteriorated Count Guy de Dampierre's urgent desire to maintain a foot in both camps is readily explicable. An unofficial naval war - between

---

[18]Robert Fawtier, *The Capetian Kings of France*, trans. Lionel Butler and R J Adam (London, 1960), 111-17; Pirenne, *Histoire*, i, 219-41, 253-61, 335-43.

[19]Alexander Stevenson, 'Trade with the south' (hereafter Stevenson, 'Trade'), in *The Scottish Medieval Town*, ed. Michael Lynch, Michael Spearman and Geoffrey Stell (Edinburgh, 1988), 184-7; Nicholas Mayhew, 'Alexander III - a silver age?' in *Scotland in the Reign of Alexander III*, ed. Norman H Reid (Edinburgh, 1990), 53-73.

[20]Joseph Stevenson, ed., *Documents illustrative of the History of Scotland, 1286-1306* (2 vols, Edinburgh, 1870) (hereafter Stevenson, *Documents*), i, nos. 24, 233, 234, 246, 248, 311, 315, 323; Gilliodts, *Cartulaire*, i, no. 102.

Normans and Flemings on one side, and English and Gascons on the other - gave Philip IV of France an excuse, in the view of his most recent French biographer, to contrive the imposition of royal control over Gascony.[21]

Relentless pressure was applied by Philip over a period of about a year, culminating in Edward I's forfeiture of the duchy of Aquitaine on 19 May 1294 (just three days after Balliol's final settlement with the count of Flanders). In retaliation, Edward introduced an embargo on trade with all parts of the French kingdom at the end of May and began preparations for war. Although the trade ban was rigorously enforced against Flanders, Edward simultaneously pressed ahead with the previously desultory Flemish marriage negotiations, as part of a general network of alliances, and reached an agreement with Guy de Dampierre at the end of August.

Intelligence of the secret marriage treaty rapidly reached the French king. On a visit to Paris, Guy was arrested and released only after Philippine had been surrendered into her godfather Philip's custody and a string of other measures had been introduced to strengthen Franco-Flemish ties.[22] Flanders' loyalty was thereby secured in the ensuing war with England, with the consequence that Edward I continued to embargo English wool supplies.

Since Flemish and Artesian cloth was made almost exclusively of English, Scottish and native wool (probably in that order), this was indeed a punitive measure. But, to be fully effective, it was necessary to ensure that the Scots complied with the English trade ban. This they refused to do. Scottish trade with Flanders and other parts of the French kingdom probably continued as before, despite English harassment.[23]

Thus matters continued until 3 March 1295 when, following Edward's example, Philip IV of France introduced a blanket ban on trade with the British Isles.[24] The timing of the French ban is significant because it was issued during a slack season in the wool trade. It must therefore have been intended primarily as a warning, aimed particularly at the Scots, who had no alternative outlets for most of their exports: since English wool, hides and sheepskins had, of necessity, swamped all other markets. Two years later the English barons claimed that nearly half of England's wealth was derived from wool;[25] with its limited arable

---

[21]Jean Favier, *Philippe le Bel* (Paris, 1978), 206-12; Sir Maurice Powicke, *The Thirteenth Century, 1216-1307* (2nd edn, Oxford, 1962), 644-9; Frantz Funck-Brentano, *Philippe le Bel en Flandre* (Paris, 1896) (hereafter Funck-Brentano, *Flandre*), 23-6.

[22]Pirenne, *Histoire*, i, 398-400; Favier, *Philippe le Bel*, 216-17; Funck-Brentano, *Flandre*, 139-51.

[23]Thomas Rymer, ed., *Foedera* (3rd edn, 10 vols, The Hague, 1739-45), Iiii, 129; Joseph Bain and others, eds, *Calendar of Documents Relating to Scotland* (5 vols, Edinburgh, 1881-1986) (hereafter *CDS*), ii, 162.

[24]Stevenson, *Documents*, ii, no. 334.

[25]Lloyd, *Wool Trade*, 1.

lands, Scotland's reliance upon the wool trade must have been significantly greater. By 10 May the Scots had secured a six-month truce.[26]

Discussion of the Scottish embassy to France in July 1295 has always focused upon Edward I's attempted coercion of Scotland. Philip's far more successful coercion has never been noted - in keeping though it is with his extraordinarily ruthless and unscrupulous conduct towards Gascony, Flanders, the Jews, the Papacy and the Knights Templar. Yet it is surely much more likely that the parliament held at Stirling early in July 1295 was convened primarily because of the need to send an embassy to France, in order to prevent reimposition of the French trade embargo on 1 November and the slump which would inevitably have followed. Given the period of notice required to summon a parliament, and the travelling time between France and Scotland, the timescale is exactly right.

That Edward I's assertion of overlordship must have bulked large in the proceedings, along with John Balliol's incompetence in defending Scottish interests, is inescapable. Doubtless these were reasons for the appointment of a governing council; but that the deciding factor was a decision to send an embassy to France, to *propose* an anti-English alliance, is convincing only if the threatened trade embargo is overlooked. The record of English chronicles, written after Edward's occupation of Scotland and concerned to emphasise Scottish perfidy, can hardly be regarded as impartial evidence.[27]

The letters of credence for the Scottish embassy to Philip IV refer to the strengthening of relations with France through a marriage alliance between Edward Balliol and a French princess, not to a treaty against England.[28] It is far from clear that a full offensive alliance was in Scotland's interest, particularly one which required the Scots both to mount an attack on England without first receiving reinforcements (unlike earlier or later campaigns) and to maintain hostilities for the duration of the Anglo-French war. But such terms were much to the advantage of Philip IV.

In this context, it is interesting to note that Guy de Dampierre was again seizing Scottish goods by July 1295, a month before the annuity fell due, and that Philip then ostentatiously took all Scottish merchants under his protection for the duration of the truce.[29] It looks very like a heavy-handed reminder to the Scots that their well-being depended upon the French king's goodwill. It is also significant that the Scottish embassy remained at the French court for nearly three months and agreed to the terms of a full offensive and defensive alliance against England only a week before the expiry of the trade truce.[30] Far from being the

---

[26]Stevenson, *Documents*, ii, no. 335.

[27]Joseph Stevenson, ed., *Chronicon de Lanercost* (Maitland Club, 1839), 161-2; Harry Rothwell, ed., *The Chronicle of Walter of Guisborough* (Royal Historical Society, 1957), 264.

[28]Rymer, *Foedera*, Iiii, 146-7.

[29]Stevenson, *Documents*, ii, nos. 337-8.

[30]Rymer, *Foedera*, Iiii, 152. Translated in: Walter Bower, *Scotichronicon*, ed. Donald E R Watt and others (Aberdeen, 1987-), 6, 45-51.

driving force behind the alliance, the Scottish government may thus be see as a hapless pawn in the struggle between Edward I and Philip IV. Neutrality had ceased to be an option. A French alliance preserved Scottish trade and could be further justified as possibly the only means of forcing the English king to renounce his suzerainty.

From Philip's viewpoint the initial outcome of the alliance was eminently satisfactory. In the next campaign season Edward I felt obliged to turn his attention from Gascony to Scotland.[31] But the English occupation of Scotland was disastrous for the Flemings. Although it was not the spark which ignited the Flemish revolt, the loss of all wool from Scotland (as well as from England) must have been a major factor in bringing Flanders to the brink of rebellion; albeit the full impact would not have been felt until the peak wool exporting season during the summer and autumn.[32]

Scotland had fallen by the summer of 1296 and Flanders rebelled in the autumn. An Anglo-Flemish truce was concluded on 2 November, which included provision for the reopening of trade links with both England and Scotland (and made specific reference to the release of wool), and a full alliance was agreed on 7 January 1297.[33] Flanders' fate mirrored that of Scotland. It was largely occupied by the French in the summer of 1297, before the arrival of Edward I at the end of August with an English army.

After the annihilation of the English army in Scotland at Stirling Bridge, on 11 September 1297, Edward was obliged to abandon his Flemish confederate in order to concentrate his forces upon the reconquest of Scotland. On 9 October he agreed a humiliating truce with Philip IV, which left Philip in possession of Gascony and enabled him to complete the reoccupation of Flanders after Edward returned to England the following March. Edward insisted upon the inclusion of the count of Flanders in the original truce, but not in its successors. When the Franco-Flemish truce expired in 1300 Guy de Dampierre and his most prominent supporters were imprisoned. Flanders was then added to the French royal domain.[34]

In the days of relatively primitive sailing ships the English Channel acted as a natural barrier between northern and southern Europe. Whilst access from the south presented few problems, prevailing winds and currents made access from the north slow and difficult. Navigation around western Britain was also hazardous. Flanders and Artois therefore occupied a pivotal position between north and south.

As the only French territories adjoining the North Sea, Flanders and Artois provided Philip IV with much the most reliable means of furnishing the Scots with the money and supplies they needed to repel the English invaders. Such ac-

---

[31]Michael Prestwich, *Edward I* (London, 1988) (hereafter Prestwich, *Edward I*), 381-5.
[32]For Philip's threatened dispossession of Guy de Dampierre, which finally triggered the revolt, see Pirenne, *Histoire*, i, 401-8.
[33]Gilliodts, *Cartulaire*, i, nos. 119, 122; Rymer, *Foedera*, Iiii, 168-70.
[34]Funck-Brentano, *Flandre*, 198-349; Pirenne, *Histoire*, i, 409-12; Prestwich, *Edward I*, 392-6.

tion may have been contrary to the Anglo-French truces,[35] but it was probably the only way Philip could ensure that the English were too preoccupied to interfere in continental affairs.

Is it coincidental that much of Scotland escaped the shackles of English occupation from 1297 to 1302, at the same time that Philip possessed Flanders? Or that Scotland was reoccupied between 1303 and 1304, after the stunning success of the next Flemish revolt, in which a seemingly invincible French army was overwhelmed and most of its cavalry massacred at the battle of Courtrai? Or that the revolt of Robert Bruce took place only after it became apparent that the Franco-Flemish peace settlement of 1305, with its reinstatement of the count of Flanders, had secured the prospect of further support?

The Flemings seized Scottish goods in Flanders at the outset of their revolt,[36] presumably as a sop to win English support in their struggle against the French king. To prevent English aid to the Flemings, Philip IV was obliged to conclude a full peace treaty with England, restoring Gascony to Edward I, in May 1303.[37] Not until Flanders had been pacified could the Scots hope for significant French aid. But, by the same token, any Flemish support for the Scots was likely to be viewed by the French king as a gesture of loyalty to himself.

As early as 10 April 1305 the magistrates of Bruges wrote to the English government insisting that Flanders was open to all nations, the Scots included, and six days later the count of Flanders did likewise.[38] The following year, when an English commission tried to claim massive damages from the French government for losses attributed to French support for the Scots from 1297 onwards,[39] an advocate for the count of Flanders insisted that the Anglo-French truces and treaty did not affect France's obligations to the Scots, under the treaty of 1295, and testified to the importance (to Flanders) of relations with Scotland. Given the concurrence of Philip IV with this view, it seems probable that Flanders continued to provide a haven for the Scots thereafter. At least, that is the implication of a memorandum, concerning the English claims and the countervailing French arguments, submitted to Edward II about 1309.[40]

Dutchmen, Flemings and Germans appear repeatedly in English records as suppliers and supporters of the 'Scottish rebels', and Flanders was the base from which they mainly operated.[41] As Franco-Flemish relations deteriorated once

---

[35]Rymer, *Foedera*, Iiii, 191-5; Iiv, 4, 24-6.

[36]Gilliodts, *Cartulaire*, i, no. 136.

[37]Favier, *Philippe le Bel*, 242, 314-15; Funck-Brentano, *Flandre*, 426, 465-6; Prestwich, *Edward I*, 397; Rymer, *Foedera*, Iiv, 24-6.

[38]Gilliodts, *Cartulaire*, i, no. 153; *Foedera*, Iiv, 39-40.

[39]*CDS*, v, no. 428.

[40]Ibid., no. 528.

[41]William S Reid, 'Trade, traders and Scottish independence', *Speculum*, 29 (1954), 210-22; idem, 'The Scots and the staple ordinance of 1313', *Speculum*, 34 (1959), 598-610; idem, 'Sea-power in the Anglo-Scottish war, 1296-1328', *Mariner's Mirror*, 46 (1960), 7-

more, the English government mistakenly hoped it could at last bring pressure to bear upon the Flemings and began a stream of protests to the count of Flanders about the trade and military aid that his territories, and Bruges in particular, were providing to the Scots.[42] Bruges had latterly been the principal centre of Scoto-Flemish trade before the Wars of Independence,[43] and it consolidated that position by becoming a focal point for Scottish relief activities.

It was perhaps during this period that a Scottish staple was first established at Bruges, in imitation of the English staple at St Omer; the institution of which, in 1313,[44] must have forced the Scots finally to abandon their trade with Artois. The same year, incidentally, that English agents reported the departure from the Zwyn (the long silted-up harbour of Bruges between Damme and Sluys) of a convoy of 13 ships, laden with arms and supplies for the Scots.[45] Although the first allusion to a Scottish staple does not occur until 1347, its context implies that the staple was by then well established.[46] And the copy of a letter of 1321, from Robert Bruce to the magistrates of Bruges, in the Dunfermline Abbey cartulary - informing them that he had granted Dunfermline Abbey its own cocket seal (entitling the abbey to collect customs duty on goods exported from its estates) and requesting the Bruges authorities to accept it as they would his own - suggests that by then Bruges was already the officially recognised centre of the Scottish export trade.[47]

Despite increasing hostility towards Flemish merchants in England and disruption of their trade, and the renewed friction between Flanders and the French crown from 1310 to 1320, the Flemings continued to maintain friendly relations with the Scots. All attempts by the English government to persuade the Flemish authorities to obstruct Scottish trade were rebuffed. The intensity of Flemish feelings in this regard is emphasised in a letter, written in 1317 by an English ambassador to Flanders, which noted that '[the Flemings] would never consent to refuse the Scots entry to their lands, or to prevent their merchants from trading in Scotland'. It therefore counselled that ships and goods seized from Flemings who were suspected of trading with the Scots should be restored, lest action be taken against English merchants in Flanders.[48]

Although it has never been remarked, Robert de Béthune, count of Flanders from 1305 to 1322, must have been Scotland's most resolute foreign supporter during the Wars of Independence. That is confirmed by the rapidity with which his grandson, Count Louis de Nevers, bowed to English demands and expelled the

---

23; James W Dilley, 'German merchants in Scotland, 1297-1327', *Scottish Historical Review*, 27 (1948), 142-55; Lloyd, *Wool Trade*, 102-14.

[42]David Macpherson and others, eds, *Rotuli Scotiae* (2 vols, London, 1814-19) (hereafter Macpherson, *Rotuli Scotiae*), i, 78, 136, 193-4; Rymer, *Foedera*, Iiv, 177; Ili, 35-6, 170-1.

[43]Stevenson, 'Trade', 187.

[44]Lloyd, *Wool Trade*, 106.

[45]*Calendar of Close Rolls, 1307-13* (London, 1892), 570-1.

[46]See below, p. 39.

[47]*RRS*, v, 458.

[48]*CDS*, v, no. 634.

Scots from Flanders in April 1323, seven months after Robert's death, in an effort to improve Anglo-Flemish relations.[49]

Since Louis had been brought up at the French court and remained under French tutelage, this implies that by then the French government was itself indifferent to the Scottish cause.[50] As Professor Nicholson has suggested, the loss of Flemish support and the Scots' exclusion from Flanders may well have been the catalyst which forced the Scots to accede to a thirteen-year truce with England at the end of the following month.[51] Measures to protect Scotland's overseas trade are a major feature of the truce because, as John Barbour (Robert Bruce's fourteenth-century biographer) noted, attacks on Scottish trade with Flanders were the one way in which the English could still seriously damage Scottish interests.[52]

The Flemings rebelled against their young count in the winter of 1323. Flanders was convulsed by civil war until King Charles IV gathered an army to occupy the county and thus imposed a peace settlement in April 1326.[53] It is therefore highly significant that the Franco-Scottish alliance was renewed the following week (for the first time since 1295) and in terms geared to securing the Scots' position in France, as well as to ensuring that Scotland and France would support each other in any conflict with England.[54] Once again it is Flanders that was central to Scottish concerns. Scottish interests were most threatened by the English through Flanders; only French influence could then provide an adequate counterbalance, and only through Flanders could French military aid readily reach Scotland.

When the English again attacked Scotland, Flanders once more became a major supplier of military aid to the Scots. In April 1333 Edward III protested to Louis de Nevers and the major Flemish towns about the arms, supplies and men being sent to Scotland from Flanders.[55] Two years later a large force was apparently fitted out by order of the French king and sent to Scotland under Flemish command;[56] and in March 1337 English agents reported that five ships were preparing to sail to Aberdeen from the Zwyn with arms and munitions for the Scots. This was followed in both May and September 1337 by royal writs to the English sheriffs warning them of the scale and frequency of aid being sent to the Scots

---

[49]Terence H Lloyd, *Alien Merchants in England in the High Middle Ages* (Brighton, 1982), 103-4; *Calendar of Patent Rolls, 1321-4* (London, 1924), 269, 276.

[50]Pirenne, *Histoire*, ii (3rd edn, Brussels, 1922), 7-9.

[51]Ranald Nicholson, *Scotland, the Later Middle Ages* (Edinburgh, 1974) (hereafter Nicholson, *Scotland*), 105-6.

[52]Rymer, *Foedera*, IIii, 73-4; John Barbour, *The Bruce*, book xix, lines 193-204.

[53]But after the French army dispersed the revolt flared up again. It was finally suppressed by another French army in 1328: Pirenne, *Histoire*, ii, 88-98.

[54]Thomas Thomson and Cosmo Innes, eds, *Acts of the Parliaments of Scotland* (12 vols, Edinburgh, 1814-75) (hereafter *APS*), xii, 5-6.

[55]Macpherson, *Rotuli Scotiae*, i, 233-4.

[56]Jean Froissart, *Chroniques*, ed. S Luce and others (13 vols, Société d'histoire de France, 1869-1957) (hereafter Froissart, *Chroniques*), 1, ccxxi.

'from Flanders and elsewhere'.[57] Thereafter there is a gap until 1355, when both Fordun and the *Scalacronica* record the despatch of a small French expedition from Sluys to Scotland.[58]

In the interim a further Flemish revolt, in 1338, had seriously damaged Scoto-Flemish relations. England initially strongly supported the Flemish rebellion. Like most fourteenth-century Flemish uprisings, the rebellion was centred upon Ghent, mainly situated as it was in imperial Flanders and thus lacking ties of loyalty to the French crown. By contrast, Bruges, Flanders' most francophile city, was an unwilling participant.[59] At what point the Scots were forced out of Bruges is unclear. The only evidence for the Scots' departure is two surprisingly late decrees of the Scottish council, on 12 November 1347: one authorising the establishment of the Scottish staple at Middelburg (25 miles to the north, on the island of Walcheren, in Zeeland); the other ordering the exclusion of Flemings from Scotland, in retaliation for the expulsion of the Scots from Flanders.[60]

In 1348, with Flemish opposition to the English alliance rapidly escalating, particularly in Bruges, the English abandoned the Flemish rebels. The Scots seem to have returned to Bruges gradually in the course of 1348,[61] although Ghent held out against Count Louis de Male until January 1349. The Franco-Scottish alliance was renewed in 1352, on the initiative of King John of France, and again in June 1359,[62] the latter renewal while negotiations were in progress for an Anglo-Flemish staple treaty.[63] This was followed in November by the first surviving Scottish staple treaty with the count of Flanders,[64] possibly the result of French pressure to ensure that Scottish interests were protected after the brief return of the English staple to Bruges in July. Like the arrangements proposed for the Middelburg staple, the comital treaty was presumably complementary to staple agreements, now lost, already made with the Bruges authorities.

Although Bruges played a vital role between 1357 and 1373, as the financial centre through which instalments of David II's English ransom were raised and channelled, there was a lull in diplomatic activity thereafter until the accession of Robert II in 1371. He promptly renewed the Franco-Scottish alliance (the first king to do so upon his succession). The treaty was couched in similar terms to its predecessors; but new guarantees were given to protect the rights, honour, profit,

[57]Macpherson, *Rotuli Scotiae*, i, 485, 490, 498.
[58]William F Skene, ed., *Johannis de Fordun, Chronica Gentis Scotorum* (2 vols, Edinburgh, 1871-2), ii, 360-1; Joseph Stevenson, ed., *Scalacronica, by Sir Thomas Gray of Heton, Knight* (Maitland Club, 1836), 302.
[59]Pirenne, *Histoire*, ii, 105-35.
[60]*RRS*, vi, 140-1.
[61]Gilliodts, *Cartulaire*, i, nos. 272-4.
[62]*APS*, xii, 8; Paris, Archives Nationales, Trésor des chartes, J 677, no. 7.
[63]Lloyd, *Wool Trade*, 209-10.
[64]Matthijs P Rooseboom, *The Scottish Staple in the Netherlands* (The Hague, 1910), appendix 10.

privileges and franchises of the subjects of both countries, and to do all in the kings' power to prevent harm from befalling them.[65]

The reasons for these new guarantees are unclear, but were probably related to a serious piratical incident at Sluys late in 1370: when French warships seized Scottish, German and other vessels, killing some of their crews, capturing others and pillaging their cargoes, on the pretext that they were enemies of France. This caused consternation in Flanders. Intense lobbying by the count of Flanders and the major Flemish towns persuaded King Charles V to release the ships, goods and men taken in the attack.[66] But the lack of French recognition which these seizures imply must have left the Scots feeling exceptionally insecure, both economically and politically. They were powerful arguments for a formal renewal and clarification of the alliance at the outset of the reign.

The next test of the alliance was also focused upon Flanders. After thirty years of relative peace, Flanders was rent by civil war between 1379 and 1385. Once more based in Ghent, the rebels rapidly overran the county, but most of it was won back for Louis de Male by a French army in 1382. As in previous revolts the rebels secured English support. An English force devastated much of western Flanders in the summer of 1383 and another was sent the following year to swell the Ghent garrison.

In January 1384 Count Louis de Male died and was succeeded by his son-in-law, Philip the Bold, duke of Burgundy.[67] Having bottled up the rebels in Ghent, Philip and the French government turned their attention to a highly ambitious plan for a two-pronged invasion of England. Preparations for this had begun as early as 1383, when Robert II had agreed to accept 1,000 French troops, arms and money, in the event of war with England.[68]

Military stores were prepared throughout northern France and a fleet was assembled in the Zwyn. The main army was to have landed in Kent, to move up through southern England, while a combined Franco-Scottish army invaded England from the north - much as Philip d'Alsace had planned two centuries before. In the event only the northern force was despatched. Jean de Vienne sailed from Sluys with an army of 1,500 men and extensive money and supplies for the Scots on 20 May 1385. The southern army was to have assembled and embarked two months later. But on the night of 14 July a large force from Ghent seized Damme, the town at the mouth of the Bruges canal, thus stopping all seaborne traffic with Bruges and rendering the Zwyn anchorages unsafe.

The planned invasion of Kent had to be abandoned and the army diverted to the siege of Damme. Consequently the Vienne expedition lost its purpose and the

---

[65]Quoted *verbatim* in the 1391 renewal, after the accession of Robert III: John Stuart and others, eds, *The Exchequer Rolls of Scotland* (23 vols, Edinburgh, 1878-1908), iii, xcvii-civ.

[66]Gilliodts, *Cartulaire*, i, no. 344.

[67]Richard Vaughan, *Philip the Bold* (London, 1962) (hereafter Vaughan, *Philip the Bold*), 19-31, 34-5.

[68]*APS*, xii, 19.

Scots found themselves facing England alone. Much of Berwickshire, Roxburgh-shire and Lothian was devastated and Edinburgh was sacked by an English army that would otherwise have been required to defend southern England. In such cir-cumstances, it is hardly surprising that the Scots soon turned hostile towards Vi-enne and his men, and that they concluded a truce with England as quickly as possible (almost at the moment that the Ghent rebels agreed to an armistice).[69] Set in context, the Scots' notorious behaviour in the campaign of 1385 appears much less rash and mean-spirited than is generally supposed.

After these unhappy events the Scottish government refused to be drawn into the next four years of ineffectual Anglo-French hostilities. A series of truces fol-lowed, which lasted until the early 1400s and included Scotland as a French ally, enabling Philip the Bold to consolidate his position in both Flanders and France.[70]

Since Philip intended to spend most of his time in Paris, as his nephew King Charles VI's principal adviser, he established a council to govern Flanders in his absence. One of the main responsibilities listed in its constitution was 'the protec-tion of the privileges granted to foreign merchants like the Scots, the Italians and the Hansards'.[71] The order is illuminating because the value of trade with both Italy and the German Hanse must have been considerably greater than with Scot-land. The precedence accorded to the Scots can only be explained in terms of the Franco-Scottish alliance, since by then the Scottish wool trade was in marked de-cline.

Space precludes any discussion of the complex issues surrounding this decline, or the upsurge in piracy which followed the renewal of Anglo-Scottish hostilities at the end of the fourteenth century.[72] Suffice it to note that they led to a break-down in Scoto-Flemish commercial relations in 1406, which was remedied by a further renewal of the Franco-Scottish alliance in 1407. In the process of this the magistrates of Bruges were dismissed by the duke of Burgundy; and the Flemish towns were forced to rescind all judicial measures taken against the Scots, to pro-vide compensation for Scottish losses in Flanders, and to extend Scottish com-mercial privileges. Similar pressure prevented a further breakdown of relations in 1416.[73]

That was almost the last occasion when the Auld Alliance could be invoked to protect Scottish interests in Flanders. The assassination of John the Fearless, duke of Burgundy, in 1419 - by supporters of the Dauphin, later Charles VII, and in the

---

[69]Vaughan, *Philip the Bold*, 35-6; Froissart, *Chroniques*, 11, xlv-lxxi; Nicholson, *Scotland*, 196-8; Alexander Grant, *Independence and Nationhood: Scotland 1306-1469* (London, 1984) (hereafter Grant, *Independence*), 41.

[70]Froissart, *Chroniques*, 11, lvii-lxii; 13, i-xxx; Vaughan, *Philip the Bold*, 37, 48-50.

[71]Richard Vaughan, *John the Fearless* (London, 1966), 19.

[72]The reasons are discussed in: Stevenson, 'Trade', 191-2; idem, 'Trade between Scotland and the Low Countries in the later Middle Ages' (Ph D, University of Aberdeen, 1982) (hereafter Stevenson, 'Thesis'), 21-6; David Ditchburn, 'Piracy and war at sea in late me-dieval Scotland', in *Scotland and the Sea*, ed. T C Smout (Edinburgh, 1992), 48-9.

[73]Stevenson, 'Thesis', 27-31, 42, 68-9.

Dauphin's presence - must have been considered in Scotland to be as great a disaster as it was in France. Many Scots, including the earls of Douglas and Mar, had served the duke of Burgundy; and, before news of the assassination reached Scotland, a Scottish army of 6,000 men had set sail, under the misapprehension that it would be joining a combined Dauphinist and Burgundian campaign to expel the English from northern France. Indeed, much of the army may have been sent to France in fulfilment of a treaty, made by the earl of Douglas in 1413, to supply the duke of Burgundy with a force of 4,000 men, if required (the earl's eldest son was one of the leaders of the Scottish expedition).[74]

After the death of John the Fearless, French interests collapsed in Flanders. His son Philip the Good created, for the first time, an essentially Netherlandish state by expanding Burgundian power into the patchwork of imperial counties and duchies to the north and east of Flanders.[75] The Flemish dimension of the Auld Alliance underwent a half-life thereafter, until a separate Scoto-Burgundian alliance was sealed in 1449. French sovereignty continued to be recognised in Flanders until after the accession of Charles the Bold.[76] But, in practice, the Scottish crown treated the Burgundian Netherlands as an independent power from the 1420s onwards and its dealings with the French government were correspondingly circumscribed. Only in the sixteenth century did the Franco-Scottish alliance regain its previous importance, by which time major direct trade links had been established between Scotland and France, following a further sharp decline in Scottish trade with Flanders.[77]

Unfashionable though it may be to stress the importance of economic affairs in the formulation of medieval foreign policy, that has to be the conclusion of this survey. Most of Scotland's export trade was geared to the Flemish market from the twelfth to the fifteenth century and the security of that trade was essential to the well-being of the Scottish economy. When subversion of Flanders became a key objective of English foreign policy, it posed a serious threat to both France and Scotland. Their interests merged: an anti-English alliance was a natural outcome.

English domination of Scotland also posed a serious threat to Flanders because the Flemish cloth industry would then have been dependent upon a monopolistic supplier (until Scottish wool was increasingly displaced by Spanish from the late fourteenth century onwards). Aid to Scotland was supplied by both the Flemings and the French government and was channelled through Flanders. Since Flanders provided the mainspring of the Auld Alliance, it should not be surprising that the main events in the alliance's early history can be linked so closely with Flemish affairs, or that periods of instability in Flanders were so damaging to the Scots.

---

[74]Vaughan, *John the Fearless*, 55, 259-61, 267-86; Grant, *Independence*, 47; Nicholson, *Scotland*, 249-50; Rymer, *Foedera*, IViii, 131-2.
[75]Richard Vaughan, *Philip the Good* (London, 1970), passim.
[76]Ibid., 19-20, 350-3; Richard Vaughan, *Charles the Bold* (London, 1973), 57-8, 73.
[77]Stevenson, 'Thesis', 74-85, 102-20, 262-3, 317-25, 330; Grant, *Independence*, 48-53; Jenny Wormald, *Court, Kirk, and Community: Scotland 1470-1625* (London, 1981), 6-7.

4

FROISSART AND SCOTLAND

Philippe Contamine

There is a variety of possible answers to the question of what knowledge of Scotland and the Scots the French of the late thirteenth and early fourteenth centuries might have had. In some regions of France at that time, and particularly in Paris, there were labourers and craftsmen, in significant numbers, whose very names ('l'Escot', 'Scot', 'l'Escote') show, or at least suggest, that they were of close or distant Scottish extraction. We can also see them appearing by the dozen in Parisian tax rolls dating from the reign of Philip the Fair (from 1292 to 1313).[1] Scottish students - and occasionally masters - belonged to the universities of Paris and Orléans, as is borne out by the creation of a Scots college in Paris in the first quarter of the fourteenth century.[2] Scottish troops served under Louis IX during his second crusade (1270).[3] At the start of the fourteenth century, Scotland was known for the export of wool, leather, cheese and tallow to Bruges.[4] Although the permanent or temporary residence of Scots in France resulted at least in indirect knowledge of their country, a much smaller number of Frenchmen were tempted to visit Scotland: the movement was largely one-way.

Here and there, reference is made to Scotland in literary works in French: for example, the *Roman de la Rose*.[5] Broadly speaking, the Scots would certainly have been considered to be Christians, but also to be foreigners who had come from afar. A case in point is this passage from Joinville about Saint Louis:

> The love he had for his people was apparent in his words to his eldest son during a very serious illness which afflicted him at Fontainebleau: 'My fine son', he said, 'I beseech you to make yourself loved by the people of your

---

[1] Cf. on this subject the documents published and studies undertaken by K Michaelson, especially his article, 'Les noms d'origine dans le rôle de taille parisien de 1313', in *Symbolæ philologicæ Gotoburgenses*, 56 (1950), 357-401.

[2] R Cazelles, *Paris de la fin du règne de Philippe Auguste à la mort de Charles V 1223-1380* (Paris, 1972), 70.

[3] Francisque-Michel, *Les Ecossais en France, les Français en Ecosse* (2 vols, London, 1862).

[4] Ch-M de La Roncière, Ph Contamine, R Delort, *L'Europe au Moyen Âge, documents expliqués*, iii, *Fin XIIIe - fin XV e siècle* (Paris, 1971), 205.

[5] Guillaume de Lorris and Jean de Meun, *Le Roman de la Rose*, ed. F Lecoy, vol.ii (Paris, 1973), 58, v.10124: here Scotland is presented as a country short of food.

kingdom, for I should prefer a Scot to come from Scotland and govern the people well and loyally than for you to govern badly for all to see'.[6]

Possibly the most topical passage on Scotland and its people is to be found in the famous encyclopedia, *De proprietatibus rerum*, composed by the Franciscan Barthélemy l'Anglais around 1235.[7] One book in this collection describes the 'provinces' (*provinciæ*), which constitute Scotland. Several extant manuscripts of this work were available for consultation in the world of French culture from the thirteenth century onwards, and more still at the start of the fourteenth century.[8] In the course of that century it was to be translated into English by John of Trevisa, and also into French, at the instigation of Charles V,[9] by Jean Corbechon, an Augustinian friar, who gave Barthélemy l'Anglais's work the title *Proprietaire des choses*. This translation, which achieved quite considerable success until well into the sixteenth century, is quoted here:

> Scotland is so called because of the Scots who live there and is the top part of the island of Great Britain; it is divided from England by arms of the sea and by rivers which flow between the two towards the west and the area opposite. It is entirely surrounded by the sea which separates it from Ireland. The Scots are very similar to the Irish in language,[10] custom and

---

[6]Jean, sire de Joinville, *Histoire de Saint Louis*, ed. and transl. N de Wailly (Paris, 1867), 12-13.

[7]*Cf.* the note *Bartholomaeus Anglicus* by C Hünenmörder and M Mückshoff, in *Lexikon des Mittelalters*, i (Munich and Zurich, 1980), col.1492-3.

[8]Some examples are: Ms.992 of the municipal library of Reims (18 June 1325: this ms. belonged to Saint-Remi Abbey in Reims; C Samaran and R Marichal, *Catalogue des manuscrits en écriture latine portant des indications de date, de lieu ou de copiste*, v, *Est de la France*, annotated by M Garand, M Mabille and J Metman, with the assistance of M-T Vernet, Paris, 1965, 285). Ms. lat.16098 in the Bibliothèque nationale, Paris (hereafter BN) (before 1306: '*Iste liber est pauperum magistrorum de Sorbona, ex legato magistri Godefridi de Fontibus*'; C Samaran and R Marichal, op. cit., iii, *Bibliothèque nationale, fonds latin (nos 8001 à 18613)*, under the direction of M-T d'Alverny, annotated by M Mabille, M-C Garand and D Escudier (Paris, 1974). Ms.172 in the municipal library of Clermont-Ferrand (1321: C Samaran and R Marichal, op. cit., vi, *Bourgogne, Centre, Sud-Est et Sud-Ouest de la France*, annotated by M Garand, M Mabille and J Metman (Paris, 1968, 165). Ms.696 in the Bibliothèque de l'Arsenal, Paris (1321: the ms. having belonged in the fourteenth century to the Carmelite friar Jean de Tostevilla; C Samaran and R Marichal, op. cit., i, *Musée Condé et bibliothèques parisiennes*, annotated by M Garand, J Metman and M-T Vernet, Paris, 1959, 107). Ms.3577 in the Bibliothèque Mazarine (1321: ibid., 313).

[9]The ms., which was in the collection of Charles V, is fr.22531 in the BN. Cf. lastly M Salvat, 'Quelques échos des rivalités franco-anglaises dans les traductions du *De proprietatibus rerum (XIIIe-XVe siècles)*', *Bien dire et bien apprendre*, 5 (1987), 101-9.

[10]Thus the relationship between Scottish and Irish Gaels was clearly perceived. None the less, it was not until the end of the fourteenth century that the difference between Gaelic-speaking Scotland and English-speaking Scotland was specified formally, in the *Chronica gentis Scotorum* by John of Fordun, priest of Aberdeen cathedral: 'They have two lan-

character, and are a courageous people, proud when confronting their enemies, who would rather die than be in servitude and say that it is a disgrace to die in one's bed, whereas it is a great honour to die killing one's enemies. The Scots are a frugal people who withstand hunger for a very long time, who rarely eat until sunset and live off milk and butter and cheese, fruit, meat and fish rather than off bread. They are a very attractive people in face and body, but their clothes render them very ugly,[11] and through their links to the English they have lost much of their original ways and their dress, and have changed for the better. All of their honesty comes from the English with whom they are in contact, whereas the wild Scots who inhabit the woods, like the Irish, take pride in keeping their former ways in dress, speech and lifestyle and are scornful towards all those who do not live as they do. The Scots want to be praised and valued above all other peoples, speak ill of all, and are envious of their neighbours. They laugh at everybody, reprove the ways of others and praise their own. They are not ashamed to lie and refuse to consider any person to be noble, good or hardy who is not one of their nation. They take pride in their misdeeds and dislike peace. In terms of the quality and abundance of its possessions, the beauty of its woods, rivers and fountains and the number of its animals, their region is not equal to England.[12]

Written by an Englishman, this picture clearly does not lack elements of criticism, but it is far from wholly negative. It portrays Scotland as a fairly poor country, and the Scots are perceived as a proud, brave, warlike people, who have received from England, for better or worse, *true* civilisation. One fact remains: even before the wars of independence, it is beyond doubt that the English considered the Scots to be a people different from themselves.

It is precisely at the moment at which Scotland found itself involved in its great national struggle against its powerful neighbour that French chroniclers, who had up to then been very non-committal about its history, began to refer to it quite regularly in their accounts in a more or less consistent fashion. The most striking example here is that of the *Chronique parisienne anonyme* [*Anonymous Parisian chronicle*]. This work, contemporaneous with Philip de Valois (1328-50), consists of two parts: the first, which covers the years 1206-1316, provides a

---

guages, Scottish and Teutonic: speakers of the latter language occupy the coastal regions and the lowlands, while the Scottish speakers inhabit the mountains and the outer islands'. (Cited in R Nicholson, *Scotland: the later middle ages*, Edinburgh, 1974, 206).

[11]Guibert de Nogent, in his *Gesta Dei per Francos* (early twelfth century) had previously observed the ridiculous character of the Scots' dress during the first crusade: 'Battalions of Scots, very proud of themselves at home and very cowardly in their country, may be seen descending bare-legged from their marshy borders, clothed in a leather coat with a pouch hanging from their shoulders, armed in a most ridiculous fashion, at least by our standards: they come to offer their services as faithful and devoted auxiliaries'. (Cited by Francisque-Michel, op. cit.).

[12]BN, fr. 22531, fo. 253r.

number of additions to the French chronicle of Guillaume de Nangis, a monk from Saint-Denis; the second, dealing with the years 1316-39, is original. Here, taking up around ten pages of the printed edition, we find the story of the whole development of the Anglo-Scottish conflict from its beginnings: 'Here you may learn and understand how and in what way the kingdom of Scotland belongs to the kings of England and why, how and when war broke out.'[13]

I want to present now an account of the most enjoyable, most attractive, most prolific, most imitated, best informed - if not the most precise - of the French chroniclers of the late Middle Ages: Jean Froissart. I do so particularly in that he was a native of Valenciennes, in Hainault region, which was outside the French kingdom at that time, and whilst he had experience of many western countries, by all accounts it was Flanders and Brabant, in short the future Low Countries, which were his preferred base. The views expressed by Froissart in a number of respects are indeed those of a northerner, in the French sense of the term.

It would be inappropriate to discuss here in detail relations between the king-doms of France and Scotland throughout the fourteenth century. It is enough to recall briefly the famous alliance of 1295 made with Philip IV the Fair and espe-cially the treaty of Corbeil in 1326 concluded by Robert I and Charles IV the Fair, the son of Philip IV. This treaty, which was subsequently renewed regularly until the sixteenth century, stipulated that the French would help and advise the Scots in the event of a war between England and Scotland and that, in return, the Scots would help the French in the event of an Anglo-French war.

We also know how, a few years later, David II had to take refuge in France with Philip VI de Valois, who welcomed him all the more willingly because they were on the eve of the outbreak of the tremendous conflict which was to become the Hundred Years War. For a time the king of France even envisaged a great expedition to Scotland (in 1337 or 1338), which would have involved transporting by sea 1,200 men-at-arms and 20,000 footsoldiers. Plans were made to order 200 large vessels, 60 fishing boats and 30 galleys. As Scotland was reputed to be a country lacking in resources, considerable quantities of provisions were to be sent: wheat, beans, meat, fish, wine - all the details are known - as well as military equipment, including no fewer than two million crossbow bolts.[14] In fact, the expedition, which was to last three months, was abandoned: instead, a small relief contingent was sent under the orders of Arnoul d'Audrehem.[15] In 1341, however, accompanied by the latter, David II returned to Scotland after a seven-year exile spent largely at Château Gaillard in Normandy.

---

[13]'Chronique parisienne anonyme de 1316 à 1339 précédée d'additions à la chronique française dite de Guillaume de Nangis (1206-1316)', ed. A Hellot, in *Mémoires de la So-ciété de l'histoire de Paris et de l'Ile-de-France*, 11 (1884), 78-87.

[14]'This is the estimate of what an attack by the Scottish army might cost in supplies and other necessities' (J Petit, *Essai de restitution des plus anciens mémoriaux de la Chambre des Comptes de Paris (Pater, Noster1, Noster2, Qui es in coelis, Croix, A1)*, Paris, 1899, 204-10).

[15]E Molinier, *Etude sur la vie d'Arnoul d'Audrehem, maréchal de France* (Paris, 1883), 8.

During the imprisonment of David II after his defeat at Neville's Cross in 1346, the French, who themselves were suffering extreme difficulties, attempted to help the Scots as far as their means allowed, financially and militarily: in 1355, a company of 50 men-at-arms was sent to Scotland under the command of Yon, sire de Garencières, who was entrusted with quite a substantial sum of money - 40,000 gold deniers - designed to persuade the Scots to break their truce with the English. In fact, the town of Berwick was taken by surprise, but not the castle, which held out.[16] After this, Garencières returned to France. Correspondingly, the earl of Douglas fought at Poitiers the following year alongside King John.[17] In 1357, David II was freed by the treaty of Berwick for a ransom of some £66,000 sterling, payable over ten years (roughly a tenth of the ransom anticipated for King John, which is an indication of the resources generally attributed at the time to the monarchies of France and Scotland, and, more generally, to the two kingdoms).

The treaty of Berwick led to a cease-fire of 27 years up to 1384. By the treaty of Calais (1360), King John the Good promised to break his alliance with Scotland; in fact, this treaty was not carried out.

In 1371 David II died, without a direct descendant. His nephew Robert the Steward succeeded him as Robert II. He was a cautious individual, and quite indifferent to knightly values. He declined the offers of financial and military aid made by Charles V in the context of the resumption of Anglo-French conflict, which did not prevent the Scots from increasing the number of their attacks on the north of England, although the truces remained officially in force. In 1384, a small expedition left France under the command of Geoffroy de Charny. The following year, a plan was devised between Robert II and the young king of France, Charles VI - in reality his uncles, the most powerful of whom was Philip the Bold, duke of Burgundy. A French fleet was to disembark in the south of England, while the Scots would launch a powerful attack in the north. In fact, this sea expedition was abandoned. But a relatively large French relief force disembarked in Scotland under the orders of Jean de Vienne, admiral of France.[18] Misunderstanding, distrust and discord between the allies soon emerged. Perhaps there was a divergence of strategy: the Scots wished above all to recapture the fortresses still held by the English in the south of the kingdom, while the French hoped to devastate the northern English counties in a spectacular and profitable expedition. Richard II organised a powerful counter-attack and the French went home in fury, disappointment and pique. So ended what Froissart calls, in the language of the period, 'li rese

---

[16]*Chronique normande du XIVe siècle*, ed. A and E Molinier (Paris, 1882), 109.

[17]Froissart, *Chroniques*, ed. Kervyn, vol. x (Brussels, 1870), 407-28 (see below, p. 52, n. 37). He had already taken part in the so-called battle of Buironfosse in 1339 (ibid., vol. iii, Brussels, 1867, 431).

[18]Terrier de Lorray, *Jean de Vienne, amiral de France, 1341-96: Etude historique suivie de documents inédits pour servir à l'histoire de la marine française au XIVe siècle* (Paris, 1878).

d'Escoce' (the Scottish campaign).[19] Certainly the comments made by Jean de
Vienne's companions did not help to improve the reputation in France of the
Scots. From then on they kept clear of the Anglo-French disputes. They did, how-
ever, put to good use the political difficulties faced by Richard II by invading
England and gaining victory at Otterburn in 1388. In the following year Scotland
was successfully included in the long-lasting truce agreed at that time between
France and England.

We can here end this survey, which shows Scotland's vested interest in being
actively involved in the Anglo-French negotiations in such a way that an eventual
reconciliation would not work out to her detriment, but which also shows the inef-
ficiency and even the weakness of the Franco-Scottish alliance. In particular Scotland did not constitute for France the 'back-door alliance' one might imagine. It
remains none the less true that the attitude of the Scots was very often modelled
on that of the French: thus, throughout most of the period of the Great Schism, the
king of Scotland acknowledged the same pope as the king of France, just as did
his other allies, Savoy and Castille.

The events which constituted the fabric of Franco-Scottish history in the fourteenth century are alluded to by chroniclers from the world of French culture in a
more or less detailed and sustained fashion. Most of them, in fact, simply report
the facts drily, without commentary or criticism.[20] And yet, even before Froissart,
whose work stands in sharp contrast to this practice, the name of another chronicler whose ideas he took up, deserves note as a primary source. Jean le Bel, a noble and warlike canon of the cathedral of Saint-Lambert of Liège, who was born at
the end of the thirteenth century and died in 1369, wrote between 1352 and 1361
a chronicle in French covering the years 1326-61.[21] As a companion of John of
Hainault, Jean le Bel took part in Edward III's Scottish expedition of 1327.
Having assembled at York, the English army penetrated Scotland as far as Aberdeen, while the Scots, in keeping with their usual tactics, retreated deep into their
impenetrable forests. The invaders were forced to suffer hunger and cold. They
retreated to York after a fruitless campaign, having failed to achieve the victory
they had anticipated. This expedition, though, has brought us, by means of Jean le
Bel, a quite detailed form of war diary. In it he mentions 'the great forest which is
called Gendours. The wild Scots there consider that the forest is so mixed and so
full of stretches of marshland that nobody dares to enter it unless he knows its
routeways very well'.[22] We find here the expression 'wild forests' used to describe
an entire area of the Scottish landscape, but one which is by no means character-

---

[19]From the German *Reise*, meaning journey.

[20]This is true of the *Chronographia regum Francorum*, ed. H Moranvillé (3 vols, Paris,
1891-7), which covers the period 1270 to 1405.

[21]Jean le Bel, *Chronique*, ed. J Viard and E Déprez (2 vols, Paris, 1904-5).

[22]Ibid., i, 273. Gendours is probably Jedburgh Forest, in the Borders. Le Bel's chronology
is somewhat confused in the above passages, which may relate to events of 1333 (ibid., i,
105).

ised by forests nowadays.[23] He describes 'good king Robert' pursued by Edward I's pack of hounds into its most secluded retreats: 'good king Edward had him chased through those great forests for three or four days by dogs and bloodhounds to seek him out and wear him down, but he could not be found'.[24] This 'wild Scotland' not only had very uneven ground, but also abounded in potholes, bogs and marshes, stones and boulders. As for the useful parts of Scotland, the Lowlands, these were for him the 'flat lands of Scotland'. During this campaign, he saw a good many castles and towns: his description of these as 'enclosed by good moats and strong palisades',[25] that is to say, not yet by stone walls, is confirmed by modern-day archaeologists of medieval Scotland. Is he referring to a personal recollection when he says of the town of Saint-John (St Johnston, now Perth) that 'good salmon is to be had' there? The site of Edinburgh castle is certainly familiar to him:

> Eldebourch was the strongest and was on a high rock from which all the surrounding land could be seen. And the climb was so difficult that it was hardly possible to reach it without resting two or three times, or without a half-laden horse.[26]

There is in particular a long passage where he interrupts his narrative to talk 'of the way the Scots are and how well they can fight'. Each detail has its importance here, every word counts:

> The Scots are bold and tough and very energetic in battle, and at that time they were quite unafraid of the English. I do not know how true that is now. And when they want to invade the English kingdom, they lead their army for twenty or thirty-two miles, day and night, which would astonish those unfamiliar with their habits. It is certain that when they set out to penetrate into England, they are on horseback, one and all, except the camp-followers who go on foot; the knights and esquires ride rouncies, and all the other common folk are on ponies. And they take no wheeled transport, on account of the various mountains which have to be crossed in that country, nor do they take any supplies of bread or wine, as their custom in wartime is such and their austerity is so considerable that they survive easily for quite long periods on half-cooked meat, without bread, and on good river water, without wine. And they have no need for pots or cauldrons, for they cook their meat in the animal's hide, after skinning it. As they know that they will find plenty of animals in the country to which they are bound, they carry no provisions except that they all carry a large flat stone

---

[23]'Actually forests - extensive tree-covered areas, as distinct from the treeless "deer forests" of Scottish phrase - are practically absent in Scotland; wooded tracts are of no great extent and are scattered, save in so far as they appear mainly upon the eastern and southern borders of the Highlands' (*Encyclopædia Britannica*, 20, Chicago, 1948, 146).
[24]Jean le Bel, op. cit., i, 111.
[25]Ibid., i, 110.
[26]Ibid., i, 276-7.

between their saddle and their 'peneau' [a small cushion placed under the saddle-flap?] and tie a sack full of oatmeal at their backs, so that, when they have eaten so much of that ill-cooked meat that their stomachs feel infirm and weak, they put the flat stone on the fire and soak a little of their oatmeal in water when the stone is hot, and make a little biscuit like an *oublie* (little cake) and eat it to soothe the stomach. And this is why it is not surprising that they make longer marches than other people since they are all on horseback, except the common folk, and take neither wheeled transport nor other trappings, as you have heard.[27]

Even though Froissart, in the prologue to his *Chronicles*, makes no attempt to hide the fact that they are based on the writings of Jean le Bel, the latter's work remained practically unknown for centuries. It was only in the mid-nineteenth century that it was discovered in one single manuscript in the library at Châlons-sur-Marne and subsequently edited.[28] This meant that many elements previously attributed to Froissart were in fact those of his predecessor, including the passage just quoted.

Froissart's *Chronicles* cover the main part of the fourteenth century and seek to recount to a readership of kings, princes, lords and knights, not only the 'great wars' fought by the kings of France and England, but also all the more or less closely related conflicts, and they constitute a world of their own. The characters run into hundreds. Colourful anecdotes abound. Froissart has an undeniable power to evoke, a feel for dialogue and vivid expressions. He likes to surprise his audience, entertain it, keep it on tenterhooks. He easily keeps several plots going at once, abandoning one subject for another before picking it up again. He is not averse to flashbacks or to digressions. In short, he is an artist, a writer - a poet, moreover, in a highly esteemed work in verse - as much as he is an historian. This is just as well, as scholars since the nineteenth century have not been reluctant to criticise his non-existent or erroneous chronology, his questionable geography, his credulity, his relative disdain for official documents, and, furthermore, the superficial and one-sided character of his historical approach, the 'artlessness of his social and political ideas', his snobbery rather in the vein of a Marcel Proust, not to mention the archaic quality of a language which has even been termed rustic. It has even been said of him that the sound of the story has caused him to forget its meaning. It should be added that, despite his flaws, Froissart always took

---

[27]Ibid., i, 50-2. Cf. Froissart, op. cit., i (Société de l'histoire de France, Paris, 1869), 208: 'They usually run into battle and when they have done this and think that men are coming towards them, they retreat': the perennial tactic of the weak. Hereafter I shall use both Kervyn de Lettenhove's edition of Froissart's *Chroniques* (25 vols. in 26, Brussels, 1867-7) (hereafter Kervyn), and the edition of the same *Chroniques* by the Société de l'histoire de France (15 vols, Paris, 1869-1975) (hereafter SHF). Both editions, designed according to different principles, have their merits: the Société de l'histoire de France edition, better in philological terms, stops at the end of the third book, while Kervyn's edition includes book iv. The former has no index, whereas the latter has one.
[28]By J Polain (Mons, 1850).

the trouble to collect new information from witnesses, some of it possibly questionable, on subjects he had already tackled, and that he was also keen to adapt his writing to the tastes of the time and bring it up to date. He produced several editions of the first books of his *Chronicles*, each of which was more or less a reflection of his attitudes at that time or perhaps of the political opinions of his patrons. Broadly speaking, in spite of everything, he was a native of Valenciennes in Hainault, outwith the French kingdom, and as such he was reputed to be significantly more favourable towards the cause of Edward III than to that of the Valois. Whatever the case, 'sire Jean Froissart', a man of the church but apparently uninterested in spiritual matters, and even less in theology, 'good old Froissart', as Montaigne says with just a hint of condescension, is a first class source, and one who is not only amazingly lively but also - as even the most superficial reading will suggest - much more varied than has often been said. Thus, in his account of the conflict between Louis de Male and the Flemish towns, this supposedly uncritical and old-fashioned spokesman of knightly values, this habitué of princely courts who was always ready to seize upon the scandals and good stories doing the rounds, is also able to do full justice to the demands of the bourgeoisie while presenting their political agenda in its full breadth and dignity.[29] All in all, his works are not lacking in humanity.

What Froissart says of Scotland is especially noteworthy as he made one, rather long stay there. Born in 1337, at the age of 19 he set sail for England where he was well received by Queen Philippa of Hainault - a compatriot of sorts, who had married Edward III. On his return, he undertook a chronicle in verse (unfortunately lost) of the wars of his day. When his piece was finished, he returned across the English Channel in 1361 to offer it to Philippa of Hainault. He remained in England for several years:

> God has favoured me in that I have been of the household of King Edward III and the noble queen his wife, Madame Philippa de Haynaut, whom in my youth I served as clerk, and to whom I offered fine compositions and treatises on love.[30]

It was at the instigation and with the written recommendation of the queen that he went to Scotland in 1365. For the love of his 'lady', the barons of that country gave

---

[29]Literature on Froissart is obviously extensive, and there can be no question of examining it here. I shall merely refer to the note of D Hoeges in the *Lexikon des Mittelalters*, iv (Munich and Zurich, 1989), col.984-5, which cites the editions and principal works, and to the *Dictionnaire des lettres françaises, Le Moyen Age*, new edition, ed. G Hasenohr and Michel Zink (Paris, s.d., 1992), 771-6 (note by Sylvie Lefèvre and Gilette Tyl-Labori). See also *Froissart: Historian*, ed. J J N Palmer (Woodbridge, 1981); and, more specifically, E Baumgartner, 'Ecosse et Ecossais, l'entrelais de la fiction et de l'histoire dans les *Chroniques* et le *Méliador* de Froissart', in *L'image de l'autre européen, XVe-XVIIe siècle*, ed. J Dufournet, A C Faiorato and A Redondo (Paris, 1992), 11-21.
[30]Cited in Kervyn de Lettenhove, *Froissart, étude littéraire sur le XIVe siècle* (Paris, 1857).

him a warm welcome, but especially so King David II, who had him as a house-hold guest for fifteen weeks, or a 'quarter of a year'. Froissart questioned him several times, especially on the subject of the battle of Neville's Cross, all the more easily as the king, who had been 'brought up in France in his youth', had an excellent command of French. This of course explains the interest of Froissart's account of this battle, in which, on the Scottish side, there were 'three thousand soldiers in armour, knights and horsemen, as well as thirty thousand men of other kinds, all of them mounted on battle horses, as no-one goes on foot in Scotland, but everyone on horseback'.[31] Amongst these innumerable troops - all of Scotland had been mobilised - there was, according to our chronicler, the contingent of a certain 'Jean des Adultilles, who governs the wild Scots', who obey him alone. In another passage, Froissart presents Scotland in its entirety as feudally dependent on the king of England, 'with the exception of those islands which mark the meeting place of Ireland and Norway, which are named the wild Scottish islands and have their own lord who is called Jehan des Adultilles':[32] This would mean that for Froissart wild Scotland, the only fully independent one, was first and foremost the Scotland of the Western Isles.

Let us return to his account of the battle. It was bitterly fought, since 'the Scots are a very good and hardy people who at that time felt profound hatred towards the English for the great harm they had done them'.[33] Even so, Froissart cannot help finding them presumptuous, too 'hot, fiery and proud', for considering themselves strong enough to defeat the English, even at the odds of one man against four. He provides details on the favourite weapon of the Scots: they 'usually carry axes with which they strike hard; and everyone, however well armed, certainly falls to the ground if he is hit firmly'.[34] 'As for the use of the bow, the Scots hardly practise it, and instead they all carry axes over their shoulders and advance quickly into battle and with these axes strike hard'.[35] Froissart also relates the following anecdote: in the battle, David II was wounded in the head by two English arrows. The arrowheads stuck, but 'with much effort, one of the arrowheads was removed through his nose'. The other one, by contrast, remained in place as long as he lived, and 'at the new moon, he usually had severe headaches'.[36]

In the king's company, Froissart visited 'the greater part of his realm,' 'as a result of which visit I learned and admired much about the ways of the Scots'. He also spent two weeks 'as a guest of Earl William of Douglas[37] [...] in a castle five

---

[31]Froissart, iv, SHF, 19-20. Cf. Jean le Bel, op. cit., i, 126: 'All the common people of Scotland use small horses when they go into battle'.
[32]Froissart, ii, Kervyn, 279. This is presumably John, lord of the Isles, active from the mid-1330s until his death about 1387.
[33]Froissart, iv, SHF, 229.
[34]Ibid., 236.
[35]Froissart, xv, SHF, 122. It is interesting to note that in the fifteenth century, at least in the armies of Charles VII, the Scots were considered above all to be archers.
[36]Froissart, iv, SHF, 235-6.
[37]The same one as had fought at Poitiers alongside King John

miles from Haindeburg which is known locally as Dalquest'.[38] Many years later, he still remembered the earl's children: a son, James, who died at Otterburn, and a daughter, Blanche. But, he adds, 'there were still more of Douglas's people in Scotland, as I have seen up to five brothers who bore the surname Douglas, all of them esquires in the household of King David of Scotland, and sons of a knight called Sir James Douglas'.[39]

All of this explains how he was in a position to verify, confirm and elaborate the account of Jean le Bel, besides, of course, adding to it the part after 1361.

Like Jean le Bel, Froissart mentions the 'good salmon' of St Johnston, adding that they could be found 'in great profusion' and that this was a 'good market town placed on a river called the Tay', or 'on a sea inlet'.[40] To describe the Scottish countryside, Froissart uses virtually the same vocabulary as Jean le Bel: a precursor of Walter Scott, he speaks of mists, mountains, difficult glens, of 'marshes, potholes and other bogs', 'rocks', 'dense woods', 'large areas of marshland and tall forests', all this inhabited by 'deer or hinds or other wild beasts which flourished in these woods and wild countryside'. On several occasions, he mentions the 'great forest of Gedours', 'strong, wild and immeasurably large, where no stranger would dare to tread', 'forests uninhabitable by those who do not know the country' and 'difficult to ride through'.[41] This can only be the forest of Jedburgh, in what are now the borders, which suggests that for him 'wild Scotland' meant not only the entire north-western part of the country and the outlying islands, but also all the land not under cultivation or used for pasture. Distinct from this wild Scotland are the 'flatlands of Scotland'[42] (he even goes so far as to speak of 'mild Scotland'),[43] which stretch from the English border up to Aberdeen.

He emphasises the rudimentary nature of Scottish rural dwelling habits. Hence, it does not matter whether the English set fire to them, 'as the Scots do not build houses of great strength: they make one fit for habitation according to their custom quite easily in less than five days'.[44] 'We rebuilt one cheaply, we only spent three days rebuilding it, as we used four or six beams and branches for the roof'.[45] They attached similarly small value to their furniture: for this reason it was not uncommon for them to burn their own houses to prevent the English from taking shelter in them, or to gather their abundant stocks of cattle and take refuge in the wild areas where they could not be pursued.

---

[38]Dalkeith, to the south-east of Edinburgh.
[39]Froissart, xv, SHF, 141, 172.
[40]Froissart, ii, Kervyn, 263; iii, Kervyn, 434; and vi, Kervyn, 21.
[41]Froissart, xxiv, Kervyn, 383-4.
[42]Froissart, ii, Kervyn, 281.
[43]Froissart, xi, SHF, 275.
[44]Froissart, iii, Kervyn, 234.
[45]Froissart, xi, SHF, 214-15. Elsewhere six or eight beams are mentioned.

Like Jean le Bel, Froissart comments on the very small number of Scottish towns surrounded by a stone wall. 'There are very few walled towns in Scotland.'[46] He agrees nevertheless that Dunfermline is a 'very beautiful small town', a 'good and well enclosed town', with - and this is quite accurate - 'an abbey of black monks[47] which is quite large and beautiful and which possesses the common burial-place of all the kings of Scotland'.

Another place he describes is Aberdeen, 'a city which lies on the sea and is at the entrance to wild Scotland'.[48] But it was Edinburgh above all which impressed our chronicler. He not only reiterates Jean le Bel's comment on the 'high mountain' on which Edinburgh Castle is built, but also details accurately both the size of the town and its role: introduced as a 'haven [port]', it is a 'large, rich town and not at all enclosed'. 'Haindebourc, the principal town of Scotland, where the king spends most of his time when he is in the country'. 'Edinburgh, for all that the king of Scotland has his seat there, as if Paris were in Scotland [variant: as if Edinburgh were to Scotland what Paris is to France], is not even a town like Tournai or Valenchiennes,[49] since there are not four hundred houses in the whole town'.[50]

It goes without saying that castles, with their double function, military and residential, greatly attract his attention. His overall analysis is revealing: even though there is, he says, 'a great profusion of castles', they are ten times less numerous than in England, which is quite a good observation. Moreover, their strategic role differs from that which they possess elsewhere, since 'the Scots have a habit when they are aware that the English are approaching [...]: they make camp and do not hide their leaders in their castles; and say that a knight shut up inside can do no more than any other man'.[51] In short, their instinctive - and calculated - reaction is to refuse siege warfare, and not give in to what has been called the siege obsession so common in the middle ages, in order to be able to carry forward a war of movement.

Many castles are not only named by Froissart but described as if he had seen them. Roxburgh, situated right on the border with England, is described as a 'beautiful castle': 'It is a castle on a rock surrounded by flat countryside and has quite deep moats, but very little of the water which falls into them remains there'.[52] Dumbarton is described as 'a very strong castle on the border of wild Scotland',[53] which is geographically correct. The description becomes even more graphic for Dalkeith Castle, 'twenty miles from Edinburgh', where, as we have seen, he was the guest of the earl of Douglas:

---

[46]Froissart, ii, Kervyn, 281.
[47]In other words, Benedictines.
[48]Froissart, ii, Kervyn, 283.
[49]His home town!
[50]Froissart, xxiv, Kervyn, 286-7.
[51]Froissart, ii, Kervyn, 281-2.
[52]Ibid., 288.
[53]Ibid., 272-3.

The castle of Dalquest is not very large but is well provided with rooms and buildings constructed in a large square covered tower[54] which need not fear any attack by machines of war or catapults. It sits on a small, well defined rock surrounded by a stream which is not very big except after abundant rainfall. And the lower court [bailey] is a little above.[55]

On Stirling Castle, Froissart has the following to report:

Struvelin is a beautiful strong castle, situated on a rock which is high on all sides except one. It is twenty leagues from Edinburgh, twelve from Dunfermline and thirty from the St Johnston (i.e. Perth).[56] It was one of the castles known in the days of King Arthur and called Smandon [correctly 'Snowdon'], and the knights of the Round Table used to return to it, as I was told when I stayed in the castle for three days with King David of Scotland.[57]

This is not the only allusion to the fabulous tales of the Round Table. On the subject of the abbey of Black Ader, 'a large abbey of black monks', Froissart explains that, 'at the time of King Arthur it was called the Black Combe because it lies in a valley and on a black stream which used to divide Scotland from England. And this abbey is guaranteed exemption from the war between the two countries (for which it has a charter)'.[58] Here too is perhaps a personal recollection: it is tempting to imagine that the worthy monks had shown him the charter in question, which guaranteed their safety in the event of war.

'Scotland is not France'.[59] Froissart's Scotland is certainly a poor country, its economy above all pastoral, almost devoid of a craft industry. Whenever the English attack, they have no choice but to take all they need with them. 'It is very difficult to find iron to shoe horses or leather to make harnesses, saddles or bridles. These things come to them ready made from Flanders and when the supply has run out, they have nothing'.[60] Even food is frugal: 'a little beer', 'oatmeal and barley bread'. Froissart stresses the discontented condescension of the French knights who accompanied Jean de Vienne to Scotland in 1385. Very poorly received by

---

[54]Similar *Wohntürme* (tower-houses), often in ruins, still remain in Scotland today.

[55]Froissart, ii, Kervyn, 294.

[56]This is all more or less correct (a league is about 2-3 miles): from Stirling to Edinburgh, thirty-seven miles; from Stirling to Dunfermline, a mere thirty or so; from Stirling to Perth, twenty-eight miles.

[57]Froissart, ii, Kervyn, 312-13.

[58]Ibid., 264. The reference must be to Coldingham Priory, Berwickshire, which was the only Benedictine monastery in the Border area. It was situated, however, about 7 miles from the Blackadder Water.

[59]Froissart, xxiv, Kervyn, 285.

[60]Froissart, x, Kervyn, 336. Evidence from archaeology suggests that Froissart's critical remarks here, which relate to aristocratic possessions, are somewhat exaggerated. Excavations have revealed active leather industries and metalworking. (See Elizabeth Ewan, *Townlife in Fourteenth-century Scotland*, Edinburgh, 1990, 30-1, 33-4.)

most of their hosts, they habitually exclaimed: 'To what sort of Prussia have our leaders brought us?'[61] Their possessions were prey to pillage at the hands of the country's 'brigands'. Even the Scottish king was nothing but a sorry gentleman: 'A big fellow with red, flayed eyes (they looked like silk), which showed that he was not a very skilful man in battle'. 'A weary knight'.[62] His predecessor, David II, when showing some French knights around his kingdom, is reported to have said: 'They saw a poor country full of woods and mist. They joked about it, laughed amongst themselves and said: "No wealthy man can be lord of a country like this".'[63]

Raids and brawls were common currency among the Scots: even in times of truce, whenever they encountered the English at fairs and markets, 'rogues' and 'wretches' in varying states of drunkenness would fight, rob, injure or kill one another. 'Some Scots are great thieves.'[64]

Against England, these people were extremely warlike, capable, despite their small number, of assembling impressive armies as every single one of them was a powerful fighter: 'The Scots are just as fond of war with the English as they are of peace, especially the Scottish *bachelerie*' - that is to say, the young noblemen. In relations with the English, 'the entire kingdom of Scotland' was in 'deadly war and deadly hatred'.[65]

Much influenced by the story of the 1385 campaign passed on by the French, Froissart went so far as to dub the Scots a people 'without honour' - the supreme insult, to the medieval way of thinking - a 'wild' people, 'too envious of the good of others'.[66] In these terms he confirms the opinion of Jean de Vienne on their military power. Admittedly they were strong enough in number, but among them 'men of substance', 'knights and esquires', were few, with no more than 500 lances. The remainder - 30,000 men - were so poorly armed that 'against English archers or armed men they would not last'.[67] All in all, their 'nature', consisting of envy towards foreigners, is close to the 'nature' of the English, according to common Valois propaganda.

These are extreme remarks, provoked by circumstantial irritation. For, a little further on, in his lengthy description of the battle of Otterburn, Froissart can only pay tribute to the Scots as hardy, untiring in battle, but courteous and generous in victory. Here again, without taking sides, he hides behind the witnesses he has consulted.

The image Froissart gives of Scotland and the Scots is far from complete. On a number of aspects he remains non-committal or silent. His description is deliber-

---

[61]Ibid.
[62]Froissart, viii, Kervyn, 243.
[63]Froissart, iii, Kervyn, 435.
[64]Froissart, xiii, Kervyn, 204.
[65]Froissart, ix, Kervyn, 123.
[66]Froissart, x, Kervyn, 404.
[67]Ibid.

ately set in a warlike context, as he means to deal with the nature and conditions of war. And yet, even within these limitations, his opinion, balanced though it may be, is far from wholly favourable. Of course, he sees himself as an impartial, neutral observer, keenly recording the evidence he can accumulate from all sides. His fundamental aim is to describe rather than to judge. But his opinion, shared by many - it was held, as we have seen, by Barthélemy l'Anglais - is that Scotland is a thankless, forbidding land where it is unwise for an army to spend the winter. Apart from their undeniable and spectacular bravery and their 'shrewdness' in combat, the Scots do show themselves to be presumptuous. And above all, they retain that element of savagery which makes them less inviting than the aristocratic Anglo-French milieu in which Froissart feels so entirely at ease.

In his exposition, at least two gaps may at first sight appear surprising. Firstly, he makes hardly a single reference to the fundamental source of the Scots' behaviour: their desire for freedom when they are threatened, if not with colonisation, then at least with servitude at the hands of their powerful and dynamic neighbours. And secondly, Froissart is very non-committal on the subject of the continuance of diplomatic links between the kings of France and Scotland. On no account could he be accused of celebrating the 'auld alliance'.

In fact, even if his political development caused him to change more or less from an anglophile into a francophile, Froissart remained to the very end an admirer of England and its leaders, if not its people. Consequently, it must not have seemed strange to him that English power should try to spread into Scotland, as this, in his view, was the legitimate influence of a civilised realm over regions which were still largely uncivilised and, in current parlance, under-developed.

Moreover, one might think that the friendly links between France and Scotland did not yet exist in the fourteenth century and that it was not until the fifteenth century that they appeared in official phraseology and, significantly, in codes of behaviour. If this was the case, then Froissart's silence would have value as evidence. This, however, would be to draw the wrong conclusions. Despite misunderstandings, these links, formed to foster the common, not to say interconnected, concerted struggle against the English enemy, were already firmly in existence at any rate at the end of the fourteenth century. The most explicit text to my knowledge is the following. As an appendix to the continuation of the *Chronique Martinienne*, a monk of the abbey of Corbie, Etienne de Conty, wrote in 1400 a 'short essay' (*brevis tractatus*) on the different kingdoms and peoples of Latin Christendom. Of all foreign nations, it is for Scotland (which he imagines two or three times smaller than England) and the Scots that he reserves the most wholehearted praise: '*Item*, that in the said kingdom there are good warriors, hardy and faithful to their king, and the Scots have always liked the French and the French the Scots, and they are catholic men, towards God and Holy Church, and always in the catholic faith, and in war they sided with the French'.[68]

---

[68]Ph Contamine, *La France aux XIVe et XVe siècles: Hommes, mentalités, guerre et paix* (London, 1981): see the first chapter of this volume, 'Une interpolation de la Chronique martinienne: le *Brevis Tractatus* d'Etienne de Conty, official de Corbie (d.1413)'.

Of course one may deplore the fact that the view which Froissart and his like held of Scotland and the Scots at the end of the middle ages was so often one-sided or even contemptuous. Without passing judgement on the bias suggested by such an attitude, it is enough to observe that it presents many analogies with con-temporaneous views of Ireland, also thought to be a wild land, and of Wales.[69]

---

[69]A French version of this text was published under the title 'Froissart et l'Ecosse' in the *Actes du colloque 'Des chardons et des lys': Souvenir et présence en Berry de la vieille alliance franco-écossaise* (Bourges, Conseil général du Cher, 1992), 30-44. It is a pleasure for me to offer all my thanks to Dr Grant G Simpson, who with his usual admirable scrutiny has supervised the translation into English of the present text.

5

THE PLACE OF GUELDERS
IN SCOTTISH FOREIGN POLICY, c.1449-c.1542

David Ditchburn

For most of the medieval period Scottish contacts with the disparate collection of Netherlandish provinces focused almost exclusively on the southerly and westerly maritime regions of the Low Countries. It was with Flanders and Artois, and latterly with Zeeland, Holland and Brabant, that Scottish contacts were at their greatest. It was to the ports, markets and fairs of these provinces that Scottish merchants journeyed. It was also with these provinces, closest in geographical proximity to Scotland, that political contacts, frequently spawned by commercial interests, developed. And, with the foundation of the university of Louvain in 1425, it was also to one of these provinces, Brabant, that Scottish students studying in the Low Countries headed. Beyond the coastal fringe of Netherlandish provinces, Scottish contacts were altogether more tenuous and for most of the medieval period Scottish links with Guelders, one of the more easterly Netherlandish provinces, were at most sporadic. In the later thirteenth century the count of Guelders was briefly involved in the wrangle over unpaid dues owing on account of his wife's earlier marriage to Alexander III's son.[1] A Scottish embassy was dispatched to Guelders in the mid-1330s on a mission of uncertain purpose.[2] And there is meagre evidence from the fourteenth and fifteenth centuries pointing at very occasional trading links between Scotland and Guelders.[3]

From the mid-fifteenth century, however, Guelders began to impinge more directly on Scottish foreign policy. The emergence of this Gueldrian dimension to

---

[1] Rijksarchief Gent, Chartes des Comtes de Flandre, Fonds St Genois, no.409. This and other documents relating to the dower lands granted to Prince Alexander's wife, Margaret of Flanders, are published in J Stevenson, ed., *Documents Illustrative of the History of Scotland 1286-1306* (Edinburgh, 1870), i, nos. 4, 5, 8, 9, 17, 24, 70, 71, 246, 248, 315, 322, 323.

[2] J Stuart et al., eds., *The Exchequer Rolls of Scotland* (Edinburgh, 1878-1908) (hereafter *ER*), i, pp.cxlvi, cxlvii, 450. Eleanor, the elder sister of Joan, David II's wife, was married to the count of Guelders in 1332. The Scottish mission to Guelders was possibly related to a request sent by Edward III of England to the duke of Guelders in 1336, which sought the cessation of trade between Guelders and Scotland. (T Rymer, ed., *Foedera, Conventiones, Litterae et Cuiuscunque Generis Acta Publica* (Record Commission, 1816-69), ii, 950). On Gueldrian involvement in Edward III's Scottish wars, see R Nicholson, *Edward III and the Scots* (Oxford, 1965), 213, 218.

[3] E.g. *Calendar of Close Rolls, 1339-41* (London, 1901), 135; D Macpherson, ed., *Rotuli Scotiae in Turri Londinensi...* (London, 1814-19) (hereafter *Rot.Scot.*), i, 569; *Urkundenbuch der Stadt Lübeck* (Lübeck, 1843-1905), vii, no.808.

Scottish foreign policy arose as a result of the marriage between James II and Mary, the daughter of Arnold, duke of Guelders.[4] This marriage, celebrated at Holyrood Abbey on 3 July 1449, established a dynastic bond between the houses of Stewart and Egmont, a bond whose repercussions were a consideration, albeit a perhaps minor consideration, in the formulation of Scottish foreign policy for the next century. The decision of James II to choose a bride from a small Netherlandish duchy with which Scotland had traditionally sustained neither close diplomatic nor close commercial relations is not as surprising as it perhaps, at first sight, appears. During the king's minority attempts were made to arrange foreign marriages for all six of James I's unmarried children, following the precedent set by the late king, when, in 1428, he had agreed to a marriage between his eldest daughter, Margaret, and the French Dauphin, the future Louis XI. In addition to the marriages contracted by James II, Isabella married Francis, son of the duke of Brittany; Mary married the son of the influential Burgundian magnate and lord of Vere, Wolfaert Borselen; and Eleanor married Sigismund, duke of Austria-Tyrol. The search for continental husbands for the two remaining Stewart sisters, Annabella and Joan, ultimately proved fruitless, though both had travelled to France in search of husbands and Annabella, from 1444 until 1456, was affianced to Louis of Geneva, the second son of the duke of Savoy.[5] In stark contrast to the policy of the early Stewart monarchs, continental matrimonial alliances appear to have become a voguish desideratum for James I's children.

The initiative behind this radical departure in Scottish matrimonial policy seems to have been orchestrated principally not at the Scottish court, but, rather, at the French court. Margaret's marriage to the Dauphin was suggested by the French. Charles VII of France was responsible for arranging Eleanor's marriage and attempting to arrange that of Joan. Brittany was allied to France when the Bretons made overtures about the hand of Isabella, while Annabella's betrothal to Louis of Geneva occurred within months of the agreement of an offensive-defensive alliance between the duke of Savoy and Annabella's brother-in-law, the Dauphin.[6] Information concerning the impetus behind Mary's marriage is jejune, but, given the Franco-Burgundian reconciliation at Arras in 1435, it is just about

---

[4]The most detailed contemporary account of Mary's journey to Scotland and the marriage celebrations is included in G du Fresne de Beaucourt, ed., *Cronique de Mathieu d'Escouchy* (Paris, 1863-4), i, 177-9. See also B Keuck, 'Wie der König von Schottland die Tochter des Herzogs von Geldern, die Nichte des Herzogs von Burgund, heiratete', *Geldrischer Heimatkalender* (1990), 90-9; C McGladdery, *James II* (Edinburgh, 1990), 41-6, 171.

[5]On the marriages of James I's daughters in general see A H Dunbar, *Scottish Kings 1005-1625* (2nd edn, Edinburgh, 1906), 191-2; A I Dunlop, *The Life and Times of James Kennedy, Bishop of St Andrews* (Edinburgh, 1950) (hereafter Dunlop, *Kennedy*), passim and especially 84-96; McGladdery, *James II*, 42-4.

[6]L Barbé, *Margaret of Scotland and the Dauphin Louis* (London, 1917), especially chapter 2; idem, 'A Stuart Duchess of Brittany' in idem, *Sidelights on the History, Industries and Social Life of Scotland* (London, 1919), 1-5; M Köfler and S Caramelle, *Die Beiden Frauen des Erzhogs Sigismund von Oesterreich-Tirol* (Innsbruck, 1982), 18-25; G du Fresne de Beaucourt, *Histoire de Charles VII* (Paris, 1881-91), iv, 223.

conceivable that this marriage too was promoted by the French. The marriage of several, if not all, of the Stewart girls was arranged to suit French, rather than Scottish, diplomatic interests. Charles VII treated the Stewart girls not as the daughters of his Scottish ally, James I, but rather as the sisters of the Dauphiness and that, certainly, explains their attraction on the European marriage market. Not surprisingly, then, the French king intended to use James II's marriage in a similar fashion and in 1447 he suggested a match between the Scottish king and Annette, the daughter of Frederick II, the duke of (electoral) Saxony.[7] Indeed, at first sight, James appears to have assented to his designated role as a marital pawn of French diplomacy. Although nothing came of the Saxon proposal, on 29 September 1448 Charles VII received a request from the king of Scots to recommend a suitable bride.[8]

This request was delivered to the French king by the three Scottish ambassadors (William, Lord Crichton; John Ralston, bishop of Dunkeld; and Nicholas Otterburn, official of St Andrews) who negotiated a reaffirmation of the Franco-Scottish alliance on 31 December 1448.[9] But Charles VII, as the Scots must have known, was unable to provide a daughter of his own to marry the Scottish king. Charles seems, therefore, to have directed the Scottish ambassadors to Brussels and the court of Philip the Good, duke of Burgundy.[10] The French king's thoughts were perhaps focusing on Philip's great-niece, Mary of Guelders, who, some years earlier, in 1442, had figured in unfulfilled French schemes for a marriage with Charles of Anjou.[11] In fact, long before James II's glib request to the French for a bride, the Scottish government had been exploring marital possibilities outwith France. Indeed, the Scottish ambassadors who had brought the king's request to France had travelled abroad armed with formal instructions to seek a bride not in France, but in Burgundy, Cleves or Guelders.[12] The Scots had perhaps merely considered it politic to formally approach their French allies before openly pursuing other options. At any rate, the king's marriage is the first clear sign of an important departure in Scottish diplomacy. It marks the first sure indication that, as the royal minority drew to a close from 1445, the Scots were mounting a more

---

[7]Ibid., iv, 362.

[8]J Stevenson, ed., *Letters and Papers Illustrative of the Wars of the English in France during the Reign of Henry the Sixth* (London, 1861-1864) (hereafter Stevenson, *Wars*), i, 221-3. See also ibid., 197-8.

[9]Paris, Archives Nationales, J678/28. On the envoys and their mission, see Dunlop, *Kennedy*, 89-96.

[10]Stevenson, *Wars*, i, 239-40.

[11]M G A Vale, *Charles VII* (London, 1974), 84. For a brief and somewhat dated biography of Mary of Guelders, see S Huschka, 'Maria von Geldern, Königin von Schottland', *Geldrischer Heimatkalender* (1989), 64-71.

[12]London, British Library (hereafter BL London), Harleian MS, 4637 III, fos. 11-12; Göttingen, Niedersächsische Staats- und Universitätsbibliothek (hereafter SA Göttingen), Cod.Ms.hist.657, xvi, fos. 316-17.

independent foreign policy and one which was less sycophantic to French interests.[13]

The preferred Scottish option was for a Burgundian match for the king. The duke of Burgundy, like the king of France, had no daughter of his own to offer the Scots, but the instructions issued to the Scottish ambassadors on 6 May 1448 indicate a shrewd appreciation by the Scots of Burgundian marital policy.[14] Philip the Good was apt to use the children of his sister, Mary of Cleves, in much the same way as Charles VII used the Stewart girls to pursue his own diplomatic ends.[15] One of Mary of Cleves's daughters, Catherine, was married to Arnold, duke of Guelders. It was their daughter, Mary of Guelders, who had spent much of her childhood at the Burgundian court, whose hand the Scots had coveted, perhaps since 1445 when James II was declared to be of majority.[16] In March 1446 both a Scottish embassy and Mary (by then thirteen years old) made visits to Bruges.[17] Whether these two visits to Bruges were connected is uncertain, but in June 1446 a Scottish embassy was being feasted at Arnhem in Guelders, while the following month a Scottish herald, accompanied by a Burgundian envoy, arrived at the court of Duke Arnold of Guelders to view the 'maiden of Guelders'.[18] Then, at some point between July 1446 and July 1447, a Gueldrian knight, Otto de Pufflich, visited Scotland, no doubt to continue the preliminary discussions about the marriage.[19] By July 1447 plans were sufficiently well-advanced for the duke of Guelders to make them public: the Gueldrian estates were summoned to meet at Nijmegen to deliberate on the matter.[20] At this point, however, plans for the marriage hit a stumbling block. The impecunious Duke Arnold could not finance his daughter's dowry from his own resources, but the Gueldrian estates declined to

---

[13]McGladdery, *James II*, 33. It was only after his marriage in 1449, however, that James II assumed direct control of affairs.

[14]This had possibly been imparted to them by the Bastard of St Pol, a Burgundian emissary to England, who, in 1446, received a safe-conduct to make a pilgrimage to Scotland. (M-R Thielmans, *Bourgogne et Angleterre: Relations Politiques et Economiques entre les Pays-Bas Bourguignons et l'Angleterre 1435-67* (Brussels, 1966), 150).

[15]C A J Armstrong, 'La politique matrimoniale des ducs de Bourgogne de la maison de Valois' in idem, *England, France and Burgundy in the Fifteenth Century* (London, 1983) (hereafter Armstrong, 'La politique matrimoniale'), 246-54.

[16]G Nijsten, *Het Hof van Gelre: Cultuur ten tijde van de hertogen uit het Gulikse en Egmondse huis (1371-1473)* (Kampen, 1992) (hereafter Nijsten, *Hof van Gelre*), 101; M Sommé, 'La jeunesse de Charles le Temeraire d'après les comptes de la cour de Bourgogne', *Revue du Nord*, lxiv (1982), 735-9.

[17]L Gilliodts van Severen, ed., *Inventaire des Archives de la Ville de Bruges* (Bruges, 1883-5), v, 297; Arnhem, Rijksarchief in Gelderland, Hertogelijk Archief (hereafter RA Arnhem, HA), inv.no.272 (Rekeningen van de overeste rentmeester Arnoldus van Goer, 1445-6), fo.142.

[18]Arnhem, Gemeetearchief, Oud-Archief van Arnhem, (hereafter GA Arnhem, OAA) inv.no.1245 (Stadsrekeningen, 1446-7), fo.7r; Dunlop, *Kennedy*, 95.

[19]*ER*, v, 273.

[20]GA Arnhem, OAA, inv.no.1245 (Stadsrekeningen 1447-8), fo.10.

grant the duke a subsidy and, instead, used the opportunity of their assembly at Nijmegen to present many other grievances to the duke. In October of the following year the matter of a subsidy for the duke was still only under discussion and ultimately it was Mary's uncle, Philip the Good, who provided the necessary funds for her marriage.[21]

The Burgundians had been quite closely involved in the marriage negotiations for some time and it was perhaps as a *quid pro quo* for his financial assistance that, on 6 September 1448, Duke Arnold granted Philip the Good plenary powers to treat upon Mary's marriage.[22] The negotiations between the Scottish and Burgundian ambassadors were concluded on 1 April 1449 and their endeavours were enshrined in the treaty of Brussels.[23] Until comparatively recently the terms of this treaty languished in obscurity but, as Dr Alexander Stevenson has since demonstrated, the treaty did far more than set forth an accord for the marriage of James II and Mary of Guelders.[24] That was merely the symbolic embodiment of a full diplomatic and military alliance between Scotland and Burgundy, which also incorporated Brittany and Guelders. The king of Scots and the troika of continental dukes bound themselves to assist each other against aggressors and to promote each other's interests by diplomatic means.

Complex and different motivations lay behind the agreement which the four allies reached at Brussels. Unlike the Saxon marriage, which the French had suggested for James II, a Burgundian marriage for the Scottish king offered the Scots implicit advantages of both a commercial and a political nature. It provided a likely safeguard for Scottish trading interests in the Low Countries, which was a matter of some urgency, given the radically transformed political geography of the Low Countries in the early fifteenth century. By the 1420s most of the secular principalities of the Low Countries had come into the possession of the Valois dukes of Burgundy. Although Scottish commercial interests in Flanders and Zeeland had been afforded a measure of protection by the 1427 treaty of Leiden[25] and by Mary Stewart's marriage to Wolfaert Borselen, a marital alliance with the ducal house of Burgundy offered further protection of these interests, not only in Flanders and Zeeland, but also elsewhere in the Burgundian Netherlands, including the increasingly commercially important provinces of Brabant and Holland.

---

[21]W J Alberts, *De Staten van Gelre en Zutphen* (Utrecht and Groningen, 1950-6) (hereafter Alberts, *Staten*), i, 197-8; J Baxter, 'The Marriage of James II', *Scottish Historical Review*, xxv (1928) (hereafter Baxter, 'Marriage'), 71-2.

[22]Ibid., 71. Philip was also empowered to arrange a marriage between Arnold's second daughter, Margaret, and Albrecht VI, duke of Austria (Armstrong, 'La politique matrimoniale', 253).

[23]BL London, Harleian MS 4637 III, fos 12-14; SA Göttingen, Cod.Ms.hist.657, xvi, fos.317-21.

[24]A W K Stevenson, 'Trade between Scotland and the Low Countries in the Later Middle Ages' (University of Aberdeen, unpublished PhD thesis, 1982) (hereafter Stevenson, 'Thesis'), 78-81.

[25]M P Rooseboom, *The Scottish Staple in the Netherlands* (The Hague, 1910), appendix, no.20.

But it was not just commercial advantages which a Burgundian match for the king offered the Scots. It also offered political benefits. The emergence of the extended Burgundian state had introduced, if not a new, then at least a vastly more powerful player into the arena of western European diplomacy, which necessitated a radical reassessment of Scottish foreign policy. The Franco-Scottish alliance had been, for over a century, the cornerstone of Scottish foreign policy. The alliance was designed as a defensive mechanism against English expansionism: the French, in theory at least, were expected to extend practical assistance to the Scots when the English threatened the Scots. But the emergence of a powerful Burgundy rendered this very simple calculation redundant. When Burgundy was hostile to France and allied to England, as it had been between 1420 and 1435, Scottish diplomacy had been paralysed. If 'nothing decisive emerged' from James I's diplomacy, it was partly because the Scottish government hesitated to commit itself to France, lest Burgundy react by imposing penalties on Scottish commercial activities in the Low Countries.[26] At the same time, the success of the Anglo-Burgundian forces in early fifteenth-century France had demonstrated the inadequacy of Scottish reliance upon the French. The hard-pressed French had been patently incapable of furnishing the Scots with aid were it to have been required. The Anglo-Burgundian alliance between 1420 and 1435 had left the Scots diplomatically hamstrung and painfully vulnerable. Some stock-taking was, therefore, necessary. While the Scots had no intention of abandoning their sentimental attachment to the French alliance, it was clearly desirable for them to reach an accommodation with the Burgundians, a ploy which was greatly facilitated by the Franco-Burgundian *rapprochement* at the Congress of Arras in 1435. The Burgundian alliance which they made in 1449 was intended to complement the Franco-Scottish alliance and to provide another safeguard against the perceived threat from England. Under the terms of the treaty of Brussels, the Scots reserved the right not to provide their new allies with aid against France; and they ensured the right to call upon Burgundian aid against England.

It was first and foremost with the Burgundians that the Scots had sought an alliance in 1449. As far as the Scots were concerned, their interest in Arnold of Guelders arose merely from the coincidence that he happened to be the father of the duke of Burgundy's niece. The inclusion of the duke of Brittany within the treaty cemented an existing friendship between James II and his brother-in-law. A separate Scottish-Breton agreement had been agreed on 22 October 1448, so the Breton incorporation within the treaty of Brussels was hardly a matter of priority for the Scots, though the 1448 agreement had stipulated that the Scots would include the Bretons in any future treaties which they made with other powers.[27] The Breton presence among the parties who concluded the treaty of Brussels is, nevertheless, intriguing and it may be assumed that Duke Francis wished to be

---

[26]R Nicholson, *Scotland : The Later Middle Ages* (Edinburgh, 1974), 302.
[27]Edinburgh, Scottish Record Office, SP7/13; the Breton treaty was ratified by the Scots on 22 December 1449 (J M Thomson et al., eds., *Registrum Magni Sigilli Regum Scotorum* (Edinburgh, 1882-1914), ii, no. 296).

included within the quadrangular alliance for reasons which were similar to those of the Scots. Breton diplomacy in the early fifteenth century was geared towards standing aloof from the Anglo-French war in order to preserve the duchy's independence, but the treasonable dealings between Francis's brother and the English had pushed Francis towards closer relations with the French.[28] In 1446 Francis performed homage to Charles VII for his duchy. By 1449, then, Brittany, along with Scotland and Burgundy, constituted part of a nexus of generally francophile powers. At the same time, Anglo-Breton relations deteriorated sharply, to the point that of all the signatories of the Brussels treaty, Francis stood in the greatest danger of English attack. In the summer of 1448 the English had strengthened their garrisons in lower Normandy, along the Breton frontier, and on 29 March 1449, three days before the treaty of Brussels was agreed, the border town of Fougères in Brittany was attacked by François de Surienne, an Aragonese captain in English pay. Francis had hitherto maintained much looser relations with the Burgundians than his father had done, but in the dangerous circumstances of the late 1440s, his desire to be incorporated within the treaty of Brussels was presumably motivated by a wish to revive his links with Burgundy, possibly with a view to acquiring Burgundian aid.

The Bretons, like the Scots, had little interest in Guelders, but, unlike the Bretons and the Scots, Duke Arnold of Guelders had little to fear from the English. Indeed, England was a potential ally of the Gueldrians. In the later thirteenth and fourteenth centuries Guelders had formed part of the *cordon sanitaire* which English kings had constructed around France and, as recently as 1435, as Anglo-Burgundian relations soured, the English attempted to resurrect the Anglo-Gueldrian alliance.[29] Arnold, then, had reasons other than anglophobia for adhering to the alliance of 1449, some of which, at least, are obvious. He could hardly have hoped for a socially more attractive match for his daughter than one with a royal house. It was also - and this was no small matter to the impoverished duke - a marriage on the cheap, since Philip the Good provided funds for Mary's dowry. But for Arnold, too, the 1449 alliance perhaps offered the prospect of political benefits: it might bring an end to Burgundian support of both Arnold's external enemies (such as the duke of Berg) and, more pressingly, the discontented elements (led by Nijmegen) within his own domains.[30]

For the Scots, the Bretons and the Gueldrians alike the treaty of Brussels held out the prospect of Burgundian aid. It is altogether less apparent what the Burgun-

---

[28]M Keen and M J Daniel, 'English Diplomacy and the Sack of Fougères in 1449', *History*, lix (1974), 375-91.

[29]F Trautz, *Die Könige von England und das Reich, 1272-1377* (Heidelberg, 1961), 133, 142, 199-203, 226-9, 233-6, 248-9, 255-9, 268-71, 277-8, 287-8, 297, 302-3, 314, 319, 337, 401-2, 408, 411; A Goodman, *The Loyal Conspiracy: The Lords Appellant under Richard II* (London, 1971), 59, 102; J Ferguson, *English Diplomacy, 1422-1461* (Oxford, 1972), 60.

[30]W J Alberts, *Geschiedenis van Gelderland* (s'Gravenhage, 1966) (hereafter Alberts, *Gelderland*), 102-6; Alberts, *Staaten*, i, 204-10.

dians stood to gain from the 'unexpected' marriage of 1449 and the alliance which accompanied it.[31] Unlike the Scots, it is difficult to see Philip the Good deriving substantial commercial benefits from the alliance. It was not necessary for the duke to entice Scottish merchants to his domains since the nature of Scottish trade was such that there was nowhere else where Scottish merchants were likely to resort. Politically, too, it is difficult to see Philip the Good deriving advantage from a formal alliance with the Scots. The anglophobic tenor of the treaty of Brussels coincided with temporary strains then evident in Anglo-Burgundian relations.[32] Nevertheless, it was hardly necessary for the Burgundians to make a formal alliance with the Scots in order to coax the Scots into an anti-English posture: such an attitude was more of a habit than a policy to the Scots. It was not, in any case, part of longer-term Burgundian policy to seek confrontation with England; against France, the real threat to Burgundian interests had Philip but noticed, the treaty of Brussels offered only very limited protection.[33] Moreover, at first sight, the marriage of Philip's niece did not bring the advantages associated with most Burgundian-inspired marriages of the period. Normally, the Burgundians chose spouses for their children in adjacent territories in order to augment Burgundian influence along Burgundy's borders.[34] Mary of Guelders's Scottish marriage appears as incongruent with such as policy.

In reaching the 1449 alliance, however, it was perhaps not primarily in the Scots that the Burgundians were interested. Given the political and commercial constellation of north-western Europe in the mid-fifteenth century, Scotland was a natural Burgundian ally, whom it was unnecessary for the Burgundians to court. The same calculation could not quite be applied to Guelders. Guelders remained an island of independence from Burgundian domination of the Low Countries. Philip the Good's ambitions were to bring those Netherlandish territories which remained outwith his control into closer dependence upon Burgundy. Cleves, for example, had become a client Burgundian state by the mid-1440s at the latest and Philip seems to have aimed at establishing a similar relationship with Guelders. Initially the prospects for this had augured well. In the 1420s Philip and Arnold of Guelders had made common cause against the claims of both Jacqueline of Bavaria in Holland and Rudolph Diepholz in Utrecht. Burgundian-Gueldrian ties were tightened when Arnold married Philip's niece, Catherine of Cleves, in 1430. By the mid-1440s, however, strains were beginning to appear in the Burgundian-Gueldrian relationship. In 1444 war had broken out between Arnold and Philip's ally, the duke of Berg. The Gueldrian defeat at Linnich provided Philip with an opportunity to meddle in Arnold's affairs and in 1445, under Burgundian influence, the duke of Cleves arranged a ten-year truce between the belligerents. By 1448 Philip was in a position to meddle further as he sought to reconcile Arnold

---

[31]Armstrong, 'La politique matrimoniale', 257.

[32]J Munro, *Wool, Cloth and Gold: The Struggle for Bullion in Anglo-Burgundian Trade, 1340-1478* (Toronto, 1972), 132-42.

[33]R Vaughan, *Philip the Good* (London, 1970), chapters 4 and 11.

[34]Armstrong, 'La politique matrimoniale', 257.

with his rebellious subjects. It is perhaps significant that Philip showed partiality not towards the unreliable Arnold but rather towards the rebels, who, in the ordinance for government drawn up by the internal opposition to Arnold on 8 October 1448, had attempted to force the duke of Guelders into concluding an alliance with the duke of Burgundy.[35] Arranging and financing the marriage of Arnold's daughter was just one means of bringing the duke of Guelders into closer dependence on Burgundy. And, in James II, Philip could offer not just an eminent and worthy husband for Arnold's daughter, but a husband who was very unlikely to find himself at odds with Burgundian ambitions in the eastern Netherlands and a husband who would have no obvious interest in shoring-up his father-in-law's position, especially since the Scottish king had renounced his claims to the Gueldrian succession.[36]

Whatever Philip the Good's aims and ambitions in concluding the treaty of Brussels, from a Scottish perspective the 1449 treaty was, at least in the short-term, a success. Throughout the 1450s Scottish-Burgundian relations remained cordial. There were no serious disputes about trading privileges, while gifts and tokens of affection were exchanged between the Scottish and Burgundian courts. More significantly James was permitted to acquire arms and armour in the Low Countries, including the great cannon Mons Meg, which Philip dispatched to James in 1457 in the company of fifty men-at-arms.[37] While Charles VII of France was unwilling to respond to Scottish requests for aid in campaigns against the remaining out-posts of English control in southern Scotland, Philip was prepared to arm the Scots.[38] Yet the Scots were able to acquire Burgundian aid without slavishly following a Burgundian line in their foreign policy, for there had been a complete transformation in international relations within a few years of the conclusion of the treaty of Brussels. England, expelled from most of its continental possessions by 1453, and then convulsed by the scrap between Lancastrians and Yorkists, relinquished the role of menace to its neighbours. Instead, neighbouring powers were given an opportunity to meddle in English affairs as the Lancastrians sought French assistance and the Yorkists turned to Burgundy. Rarely was the diplomatic configuration of western Europe as favourable to Scottish interests as it was in the 1450s and early 1460s. Courted by Lancastrians, Yorkists and their allies alike, James II was able to play off all sides against each other in furtherance of Scottish interests. It was a policy which Mary of Guelders continued after her husband's death in 1460 and one which, as Dr Macdougall has demonstrated, in a convincing refutation of the old slur that the queen was degen-

---

[35]Alberts, *Staaten*, i, 204-14.

[36]Baxter, 'Marriage', 71.

[37]Stevenson, 'Thesis', 82-3; *ER*, v, 382, 552; vi, 386-7; C Gaier, 'The Origin of Mons Meg', *Journal of the Arms and Armour Society*, v (1967), 425-31.

[38] Stevenson, *Wars*, i, 332-53.

erate, she pursued with considerable success.[39] This lack of forthright commitment to Burgundian interests was hardly what Philip the Good can have bargained for when he concluded the treaty of Brussels in 1449, but he could take some consolation from the fact that Scotland did not fall wholeheartedly into the Lancastrian camp. The chances of this happening were, perhaps, somewhat greater than historians have traditionally recognized since, despite her actually astute direction of foreign affairs, Mary's instinctive sympathies may not have been pro-Yorkist and pro-Burgundian (as is usually assumed) but, rather, quite the opposite. It was, perhaps, out of fear of her intentions that in 1460-1 Philip the Good had felt the need to prod the Scottish queen into a Yorkist foreign policy.[40] To account for this we must return to the continent.

If Philip the Good's principal motive in agreeing to the treaty of Brussels related to his ambition of extending Burgundian influence in the Low Countries, then in no other respect was the treaty a more miserable failure. As early as 1450 Philip and Arnold were at loggerheads over a disputed election to the see of Münster. In 1455 a disputed election at Utrecht provided further fuel for antagonism between Philip and Arnold, as Philip's attempt to install his illegitimate son David as bishop were stoutly resisted by Arnold. In support of David's candidature, a Burgundian army marched provocatively across Gueldrian territory in 1456 to besiege the town of Deventer in the *Sticht*. By the mid-1450s Arnold had openly espoused those forces attempting to resist further Burgundian domination of the Netherlands. But it was from a position of acute internal weakness that he had done so. The tensions between Arnold and many of his subjects, which had stalled the marriage negotiations in the 1440s, rumbled anew in the later 1450s. Moreover, Arnold's relations with his son, Adolf, and his wife, Catherine of Cleves, were nothing short of appalling, as Adolf and his mother connived with the Burgundians to oust Arnold and replace him with Adolf.[41] Quite how Mary of Guelders reacted to these events in her homeland is difficult to discern. No doubt she discussed news from home with the Gueldrian servants whom she retained in Scotland; and no doubt Arnold's view of events in Guelders was communicated to his daughter by messengers including the ducal envoy who met the queen's chamberlain at Veere in 1461.[42] There are hints, however, that Mary was not unsympathetic to Arnold's plight. It was presumably at the queen's instigation that her second son, the six-year old Alexander, duke of Albany, was sent off to Guelders,

---

[39]N Macdougall, *James III: A Political Study* (Edinburgh, 1982) (hereafter Macdougall, *James III*), 51-61; D Laing, 'Remarks on the Character of Mary of Guelders...', *Proceedings of the Society of Antiquaries of Scotland*, iv (1860-2), 566-77.

[40]Kennedy, *Dunlop*, 214-15; Macdougall, *James III*, 60.

[41]Alberts, *Gelderland*, 105-10; Alberts, *Staten*, i, 235-64; Vaughan, *Philip the Good*, 224, 230, 292-3.

[42]*ER*, v, p. lxxviii; Dunlop, *Kennedy*, 224; I A Nijhoff, ed., *Gedenkwaardigheden uit de Geschiedenis van Gelderland* (Arnhem, 1830-75) (hereafter *GGG*), iv, pp xcv-vi. For a Scottish envoy to Guelders in 1451, see *Rot.Scot.*, ii, 343.

where he resided between 1460 and 1464.[43] And if so, this was a public display of confidence in her beleaguered father. For his part, Arnold instructed that bells toll and that masses be said for his daughter when news reached him of her death in 1463 and these immediate solemnities were followed almost three weeks later by a symbolic performance of funeral rites for Mary in Arnhem.[44] While this bespeaks conventional piety and the propaganda uses to which even funerals could be put by later medieval princes, it also points towards a paternal affection for Mary which was rapidly disintegrating in respect of her brother.

While the Scots could be relatively pleased with the way in which the treaty of Brussels had worked in the 1450s and early 1460s, Scottish-Burgundian relations took a turn for the worse from the mid-1460s. Attempts to draw up a new military alliance in 1465 seem to have come to nothing and Dr Stevenson has alluded to several diplomatic and commercial reasons in explanation.[45] To these one might also add Scottish disquiet at events in Guelders. At Christmas 1464 members of the Egmont family had assembled at Grave in another unsuccessful effort to effect a reconciliation between Arnold and Adolf. In January 1465 Adolf kidnapped his father and proceeded to incarcerate him for five years. Adolf's actions acquired international opprobrium and caused Philip the Good much embarrassment since he had actively promoted Adolf's cause, arranged his marriage and made him a member of the Order of the Golden Fleece. The Scottish government was one of many which, incensed at the treatment of Arnold, dispatched curt letters of complaint to the towns of Arnhem and Nijmegen, Adolf's staunchest supporter, though, as far as can be discerned, the Scots remained otherwise aloof from the unfolding civil war.[46] Ultimately, in February 1471, Arnold was released, though further attempts by Philip the Good's successor, Charles the Bold, to effect a reconciliation between Arnold and Adolf failed. These foundered, according to Philip de Commynes, who was involved in the Burgundian attempt to reconcile father and son, on Adolf's insistence that he 'would rather throw his father head first into

---

[43]The 'son of the king of Scots' was recorded at Bruges, presumably *en route* for Guelders, in 1460 (*IVB*, v, 504). In the following years Albany was recorded on several occasions in Gueldrian records (Nijsten, *Hof van Gelre*, 320, n.107). The 'prince of Scotland' was still in Arnhem in 1464, when Boece states that Albany 'was then living in Guelders' (GA Arnhem, OAA, inv. nr 1248 (Stadsrekeneningen 1464-65), fo.7; J Moir, ed., *Hector Boetii, Murthlacensium et Aberdonensium Episcoporum Vitae* (New Spalding Club, 1894), 45) For Albany's return to Scotland, see Macdougall, *James III*, 62-3

[44]RA Arnhem, HA inv.nos. 4.22, 4.23 (Archief der Graven en Hertogen van Gelre); Duke Arnold had also instructed public mourning on hearing of the death of James II (Nijsten, *Hof van Gelre*, 274).

[45]Stevenson, 'Thesis', 83-7.

[46]RA Arnhem, HA, inv. 20, i, fos.44, 140. See also Nijsten, *Hof van Gelre*, 150. For events in Guelders between 1465 and 1473, see Alberts, *Gelderland*, 114-20; Alberts, *Staten*, ii, chapters 1 and 2.

a well and follow him there than make such an agreement'.[47] The tables were turned as Charles restored Arnold and threw Adolf into prison.

Arnold's first consideration was now to exclude his imprisoned son from the Gueldrian succession. The old duke had, it is true, reason to thank Charles the Bold for effecting his release, but many of Arnold's difficulties stemmed originally from his overt hostility to Burgundian ambitions of aggrandizement in the Low Countries. Accordingly, it was not, in 1472, to the Burgundians that Arnold turned for help in excluding Adolf but rather to his Scottish grandson, James III. Arnold proposed to confer Guelders and Zutphen on the Scottish king or one of his brothers, possibly Alexander, who, as a youngster, had spent some years at the ducal court.[48] It was only with no word forthcoming from Scotland, and little prospect of French aid,[49] that Arnold gradually turned more and more to reliance upon the Burgundians in order to exclude Adolf from the Gueldrian succession. Charles the Bold was named as guardian of Guelders on 7 December 1472. The duchy was then mortgaged to Charles and three days before his death in February 1473 Arnold finally named the duke of Burgundy as his heir. At long last Burgundian policy towards Guelders seemed in imminent expectation of fulfilment. In the summer of 1473 a Burgundian army entered the Egmont lands and within weeks the duchy of Guelders and its dependent county of Zutphen were forcibly incorporated within the Burgundian state.[50]

Arnold's attempts to palm Guelders and Zutphen off onto the Scots had presented the Scottish government with an awkward problem. James III was not opposed to the pursuit of an expansionist foreign policy. His overseas ambitions had been fortified by the knowledge that years of hectoring the Danish-Norwegian government about the status of the Northern Isles had very recently succeeded in bringing Orkney and Shetland to the Scottish crown. By February 1472, just as the attempts to acquire Orkney and Shetland reached a climax with the crown's formal annexation of the isles, Brittany emerged as the king's next target. Much to the dismay of the clerics in parliament, James seems to have proposed departing for Brittany to make good his tenuous claims to the duchy.[51] The offer of the Gueldrian succession, which presumably arrived in Scotland late in 1472, came to

---

[47]S Kinser, ed., *The Memoirs of Philippe de Commynes* (Columbia, 1969-73) i, 250. For a critique of Commynes' comments on Guelders, see J Dufournet, *La Destruction des Mythes dans les Memoires de Philippe de Commynes* (Geneva, 1966), 441-2.

[48]M Napier, *Memoirs of John Napier of Merchiston* (Edinburgh, 1834), 514.

[49]A B Hilds, ed., *Calendar of State Papers and Manuscripts existing in the Archives and Collections of Milan*, i (London, 1912), no.245. It would seem from this Milanese report that Arnold had been attempting to arrange a French marriage for his youngest daughter, Catherine, who never ultimately married but did emerge as regent of Guelders in 1477.

[50]W J Alberts, 'De Eerste Bourgondische Bezetting van Gelre (1473/1477)' in W J Alberts and F Ketner, eds., *Nederrijnse Studien XIIIe-XVe Eeuw* (Groningen, 1954) (hereafter Alberts, 'Bezetting'), 57-81; Alberts, *Gelderland*, 117-20; Alberts, *Staten*, ii, chapter 3; R Vaughan, *Charles the Bold* (London, 1973) (hereafter Vaughan, *Charles the Bold*), 117-21.

[51]T Thomson and C Innes, eds., *The Acts of the Parliaments of Scotland* (Edinburgh, 1814-75) (hereafter *APS*), ii, 102; Macdougall, *James III*, 92-6.

a king who was quite prepared to contemplate foreign adventures. Nevertheless, there were a great many practical problems in pursuing the Gueldrian offer. A legal obstacle existed in James II's renunciation of Stewart claims to the Gueldrian succession.[52] Even more importantly, there was virtually no possible source of foreign support had the Scottish king decided to pursue his claim. While there was considerable opposition within Guelders, especially in the towns, towards a Burgundian takeover, William of Egmont, Arnold's brother and chief supporter in the civil war, had long since reconciled himself to the Valois cause. Of Guelders's neighbours, the Burgundians would clearly have opposed Scottish intervention and many of the other small lower Rhenish principalities were Burgundian client states. In the Empire, Frederick III was to declare himself content to see Guelders fall under Burgundian control.[53] The Anglo-Burgundian alliance of 1466 ruled out any prospect of English support for the Scottish king, while Louis XI had demonstrated a strong aversion to Scots ever since his disastrous marriage to Margaret Stewart and he was unlikely to intervene on behalf of the Scottish king unless it suited French interests. In fact, the French king, along with the Gueldrian towns, was committed to the support of the still imprisoned Adolf.[54]

James III was diplomatically isolated. Yet, in 1473, the Scottish parliament was still convinced that the king was about to depart for the continent and the parliamentary records of this date include mention of royal claims on both Saintonge, in France, and Guelders.[55] The parliamentary records do not, however, state explicitly where the king proposed to journey; and the acquisition of Guelders seems to have been dangled in front of the king by the estates in an effort to persuade him of the gains which might be acquired by abandoning his apparently blunt and perhaps bellicose intentions (in Saintonge?) in favour of more subtle diplomatic negotiation. In the event James did nothing militarily and little diplomatically. He delayed until it was too late in responding to his grandfather's offer. A Scottish embassy, issued with instructions before the parliamentary debate of July 1473, did turn up in the Low Countries and congratulated Charles the Bold on his efforts to reconcile Arnold and Adolf.[56] But the duke ignored the further Scottish request for 'supportatione, aide, and supplie ... in the recovering of his [James III's] richt' to Guelders.[57] More surprisingly, at least for those who hold that James III displayed megalomaniac tendencies in his foreign policy, the matter was never apparently pursued by the Scottish king, even in the far more propitious circumstances which prevailed after the death of Charles the Bold in 1477. For

---

[52]Baxter, 'Marriage', 71.
[53]Alberts, 'Bezetting', 52-7; Vaughan, *Charles the Bold*, 115-18. Frederick III confirmed the Burgundian acquisition of Guelders on 6 November 1473 (M A Deshaisnes and J Finot, eds., *Inventaire Sommaire des Archives Departementales anterieures à 1790: Nord: Archives Civiles: Série B* (Lille, 1899-1906) (hereafter *ISADN*), i(2), 372.
[54]Vaughan, *Charles the Bold*, chapter 2 and 116-18.
[55]*APS*, ii, 103-4.
[56]*ISADN*, 372; Vaughan, *Charles the Bold*, 118.
[57]Napier, *Memoirs*, 514.

commercial and wider diplomatic reasons James III's sensible priority was to remain on good terms with the Burgundians.

If Guelders had been something of an embarrassment to James III it reemerged in similar guise after the death of Charles the Bold. In Guelders an opportunity had presented itself to cast off Burgundian domination as Charles's heiress, Mary, and her husband, Maximilian Habsburg, weathered a storm of external aggression and internal dissent. But it was a struggle conducted in the absence of an Egmont duke. Adolf, liberated in 1477, had died shortly afterwards at the battle of Courtrai. His heir, Charles, had been captured by the Burgundians at Nijmegen in 1473 and remained with them until his capture by the French at Béthune in 1487. It was also a struggle from which the Scottish government remained aloof, though the exiled duke of Albany, who had spent part of his childhood in Guelders, was involved in attempts to secure French assistance for the return of Charles to Guelders.[58] Eventually, in March 1492, Charles did return, though his position remained precarious. Maximilian and his son, Archduke Philip the Fair, were not reconciled to the loss of Guelders from their Burgundian inheritance. They refused to recognize Charles as duke and mounted several military campaigns, most notably in 1505, against the restored duke.[59] In these dangerous circumstances Charles looked for assistance from any conceivable quarter, including his cousin and ally, James IV of Scotland.[60] Throughout his reign James IV displayed little enthusiasm for coming to his tiresome cousin's aid. In June 1505, for example, with Burgundian forces once again in possession of much of Guelders, James declined to send military assistance to Charles on the grounds that Charles was sheltering Edmund de la Pole, a leading Yorkist enemy of James's father-in-law, Henry VII of England.[61] This excuse was no longer tenable by July 1505, once de la Pole had passed into the possession of Archduke Philip,

---

[58]A J de Mooy, ed., *De Gelderse Kroniek van Willem van Berchen* (Arnhem, 1950), 157. For events in Guelders between 1477 and 1492 generally, see Alberts, *Gelderland*, 122-30; Alberts, *Staten*, ii, chapters 4 and 5.

[59]For events in Guelders during Charles's reign from 1492 to 1538 see P J Meij, 'Gelderland van 1492-1543' in J J Poelhekke et al., eds., *Geschiedenis van Gelderland 1492-1795* (Zutphen, 1975) (hereafter Meij, 'Gelderland') and J F A L Struik, *Gelre en Habsburg 1492-1528* (Arnhem, 1960).

[60]The duke of Guelders was named as an ally of the Scottish king in the 1502 Anglo-Scottish Treaty of Perpetual Peace (T Rymer, ed., *Foedera...*(London, 1704-35), xii, 793-800). It is not certain when James and Charles first communicated with each other, but they were certainly in contact by 1500 (RA Arnhem, HA, inv.nr.8, fo.83; M Livingstone et al., eds., *Registrum Secreti Sigilli Regum Scotorum* (Edinburgh, 1908-), i, no. 511).

[61]R K Hannay and R L Mackie, eds., *The Letters of James the Fourth 1505-13* (Scottish History Society, 1953) (hereafter *James IV Letters*), no. 14. Edmund de la Pole, duke of Suffolk, a Yorkist fugitive from England, had been detained by Charles in 1504. Charles's uncertain intentions with his captive were a cause of acute concern to Henry VII. See G A Bergenroth, ed., *Calendar of Letters, Despatches and State Papers relating to...England and Spain*, i (London, 1862), nos.394, 401, 402, 429, 450; J D Mackie, *The Earlier Tudors 1485-1558* (Oxford, 1952), 167-71.

but others were found: in September 1505, July 1506, and again in January 1507 (on the realistic grounds that 'the distance separating them prevented assistance') James evaded providing a Scottish military commitment to Guelders.[62]

While James would not countenance armed intervention in Guelders, he was prepared to extend diplomatic support to his cousin. Twice - in 1507 and in 1509 - though with little success, James donned the garb of a prospective mediator between Charles and the Habsburgs, initially at his own volition and latterly at papal instigation.[63] In addition James made representations on his cousin's behalf to other powers. In 1507 the Scottish king wrote meekly to Maximilian (with whom he was simultaneously attempting to make an alliance) and requested 'a more gracious treatment of his kinsman'. With his father-in-law, James was more belligerent. In January 1507 James sought to dissuade Henry VII from collaboration with the Habsburgs in an attack on Guelders by threatening, in such an eventuality, to invade England on his cousin's behalf. He also pointedly reminded Henry of their common dynastic interest in Guelders: to connive at Guelders adsorption within a Habsburg-Burgundian state could be to the long-term detriment of James's children and Henry's grandchildren.[64] Henry VII's ultimate inaction over Guelders perhaps owed something to his son-in-law's threats, though it seems unlikely that the naturally cautious English king would in any case have embroiled himself in a military campaign in the Netherlands. The more bombastic Henry VIII, however, ignored James IV's request to leave Guelders in peace and joined Margaret of Savoy, the regent of the Burgundian Netherlands, in an attack on Guelders in 1511.[65] While James attempted to dissuade the Habsburgs and the English from attacking Guelders, elsewhere he attempted to solicit support for his cousin. The Scottish king's appeals to King Hans of Denmark were, both for geographical reasons and on account of Hans's own problems with the rebellious Swedes, unlikely to produce results.[66] Appeals to the French by contrast were unnecessary since the Habsburgs were a menace to Guelders and France alike. In the treaty of Senlis, agreed within a year of Charles's release from French captivity, Charles was styled as an ally of the French king, Charles VIII.[67] Louis XII, after his accession to the French throne in 1498, continued to lend both diplomatic

---

[62] *James IV Letters*, nos. 17, 34, 73.

[63] In 1507 James offered Maximilian the services of Robert Forman and Lyon King of Arms to facilitate a settlement (ibid., nos. 71, 72, 73). Maximilian was informed of the arrival at Mechelen, and intentions, of the two Scottish envoys in February 1507 (*GGG*, vi, no. 595). For the expenses of Forman and Lyon, see T Dickson and J B Paul, eds., *Accounts of the Lord High Treasurer of Scotland* (Edinburgh, 1877-1916), iii, 361-2. For Pope Julius II's attempts to mediate between the Gueldrians and the Burgundians, see *GGG*, vi, no. 648.

[64] *James IV Letters*, nos. 70, 71.

[65] Ibid., no. 560.

[66] Ibid., nos. 73, 166. Somewhat earlier, in 1479, Hans's father, King Christian, had, however, written to Maximilian in support of Adolf's children (RA Arnhem, HA, inv.nr.8, fo.119).

[67] Meij, 'Gelderland', 18.

and military support to Duke Charles, mediating a peace treaty between the duke of Guelders and Julich in 1499, concluding a formal treaty of alliance with the Gueldrians at Mezieres in 1506 and dispatching troops to Guelders in the same year.[68]

It could, then, be argued that James IV's Gueldrian policy was of very limited success, since nobody, except possibly Henry VII, took much notice of the Scottish king's strictures on the subject of Guelders. James did not persuade the Habsburgs to abate their assaults on Guelders; and he deserves no credit for persuading the French to support Guelders. Nevertheless, in formulating his Gueldrian policy, James IV had, like his father, to strike a balance between commercial and dynastic interests. Although, by the early sixteenth century, Scottish trade was less exclusively focused on the Low Countries than it had once been, the level of trade with the Netherlandish provinces remained significant.[69] It was still important to maintain good relations with the Habsburg-Burgundian state. Against this, there was perhaps a moral obligation to help a kinsman in distress. Moreover, so long as Duke Charles remained unmarried and without a legitimate heir there was still a potential Scottish interest in the Gueldrian succession. But this was an interest of which James preferred to divest himself. While it was mentioned in his dealings with Henry VII, to underline Scottish concern at developments within Guelders, James was also bluntly urging Charles to marry: the production of an Egmont heir would release James from some of his awkward interests in Guelders.[70] As it was, dynastic interests in Guelders still played second fiddle to wider commercial and political interests in the formulation of the king's attitude to Guelders. Seen in this light James IV's diplomacy was altogether more successful and, whatever one thinks of other aspects of the king's foreign policy, his approach to Guelders was consistently sensible. He made no rash promises or commitments to his cousin which he was later to regret. As a consequence, however, it can have come as little surprise to James that Charles did not provide the Scots with aid against the English in 1513.

The sentimental concern which James IV at times expressed for his kinsman's welfare - even if it stopped short of sending Scottish troops to assist him - was abandoned during James V's reign. To judge from the published volume of his correspondence, the hard-headed James V was not in the slightest interested in Charles of Guelders's ongoing plight. Charles had apparently abandoned hope of securing Scottish aid. The volume contains no letters from the duke to the king and but one terse complaint from Scotland to Guelders about piracy.[71] There are, however, slight signs of a *rapprochement* after the death of Charles in 1538, when

---

[68] Paris, Archives Nationales, J577/2; Meij, 'Gelderland', 30-3.

[69] A W K Stevenson, 'Trade with the South' in M Lynch, M Spearman and G Stell, eds., *The Scottish Medieval Town* (Edinburgh, 1988), 199-201.

[70] *James IV Letters*, nos. 34, 70.

[71] R K Hannay and D Hay, eds., *The Letters of James V* (Edinburgh, 1954), 34. (The complaint relates to an incident in Frisia, a province to which Duke Charles of Guelders was attempting to assert a claim from 1514.)

William of Cleves succeeded to Guelders and Zutphen, possibly because, as an ally of the French, briefly Henry VIII's brother-in-law, and as duke of Cleves, Mark, Julich and Berg, as well as Guelders, William was an altogether more powerful figure than Charles had ever been. In 1541 James and William exchanged correspondence, the king congratulating the duke on his marriage.[72] At the same time the king and Cardinal Beaton began to explore the possibility of establishing a formal alliance with William, though nothing decisive seems to have emerged from the first tentative moves in this direction before James V's death in 1542.[73] The following year imperial troops crossed into Duke William's territories. Abandoned by the French, William submitted at Venlo on 7 September 1543 and renounced his rights to Guelders and Zutphen in favour of the Emperor Charles V. The Habsburgs had finally won control of the recalcitrant duchy.

It had never been a fundamental objective of Scottish foreign policy to seek an alliance with Guelders or *vice versa*. The Scots had neither commercial nor political interests in the eastern Netherlandish duchy, while the Gueldrians were more concerned with the affairs of the lower Rhenish region than with the diplomacy of the North Sea littoral. That an alliance between Scotland and Guelders had come about in 1449 was purely by dynastic accident. The civil war within Guelders, and the staunchly anti-Burgundian attitudes which surfaced there in the fifteenth and early sixteenth centuries, gave life to the dynastic bond between the Stewarts and the Egmonts when it might otherwise have been forgotten. On numerous occasions the Scottish crown was presented with opportunities to involve itself in the duchy's concerns and one might have expected a Scottish monarchy determined to play a pervasive role in European diplomacy to have readily involved itself in Gueldrian affairs. It did not. There was no grandiose lack of realism with regard to Guelders. With remarkable consistency between 1449 and 1543 dynastic obligations to, and interests in, Guelders were evaded in favour of maintaining a Burgundian alliance.

The early sixteenth century ceiling of St Machar's Cathedral in Aberdeen, with its heraldic designs, provides a simple but accurate indication of how Scots viewed Christendom in the 1520s.[74] There was a place for Guelders in this world view. The arms of the duke of Guelders were selected for inclusion in the display but his arms were depicted last in the line of a dozen coats-of-arms belonging to foreign rulers. Those of Charles V, emperor, and ruler of most of the rest of the Netherlands, took precedence over all the others.

---

[72] G E Bers, ed., *Die Allianz Frankreich-Kleve während des Geldrischen Krieges (Jülichsche Fehde) (1539-1543): Urkunden und Korrespondenzen* (Cologne, 1969), 136-7, 157, 172-3.
[73] Ibid., 353.
[74] D McRoberts, *The Heraldic Ceiling of St Machar's Cathedral, Aberdeen* (Aberdeen, 1976).

6

NORTHERN WOOLS AND NETHERLANDS MARKETS AT THE CLOSE OF THE MIDDLE AGES[1]

Ian Blanchard

In 1496, Philip the Fair, count of Flanders, concluded with Henry VII, king of England, a far-reaching political and economic peace treaty which has been named the *Magnus Intercursus*. This treaty and the subsequent liberalization of the English cloth trade contributed significantly to a trade boom which during the years from about 1492 to about 1523/6 established Antwerp as the metropolis of a transformed western European commercial network.[2] Attracted by the availability of increasingly cheap commercial credit on the Antwerp Bourse, merchants flocked to the fairs of Brabant.[3] Textiles, of both Low Country and English origin, figured large amongst the goods which attracted their attention at the marts. Particularly with regard to the products of the Anglo-Netherlands 'heavy' drapery, manufacturers at centres like Menin, Armentières, Meteren, Courtrai and Wervicq in Flanders and Leiden in the northern Netherlands, or their English counterparts, found a ready market for their wares at the fairs during the years of that boom (fig. 1).[4]

---

[1]The present study utilizes materials presented more fully in my forthcoming *The International Economy in the 'Age of Discoveries', 1470-1570*, vol. i: *The English Merchants' World*. The research for this study was funded by the Economic and Social Research Council (Grants HR 8205 and B 0023002/1, 1982-5 and R-000232851, 1991-3).

[2]Useful introductions to the changes of these years will be found in Ralph Davis, 'The rise of Antwerp and its English connection, 1406-1510' in Donald C Coleman and Arthur H John, eds, *Trade, Government and Economy in Pre-Industrial England: essays presented to F J Fisher* (London, 1976), 2-20, and Herman van der Wee, *The Growth of the Antwerp Market and the European Economy (fourteenth-sixteenth centuries)* (3 vols, The Hague, 1963), ii, 113-42.

[3]Herman van der Wee and Ian Blanchard, 'The Habsburgs and the Antwerp money market: the exchange crises of 1521 and 1522-3' in Ian Blanchard, Anthony Goodman and Jennifer Newman, eds, *Industry and Finance in Early Modern History: essays presented to George Hammersley on the occasion of his 74th birthday* (Stuttgart, VSWG Beiheft 98, 1991), which may be set in a broader context of changes on international capital markets by reference to 'International capital markets and their users: introduction', in the same volume.

[4]Figure 1 sources: Netherlands textile output (in cloths): H E de Sagher, J-H de Sagher, H van Werveke and C Wyffels, eds, *Receuil de documents relatifs à l'histoire de l'industrie drapière en Flandre*, 2e partie: *Le sud-ouest de la Flandre depuis l'époque Bourguignonne* (3 vols, Brussels, 1951-66), ii, nos 257, 263-4, 274, 284, 630-1; iii, nos 409, 415, 459, 475 (hereafter de Sagher, *Documents*). R van Uytven, 'La Flandre et le Brabant, "Terres de Promission" sous les Ducs de Bourgogne?', *Revue du Nord*, xlviii (1961), 294. E Coor-

In part the effectiveness of the Netherlands merchants in promoting their trade in these Low Countries' textiles during this period rested on their relationship with these suppliers - the heavy cloth producers of the 'grande draperie'. These were manufacturers who, by utilising the facilities of a well-developed industrial wool market, were in a position to respond quickly and effectively in satisfying the merchants' constantly changing requirements. That wool market was centred on Bruges rather than Antwerp, and throughout the years of the boom and beyond, it maintained a basically stable organizational form. As a result producers enjoyed a great freedom of action which enabled them to draw their supplies of wool through an international commercial system which operated on the basis of a multinational resource base and was capable of maintaining steadily increasing supplies of raw materials at constant prices.

I

At the end of the fifteenth century, the market for fine wools already had a long history behind it and throughout the years 1492-1523/6 and beyond maintained a basically stable organizational form. During these years, the English continued their long-established trade in fine wools at Calais.[5] Year after year, when unim-

---

naert, *Un centre industriel d'autrefois: la draperie-sayetterie d'Hondeschoote (XIVe-XVIIIe siècles)* (Paris, 1930), app. 4, 485-9. O Mus, 'De verhouding van der waard tot de drapier in de Kortrijkse draperie op het einde van 15e eeuwe', *Annales de la Société de l'Emulation de Bruges*, xcviii (1961), 163. N W Posthumus, *De Geschiedenis van den Leidsche Lakenindustrie*, vol. 1: *De Middeleeuwen (Veertiende tot Zestiende Eeuw)*, ('s Gravenhage, 1908), based on data from *strikerije* in Bijlage vi a, 467. R Sprandel, 'Zur Tuchproduktion in der Gegend von Ypres', *Vierteljahrschrift für Sozial- und Wirt-schaftsgeschichte*, liv (1967), derived from de Sagher, *Documents*, vol. ii. English cloth exports, measured across trade fluctuation peaks (x 10 cloths): E M Carus-Wilson and O Coleman, *England's Export Trade, 1275-1547* (Oxford, 1963), 111-19.

[5] The organization of the English trade revealed in the Cely papers (1472-88) is described in the classic studies of Eileen Power: 'The English wool trade in the reign of Edward IV', *Cambridge Historical Journal*, ii (1926-8), 'The wool trade in the fifteenth century', in E Power and M M Postan, eds, *Studies in English Trade in the Fifteenth Century* (London, 1933) and *The Wool Trade in English Medieval History* (Oxford, 1941); by Alison Hanham in numerous articles, e.g. 'Foreign exchange and the English wool merchant in the late fifteenth century', *Bulletin of the Institute of Historical Research*, xlvi (1973), 'Profits on English wool exports, 1472-1544', ibid., lv (1982), and her excellent *The Celys and their World: an English merchant family of the fifteenth century* (Cambridge, 1985) (hereafter Hanham, *The Celys*); and by T H Lloyd, *The English Wool Trade in the Middle Ages* (Cambridge, 1977). Many of the original letters have also been published in H Hall, 'The English Staple', *Gentleman's Magazine*, cclv (1883), H E Malden, ed., 'The Cely Papers: selections from the correspondence and memoranda of the Cely family, merchants of the Staple, 1475-88 (Camden Society, third series, i, 1900), and A Hanham, ed., *The Cely Letters, 1472-88* (Early English Text Society, cclxxiii, 1975). Subsequent descriptions of the organization of the trade will be found in Richard Hill's Commonplace Book of 1506 (Oxford, Balliol MS. 354); the enormous collection of Johnson Papers (1534-52), of which only the letters have been edited by B Winchester, ed., *The Johnson Letters, 1542-*

peded by political restraint or embargo, the English wool fleet sailed for the Staple.[6] There successive generations of Staplers conducted their business in much the same way as had the famous English Cely family: they unloaded the ships and registered their consignments with the collectors or wool-packers, sorted their wares into 'old' and 'new' wools, transported the product to the Calais mart and there, usually extending credit, sold it.[7] Their principal customers throughout the period remained the wool merchants of Flanders and Burgos, trading in Bruges, who, on acquiring the prized high-quality English wools, arranged for their transport by land or sea to that city, whence they were sold on to customers in the heavy drapery districts of the Low Countries.[8] These Bruges merchants also handled the large cargoes of fine Spanish wool which arrived with Basque iron aboard the Biscayan fleet that anchored in the Ecluse during June each year, as well as the lesser cargoes shipped from the south-western Spanish ports.[9] By far

---

52 (unpublished London Ph D thesis, 1953), whilst the accounts (Public Record Office, SP1/185, 196, 244; SP 46/5-7, copies of which are in the author's possession) remain amongst the MS collections of State Papers, and E E Rich, ed., *The Ordinance Book of the Merchants of the Staple* (Cambridge, 1937), relating to conditions in 1565. A comparison of these studies reveals a basic stability of organizational form in the trade throughout the period of this study and, in spite of the subsequent loss of Calais, beyond.

[6]The remarkably fine series of London wool customs records which link the periods covered by the Cely (1472-88) and Johnson (1534-52) papers (viz. Public Record Office E 122/73/4; 78/5, 8, 10; 79/9, 17-18; 81/11, 13; 82/1, 5-6; 83/3, 8, 16; 85/10; 166/12; 195/27; 203/6; 204/1-9) reveal both the changing personnel involved in the trade and the long-term stability in its organization.

[7]Credit terms were used to maintain price stability over time. On a depressed market prices were maintained and abatements were made by lengthening credit terms. On a rising market prices were not enhanced but credit was shortened.

[8]Small consignments of high-quality wool were also sold direct to clothiers but most Staplers probably followed the practice of the Celys and Johnsons, selling large consignments (30-60 Calais sacks) to the Bruges merchants.

[9]Burgos in Northern Castile and its merchant community dominated the northern Spanish wool trade, controlling the internal supply network and both ends of the external trade between the Cantabrian coast and Flanders or France; see C R Phillips, 'The Spanish wool trade, 1500-1780', *Journal of Economic History*, xlii, 4 (1982), 789-91; J Marechall, 'La colonie espagnole de Bruges du XIVe au XVIe siècle', *Revue du Nord*, xxxv (1953), 5-40; W R Childs, *Anglo-Castilian Trade in the later Middle Ages* (Manchester, 1978), 215-16; and C Verlinden, 'A propos de la politique économique des ducs de Burgogne à l'égard de l'Espagne', *Hispania*, x (1950), 681-715. As J H Edward's paper 'El comercio lanero en Córdoba bajo los Reyes Católicos', presented at I Congreso de Historia de Andalusía in December 1976 (subsequently published in the *Acta* of the Congress, Madrid 1978, i, 423-8) shows, they also dominated the Cordoban market from 1471 to 1514, although here they met with competition from the merchants of Seville and Genoa; R Pike, *Aristocrats and Traders: Sevillian society in the sixteenth century* (Ithaca, New York, 1972), 61, 123-6. On the arrival of these fleets in the Ecluse during the years 1486-1500, see L Gilliodts van Severen, ed., *Inventaire des Archives de Bruges: Série Treizième a seizième siècle* (6 vols, introduction and 2 indices, Bruges, 1878-85) (hereafter Gilliodts, *Inventaire*), iv, 450, vi, 275-6.

the largest part of the trade in fine English and Spanish wools thus passed through Bruges, whose merchants distributed the product in the Netherlands. Not surprisingly in these circumstances, Scots merchants, trading out of Middelburg, also reserved their better quality wools for this trade with the Bruges merchants. Annually, when the Edinburgh wool fleet arrived at Middelburg and its Aberdeen counterpart anchored at Veere, one of the first tasks of the Scots merchants and factors was to sort and grade the incoming cargoes. Thereafter, whilst the greater part of their wools was distributed elsewhere, the best was sold to these same Bruges merchants and trans-shipped by *schout* to the Damme, a satellite port of Bruges.[10] This fine wool trade was thus already at the beginning of the sixteenth century handled by merchants who could avail themselves of the facilities of a well-developed and organizationally stable wool market which at that time and subsequently operated to isolate consumers from the effects of supply-source price fluctuations.[11]

In their operations these wool merchants, moreover, proved remarkably effective. During the first great cycle in the Anglo-Netherlands cloth trade (1492-1523/6), which was dominated by the products of the heavy drapery, they were able to supply Netherlands manufacturers with an ever increasing quantity of fine wools at stable prices. As trade in the Anglo-Netherlands heavy draperies increased, the Netherlands production of these cloths also increased (fig. 1), drawing on a steadily growing supply of imported fine wools.[12] Initially, in the after-

---

[10]A vivid picture of the Scots wool trade during the years 1492-1503 can be constructed from Cosmo Innes, ed., *The Ledger of Andrew Halyburton, Conservator of the Privileges of the Scotch Nation in the Netherlands, 1492-1503* (Edinburgh, 1867) (hereafter *Halyburton's Ledger*); W S Unger, *De Tol van Iersekerood, 1321-1572* (The Hague: Rijks Geschiedkundige Publicatien, Kl. Ser. xxix, 1939) and Scottish Record Office, (hereafter SRO) E 71/1/1, which may be set in a longer time perspective by reference to J Davidson and A Gray, *The Scottish Staple at Veere* (London, 1909) and M P Rooseboom, *The Scottish Staple in the Netherlands* (The Hague, 1910).

[11]On domestic English wool prices see P Bowden, 'Statistical Appendix' in J Thirsk, ed., *The Agrarian History of England and Wales* (Cambridge, 1967), iv, 840-4, and T H Lloyd, *The Movement of Wool Prices in Medieval England* (Cambridge: Economic History Review Supplement, no. 6, 1973). The figures derived from this latter work have, however, been recalculated to overcome the statistical deficiencies of their original presentation, on which see *History*, lx, 198 (1975), 110-11. On sales prices in the Low Countries in the years to 1532 see J H Munro, 'Wool price schedules and the qualities of English wools in the later middle ages, c. 1270-1499', *Textile History*, ix (1978), Hanham, *The Celys*, 145-7, *Letters and Papers, Domestic and Foreign, Henry VIII*, viii, app. 20/1-5.

[12]On the English wool trade see E M Carus-Wilson and O Coleman, *England's Export Trade, 1275-1547* (Oxford, 1963), 69-74, 122-39, and J D Gould, *The Great Debasement: currency and the economy in mid-Tudor England* (Oxford, 1970), app. C, 182. Statistical materials for the Spanish wool trade pose greater problems. Consistent and continuous data are only available from the reign of Philip II and have been presented in the studies of Henri Lepeyre: 'Le commerce des laines en Espagne sous Philippe II', *Bulletin de la société d'histoire moderne*, série ii. xiv (1955), 'Les exportations de laine de Castille sous le regne de Philippe II', in M Spallanzi, ed., *La lana come materia prima: I fenomeni della*

math of a crisis in 1486-92, the main source of such wools was England, but as the first trade upswing of the new cycle approached its peak in 1495-6 the price of English wool at Calais began to edge upwards.[13] At this point, therefore, the Bruges merchants shifted to a 'new' supply source. By 1499-1500 Spanish wool (about 4,000 English sacks annually) once more found a place on the Bruges market, re-establishing its pre-crisis position in the trade and creating a new market equilibrium between the two products.[14] Henceforth, from 1497 to 1523, the English wool trade continued, but during each successive boom (1505-9, 1514-15 and 1518-19) sales, at about 7,000-7,500 sacks a year, never again achieved the levels of 1495-6.[15] Indeed, when crises beset the heavy cloth trade (1497-1503, 1509-13, 1516-17 and 1520-3) the figures amounted to no more than 4,000-5,000 sacks a year. The English now had to share the market with Spanish wool which, over the same period (from 1497 to 1523), was imported in quantities of between about 4,000 and 6,000 English sacks a year.[16] In aggregate, however, the shift in sources of supply allowed the wool boom to continue, imports rising to almost 10,500 sacks in 1508/9. It also allowed the market price of fine wools to once again fall in 1499 to pre-1496 levels and thereafter to remain at that price to 1523.[17] The heavy-cloth manufacturers of the Low Countries were thus able to alter continually both the quantities and types of wool they purchased, vary their

---

sua produzione e circulazione nei secoli XIII-XVII (Florence: Instituto internazionale di storia economica 'F Datini' Prato: Pubblicazioni, serie ii, 1, Atti dell 'Prima settimana di studi' [18-24 aprile 1969], 1974), 221-39, subsequently expanded in chapter iv of *El comercio exterior de Castillo a través de la aduanas de Felipe II* (Valladolid, 1981); J Israel, 'Spanish wool exports and the European economy, 1610-40', *Economic History Review*, second series, xxxiii, 2 (1980), and C R Phillips, 'The Spanish wool trade, 1500-1780', *Journal of Economic History*, xlii, 4 (1982). This latter excellent study also draws together the scattered statistical materials available for the years to 1564 which may be further supplemented for the closing years of the fifteenth century from Gilliodts, *Inventaire*, vol. 4, 450, and vol. 6, 275-6, and J Finot, *Etude historique sur les relations commerciales entre la Flandre et l'Espagne au moyen age* (Paris, 1899), 223.

[13]Hanham, *The Celys*, table 2, 146.

[14]Gilliodts, *Inventaire*, vol. 4, 450 and vol. 6, 275-6. In 1486-7, as the previous trade boom gave way to crisis conditions on Low Country markets, on average six Andalusian and Biscayan ships a year put into the Ecluse. In 1499-1500 they numbered on average four to five a year. Assuming that, as later, these ships carried about 750-800 sacks of wool each (see T Mazo Solano, 'El comercio de lanas por el puerto de Santander con Flandes y Francia en los años 1545-51', *Aportación al estudio de la historia económica de la Montaña* (Santander, 1957), 316-48), then the trade at this time amounted to about 4,000 sacks a year.

[15]When English exports amounted to slightly more than 9,000 sacks a year.

[16]In boom conditions (such as characterized the years 1505-9) Spanish wool exports amounted to about 6,000 sacks a year (C R Phillips, as in n. 12 above, 778-9).

[17]It is surely significant in this context that the 1499 Netherlands wool price schedule was actually published for current use in 1523 (see J H Munro, 'Wool price schedules...' (as in n. 11 above), 154-5).

production patterns and satisfy the merchants' changing requirements during these boom years.

Such then is the well-known story of the fine wool trade and its markets in the Netherlands during the period of Antwerp's rise to international ascendancy.

II

Far less familiar is the subject of this paper: the trade in coarse northern wools and wool-fells, which were the raw materials for the 'light' cloths of the Netherlands 'slight' or *slechte draperie*. These cheap cloths, the product of both woollen and worsted manufactories, were sought by merchants whenever they were faced with difficult market situations which forced them to be highly price competitive. Thus in the Baltic, where progressive debasement during the years 1486-97 and 1515-27 tended to cause an over-pricing of western European commodities, it was only these cheap and shoddy wares which could be vended. At these times the ships which carried English cloths from London to the Netherlands, after disembarking these wares from transmission overland to the east, then sailed on to the northern sea, carrying cheap East Anglian 'doucken' to customers in the lands bordering the Baltic.[18] There, however, these cheap English cloths had to compete with the products of Low Countries' *slechte draperie*: Naarden cloths (production about 9,000 cloths) and above all the 'doucken' of the Flemish towns of Dixmude, Tourcoing (production 4,000 cloths) and Poperinge (production 5,000 cloths).[19] In

---

[18]'Doucken': essentially these cloths, weighing between 1.0 and 1.1 lbs per square yard, were debased 'heavy' draperies utilising either (a) the cheapest varieties of wool or (b) the refuse of the clip and inferior fells - flocks and thrums (the waste ends of wool or yarn); lentynware (the skins of lambs that died shortly after being dropped in the spring); morlings (the fells of sheep that died of disease) and shorlings (broken wool). In the tight labour conditions of the 1510s these were supplemented by *étamettes* or 'tammies', a worsted utilising the same low quality wools as other products of this genre, which being woven on a narrower loom required less labour to produce. On the English production of these cloths see Norfolk and Norwich Record Office, City Records, Press B, Case 10b, and, on the increasing use of the 'stamyn' loom in the 1510s, Press E, Case 17: Second Worsted Weavers' Book, fo. 28. Both the 'doucken' and the various types of worsted utilised 'mentill' warp, small 'ouffe' and 'hevyll' yarn spun from the wool of butcher's fells: Press D, Case 16d-2, fo. 169v). Concerning labour market conditions at this time see I Blanchard, 'Population change, enclosure and the early Tudor economy', *Economic History Review*, second series, xxiii, 3 (1970), 431, and for a careful analysis of the tangled evidence concerning the nature of the *étamette*, D C Coleman, 'An innovation and its diffusion: the new draperies', *Economic History Review*, second series, xxii, 3 (1969), 420.
[19]On Naarden see A C J de Vrankrijker, 'De textielindustrie van Naarden', *Tijdschrift voor Geschiedenis*, li (1936), 154, and its markets in the Baltic: *Hansisches Urkundenbuch* (hereafter *HUB*), ed. W Stein (vols 8-11) (Munich, 1916, and Weimar, 1939): 10, no. 158; 11, no. 1211; *Liv-, Est- und Curländisches Urkundenbuch* (hereafter *Livl. UB*), ed. P Schwartz (series i, vols 10-12), L Arbusow (series ii, vols 1-3) (Riga-Moscow-Leipzig, 1884-1914): i, 11, no. 753 and ii, 2, no. 627. The Flemish industry and its relations with the Hanse is the subject of a number of studies: M Braure, 'Etudes économiques sur les Châtellenies de Lille, Douai et Orchies...', *Revue du Nord*, xv (1928), 188; H E de Sagher,

relation to other markets such cloths were normally sought by merchants on those occasions when financial crises affecting Antwerp's Bourse (in 1486-92, 1497-1503, 1509-13, 1516-17 and 1521-3) depressed the trade in 'heavy' draperies at the marts. This intermittent trade, which particularly affected Flemish worsted manufacturers at centres like Hondeschoote (production about 6,000-9,000 cloths) and Nieuwkirke (about 3,000 cloths),[20] thus in the short term moved counter-cyclically to that in the 'heavy' draperies, but in the long term, under the influence of cheap money, experienced analogous conditions to those prevailing in the 'heavy cloth trade.

Thus during the years 1492-1523/6 Netherlands 'doucken' and worsted manu-factures were affected by two major changes in market conditions. They shared in the trade boom which was contemporaneously transforming the position of pro-ducers of the 'heavy' drapery, but, finding a ready market for their wares only in crisis conditions, operated at a lower level of activity at least until about 1515. From that time, however, these cheap cloths began to displace their more expen-sive counterparts on the important Baltic market, thereby promoting a major trade boom and increase in the production of these cheap cloths.

To facilitate this expansion in 'light' cloth production, which elevated these wares into the ranks of the 'grande draperie', manufacturers were forced to aug-ment their normal supplies of local wools. To this end they drew on the coarse wool and fell trade which was, as the sixteenth century opened, a temporally in-termittent business organized through a rather informal and regionally frag-mented commercial network. Even as the new century began, there was a turmoil of crisis conditions at Antwerp, which during the years 1497-1503 afforded pro-ducers of *slechte draperie* new opportunities to promote their trade to central and eastern Europe.

The main features of their supply systems may be discerned. In the western Netherlands the marts of the Scheldt estuary provided the major focus for this sup-

---

'Une enquête sur la situation de l'industrie drapière en Flandre à la fin du XVIe siècle', *Etudes d'histoire dédiées à la mémoire de Henri Pirenne par ses anciens élèves* (Brussels, 1937), 11; H van Werveke, 'Die Stellung des hansischen Kaufmanns dem flandrischen Tuchproduzenten gegenüber', in H Aubin et al., *Beiträge zur Wirtschafts- und Stadt-geschichte: Festschrift für Hektor Amman* (Wiesbaden, 1965), 298-9, whilst on these rela-tionships and market conditions in the Baltic see *HUB* 9, nos 558, 744; 10, nox. 49, 704; *Die Recesse und andere Akten der Hansetage* (hereafter *HR*), series i, ed. W Junghans (vol. 1) and K Koppmann (vols 2-8) (Leipzig, 1870-97); series ii, ed. G Freiherr von Roppe (Leipzig, 1876-92); series iii, ed. D Schäfer (vols 1-7) and D Schäfer and F Teschen (vols 8-9) (Leipzig, 1881-1913); series iv, vol. 1, ed. G Wentz (Weimar, 1941): iii, 2, nos 162, 164; 3, no. 10; *Livl. UB*, ii, 2, no. 113.

[20]To afford comparisons of production between the relatively well documented Flemish worsted manufactories of Hondeschoote and Nieuwkirke (on which see sources listed in n. 4, above) and the rather fragmentary data available on the cheap woollen manufactories of Naarden, Dixmude, Tourcoing and Poperinge (on which see sources listed in n. 17, above), all figures presented here relate to output during the first decade of the sixteenth century.

ply system. In part, it catered for the requirements of manufacturers in the cloth-making districts of Flanders located to the west of Ypres, supplementing on this occasion the producers' normal native wool supplies drawn from Flanders and particularly Les Quatre-Métiers, Artois and Boulonnais, and Hainault. In this instance manufacturers also obtained some of the increased supplies of wool through contracts with one group of their major customers, the 'Easterlings' or Hanseatic merchants who at this time, as during previous crisis years (1486-92, for instance), may be discerned importing to Flanders 'Ostland' wool from Pomerania, Poland and Silesia.[21] Equally important, however, were the supplies which the manufacturers obtained from merchants operating under the umbrella of the older wool trading system. For the 'doucken' makers of Dixmude, Poperinge and Tourcoing this meant having recourse to the Scots.[22] For these Scots merchants, however, this trade with the Flemings was only one aspect of a multi-layered commercial system which encompassed many other elements in the western Netherlands wool trade. As has already been indicated they were also involved in the fine wool trade at Bruges. Further they sold fells to the manufacturers of Ghent and Mechelen and, far more importantly, to the Hollanders (of the Hague, Hoorne and Delft) who were also major purchasers of such wares at Calais.[23]

The principal west Netherlands producers of light draperies for the export market, therefore, in Holland and the cloth-making districts of Flanders to the west of Ypres, had access to a well-organised industrial wool market wherein Scots and Newcastle merchants, Easterlings and Staplers, operating under a traditional wool trading system, were able to supply coarse wools and fells wherever and whenever they were required. This pattern of commercial activity, first revealed in 1497-1503, repeated itself thereafter during the next quarter of a century as occasion dictated.

These light cloth producers' counterparts in the eastern provinces of the Netherlands also enjoyed access to a similar well-organized, regional wool market, in this instance centred on Frankfurt.[24] Through the fair in this town passed Rhenish wools which, since the decline of the local cloth industry in the late fifteenth cen-

---

[21]See W S Unger, *De Tol van Iersekerood*, (as in n. 10, above), and H van Werveke, 'Die Stellung des hansischen Kaufmanns...' (as in n. 19, above).

[22]See *Halyburton's Ledger*, 14, 17, 24, 29, 42, 44, 46, 66, 68, 77, 79, 82, 111, 113, 115, 118, 126, 131, 136, 143, 177, 188, 193, 195, 199, 207, 219, 221-2, 228-9, 231, 241, 244. An analysis of this branch of the trade reveals a marked increase in activity during the years 1497-1503. It is perhaps worth noting that at this time the 'say' manufacturers of Hondeschoote continued to operate solely on the basis of native wools, the drapers buying 'fleeces, packets of a few pounds at the local centres of Bergues, Loo, Dixmude...', E Cornaert, *Un centre industriel...* (as in n. 4, above), 192.

[23]On Scots sales of fells and low quality wools to the Hollanders, see *Halyburton's Ledger*, 19, 21, 23, 40, 42, 44, 46, 53, 64, 68, 71, 76, 90, 112, 209, 211. on the purchases of these wares at Calais, Hanham, *The Celys*, 159-63, and E Power, 'The wool trade in the fifteenth century' (as in n. 5, above), 60-1.

[24]A Dietz, *Frankfurter Handelsgeschichte* (5 vols, Frankfurt am Main, 1910-25), i, 254-62.

tury, were distributed north to Utrecht, Naarden and Amersfoort[25] or west to Lo-
tharingia and Aachen. From Hesse and the lands of Hesse-Cassel wools and dye-
stuffs, collected at Fritzler, Frankenberg and Sprangenberg, were also brought to
Frankfurt for redistribution to Nürnberg and Ulm; Epinal and St Nikolasport in
Lotharingia; Sedan, Arras, Tournai and Mons, and Maastricht and Aachen.[26]
Finally, these local, middle-German wool supplies were on occasion supplemented
at Frankfurt by more exotic produce, as merchants out of Leipzig brought Lausitz,
Bohemian, Silesian and Polish wools, and others from Naumberg transported
Thuringian wools to the fair, where they were bought by manufacturers from
Maastricht, Aachen, Malmedy and Trier. The principal east Netherlands producers of light draperies for the export market - in the cloth-making districts of eastern Holland and Gelderland, and Ardenne-Lotharingia - thus also, like the
equivalent producers in the west of the country, frequented a well-organized industrial wool market, wherein German merchants were able, for the next quarter
of a century, to supply coarse wools and fells as they were required.

The trade boom of the years 1492-1523/6 was occasionally stayed (in 1497-
1503, 1509-13, 1516-17 and 1521-3) by financial crises, and particularly from
about 1515 to 1526 when Baltic currencies underwent major debasements, causing the products of the light-cloth manufactory to come to the fore. In these circumstances, however, cloth makers in this sector of the Netherlands industry
found themselves well provided with the market facilities described above, which
enabled them to secure supplies of the coarse wools and fells they required. Unfortunately, because of the informal and fragmented structure of these markets and
the temporal instability of activity therein, it is impossible to provide a complete
statistical overview of this trade. Only within the western Netherlands commercial
network, centred on the Scheldt, is such an overview possible (fig. 2).[27] The picture of the trade revealed is a complex one. During the years 1497-1515 northern

---

[25]A C J de Vrankrijker, 'Naarden...' (as in n. 19, above), 155, whilst Dietz, op. cit., 260,
provides evidence that these wools were also via Hamburg drawn into the 'Ostland' wool
trade.

[26]M H Ammann, 'Der Hessische Raum in der mittlelalterlichen Wirtschaft', *Hessisches
Jahrbuch für Landesgeschichte*, viii (1958).

[27]Figure 2 sources: English fells, traded through the Calais Staple: P Ramsey, 'Overseas
trade in the reign of Henry VII: the evidence of customs accounts', *Economic History Review*, second series, vi, 2 (1953), 181, and G Schanz, *Englische Handelspolitik gegen Ende
des Mittelalters mit besonderer Berücksichtigung des Zeitalters der beiden ersten Tudors
Heinrich VI und Heinrich VIII* (2 vols, Leipzig, 1881), ii, 76-85, which distinguish the
trade in fells and wool. Newcastle wool and fells: E M Carus-Wilson and O Coleman,
England's Export Trade (as in n. 4, above), 69-74, 122-39. Scots wool: *Rotuli Scaccarii
Regum Scotorum* (Edinburgh, 1889-97), vols xii-xviii; and, for a description of the Scottish customs system, see A Murray, 'The Exchequer and Crown Revenue of Scotland,
1437-1542' (unpublished Edinburgh Ph D thesis, 1961), 142-6. 'Ostland' wool: Wo-
jéwodzkie Archiwum Panstwowe w Gdansk Komora Palowa, Pfahlkammerrechnung 300,
19/7-11, encompassing Polish exports through the Sound and thus a minimum figure, excluding exports from Pomerania and central Germany via Hamburg.

British, that is Scottish and Newcastle, coarse wools and fells dominated the markets of the Scheldt. These sources supplied annually 2,000-2,250 sacks during booms in the trade (in 1497-1503 and 1509-13) and 1,600-1,750 sacks during intervening slumps (in 1504-8 and 1514-15). These supplies were further augmented by the trade in English fells, through the Calais Staple, which amounted annually in boom years to about 1,800 sacks and in slumps to 1,250 sacks - at least until 1514-15. Throughout the period 1497-1515, therefore, Scottish and English produce dominated Netherlands markets for coarse wool and fells, the trade rising to some 4,000 sacks a year in boom conditions and stabilizing at 3,000-3,500 sacks during the intervening slumps.

Progressive debasements of the Baltic currencies during the years 1486-97 and 1515-27, however, served to alter significantly trade patterns at these times. By undermining the position of the Leiden 'heavy' draperies on northern markets and causing merchants to acquire, in 'normal' conditions (during 1493-6, 1514-15 and 1518-20) at Antwerp, the 'light' cloths of the Hague, Hoorne and Delft to sell there, they caused an augmentation in the demand for fells, particularly English, at a time when the market for this produce was normally depressed. Debasement, in lowering the foreign-exchange price of Baltic produce on Low Country markets, also introduced a new competitor into the trade - 'Ostland' wool. As a result the market was transformed. The English trade, via the Calais staple, increased to some 2,000-2,750 sacks a year. The northern British trade, on the other hand, declined to 600-1,500 sacks as its position on Netherlands markets was usurped by 'Ostland' wool, some 500-600 sacks of which were imported at these times.

Patterns of commercial development in the northern coarse-wool and fell trade were thus far more complex than in the better-known commerce in fine wools. Yet it was no less efficient in meeting the raw material requirements of those Netherlands producers of the *slechte draperie* who by the close of the 1492-1523/6 trade-cycle had established themselves on a position of parity with the previously important heavy cloth producers. In the coarse-wool and fell markets of the western Netherlands alone supplies which between 1493 and 1515 had fluctuated between about 3,500 and 4,000 sacks a year thereafter increased to 5,000 sacks in 1518-20. If analogous conditions prevailed on the Frankfurt market, then the coarse-wool and fell trade had finally come of age and had for the first time also established itself on a position of parity with the previously important and better known fine wool trade.

III

In the case of the Netherlands *slechte draperie* and its associated raw material supply system, therefore, 1520 marked the beginning of a new era. Henceforth, following the exchange crises of 1521 and 1522-3, whilst production of the Anglo-Netherlands 'heavy' drapery underwent a process of terminal decline, the 'light' draperies went from strength to strength. Those crises and the monetary disorders of 1531-2, however, ensured a transformation of its wool supply system. The establishment of a 'hard' currency system in the Baltic, based on the Joachimstaler, caused the trade in 'Ostland' wool to collapse and the northern British, and particularly Scots, trade to re-establish itself. Inflationary pressures undermined the English wool trade and again ensured its subordination to its Scots counterpart. In part, therefore, pre-existing trading patterns re-asserted themselves, but, with a total commerce still in 1540-1, at the height of the contemporary trade-cycle, below the levels of the previous cycle, this 'traditional' trade could no longer satisfy the requirements of 'light' cloth producers and was eclipsed - by those innovating farmers who were contemporaneously transforming Netherlands agriculture and its associated wool supply system.

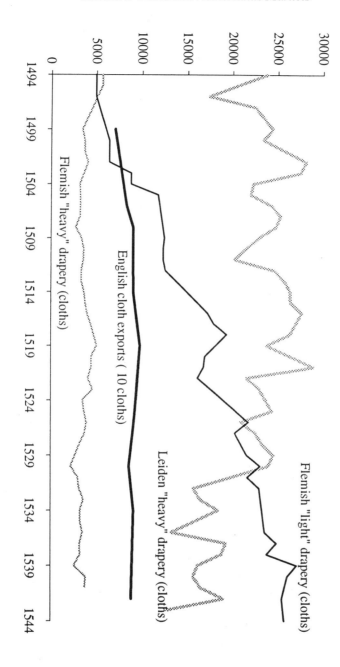

Figure 1. Anglo-Netherlands Textile Industry

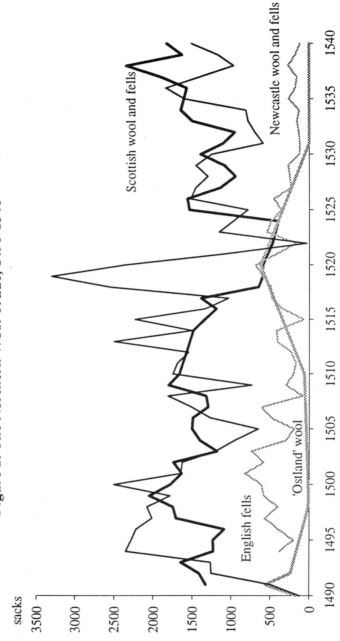

Figure 2. The Northern Wool Trade, 1490-1540

7

SCOTTISH PATRONS
AND NETHERLANDISH PAINTERS
IN THE FIFTEENTH AND SIXTEENTH CENTURIES

Lorne Campbell

In 1438 certain inhabitants of Hull seized from Coenrardus de Eyke, burgess of Haarlem, 'a panel decorated with the most beautiful pictures', valued at twelve nobles, and other merchandise, valued at one noble, which Coenrardus had brought 'de partibus Scothie'.[1] It comes as a surprise to find a Netherlander exporting from Scotland a beautiful and valuable painting, for it seems a reversal of the natural order of things. The panel, however, may not have been painted in Scotland. Coenrardus de Eyke may have brought it from the Low Countries to sell in Scotland but, in 1437-8, immediately after the assassination of James I, he may have been unable to find a Scottish purchaser. Perhaps he was taking it back to the Netherlands when he had his unlucky and violent encounter with the men from Hull.

According to Bower, James I was himself a gifted painter and, according to Hector Boece, he 'brocht oute of Ingland and Flanderis ingenious men of sindry craftis to instruct his pepill in vertewis occupacioun'.[2] Though there is no documentary evidence that James brought Netherlandish painters to Scotland, a drawing in the 'Recueil d'Arras' may be a copy after a lost portrait of James I by a Netherlandish painter (see plate 1). The 'Recueil d'Arras' is a volume of portrait copies, evidently drawn by Jacques Le Boucq, a herald of Valenciennes, and put together in the 1560s, apparently for Alexandre Le Blancq, a gentleman of Lille.[3]

---

[1]'... Incole Hullenses sibi abstulerunt et violenter rapuerunt unam tabulam picturis pulcherrimis exornatam valoris duodecim nobilium et plura alia mercimonia, que de partibus Scothie apportaverat, pro quibus tredecim nobilia exposuit ...': H J Smit, *Bronnen tot de geschiedenis van den handel met Engeland, Schotland en Ierland*, i, *1150-1485* (Rijksgeschiedkundige publicatiën, nos 65, 66, 2 vols, The Hague, 1928), ii, 801.

[2]D E R Watt, *Scotichronicon by Walter Bower*, viii (Aberdeen, 1987), 309; W Seton, R W Chambers, E C Batho, H W Husbands, eds, *The Chronicles of Scotland, compiled by Hector Boece, translated into Scots by John Bellenden 1531* (Scottish Text Society, 3rd ser., 10, 15, 2 vols, Edinburgh, 1938-41), ii, 393.

[3]On the 'Recueil d'Arras', Bibliothèque municipale, Arras, MS 266, see L Quarré-Reybourbon, 'Trois recueils de portraits', *Bulletin de la Commission historique du département du Nord*, xxiii (1900), 5-42, 67-95; L Campbell, 'The Authorship of the *Recueil d'Arras*', *Journal of the Warburg and Courtauld Institutes*, xl (1977), 301-13. The drawing of James I is reproduced in L Campbell, *The Early Flemish Pictures in the Collection of Her Majesty The Queen* (Cambridge, 1985) (hereafter Campbell, *Early Flemish Pictures*), fig. 12.

It contains a surprising number of portraits of Scots and of knights who had performed remarkable feats of valour in Scotland.[4] I do not know why the compilers of the 'Recueil' took so strong an interest in Scottish affairs, or how they obtained the originals which they copied. On folio 18, the drawing inscribed 'Jacques Roy descoce' appears to be an accurate copy of a portrait painted in the 1430s in the most up-to-date Netherlandish style and provides a possible indication that James had brought to his court a painter well versed in the latest developments in the Low Countries.

On the next folio of the 'Recueil' is the mysterious drawing of 'Legyptienne quy Rendist santè part art de medecine au Roy descoce abandonnè des medecins' (see plate 2). I do not know which king this was; four folios have been removed from the Arras manuscript between the drawings of James I and the gypsy woman, so that there is no real reason to associate her with James I (and, incidentally, four copies of Scottish portraits have gone missing).

James II's queen, Mary of Guelders, had been brought up at the Burgundian court;[5] her son James III was a friend of Anselm Adornes, an important Netherlandish patron;[6] but there is no direct evidence that either Mary or James III took an interest in Netherlandish painting. In 1502, however, James IV received at his court the Netherlandish painter Meynnart Wewyck, who worked for Henry VII of England and who brought from England portraits of Henry, his queen, Prince Henry and Margaret Tudor.[7] In 1504-5, possibly because the esteemed court painter David Pratt had just died, James asked Andrew Haliburton, Conservator of the Privileges of the Scots in the Netherlands, to send him a painter. Haliburton was well placed to find a suitable painter, for he was the son-in-law and brother-in-law of the illuminators Sanders and Simon Bening and was related through them to the Antwerp painter Goswijn van der Weyden. Goswijn was the grandson of Rogier van der Weyden, while Sanders Bening had married Catherine van der Goes, who was almost certainly related to Hugo van der Goes. Andrew Haliburton

---

[4]All the portraits are listed by Quarré-Reybourbon, 'Trois recueils', 67-83. Those with Scottish connections are on fols. 18, 'Jacques Roy descoce'; 19, 'Marguerite dangleterre Royne descoce ...'; 20, 'Sire bernard stuart Lord ofobeny escossois ...'; 21, 'Jacques Roy descoce'; 22, 'Legyptienne ...'; 25, 'Sandre aliberton co[n]bastit en ung camp en la ville de Edimbourg ...'; 243, 'Messire Jehan de compans ... vint en escoche pour faire combat a pied ...'; 244, 'Ung chevallier darthoys nommè beauffort vint en escoce pour exercer armes ...'; 246, 'Messire Anthoyne darses ... vint en escoce ... pour faire joustes ...'; 256, 'Larchevescque de St Andrieu filz b' du Roy descoce quy fut occis a la battaille avecq son pere co[n]tre les anglois'. The drawing of Sir Bernard Stewart, seigneur d'Aubigny, is reproduced in Gordon Menzies, ed., *The Scottish Nation* (London, 1972), plate 7.

[5]Monique Sommé, 'La jeunesse de Charles le Téméraire d'après les comptes de la cour de Bourgogne', *Revue du Nord*, lxiv (1982), 731-50, 735-6.

[6]Alan MacQuarrie, 'Anselm Adornes of Bruges', *Innes Review*, xxxiii (1982), 15-22 and references.

[7]M R Apted and S Hannabuss, *Painters in Scotland 1301-1700, A Biographical Dictionary* (Scottish Record Society, n.s. 7, Edinburgh, 1978) (hereafter Apted and Hannabuss, *Painters*), 68-9; Campbell, *Early Flemish Pictures*, xv and references.

was therefore connected by marriage with three of the principal artist families of the Low Countries and he duly sent to Scotland 'Piers the painter', who worked at the Scottish court from 1505 until 1508, when he received a grant of money to 'pas in Flandrez'.[8] It is just possible that Piers may have been Peerken Bovelant, who had been apprenticed to Goswijn van der Weyden at Antwerp in 1503.[9] Drawings in the 'Recueil d'Arras' may once again preserve the appearances of portraits executed by a Netherlandish-trained artist during the period of Piers's activity in Scotland. These are of James IV himself, his queen and his illegitimate son, Alexander, who was born in about 1493, who in 1504 had been made archbishop of St Andrews and who left Scotland for Italy in 1507.[10]

The Arras drawing of James resembles quite closely the copy made by Daniel Mytens for Charles I after a now lost 'Auncient water cullored peece' of James IV which had been in the collection of Henry VIII.[11] Mytens also copied for Charles I in full-length a portrait in half-length which was then believed to represent Margaret Tudor and which also came from Henry VIII's collection.[12] Described in the 1542 and 1547 inventories of Henry's pictures simply as 'the picture of a woman with a monkey on her hand', it may not have been a portrait of Margaret after all. The costume in Mytens's copy is of the 1510s. Even if the original portrait was of Margaret Tudor, it can have had nothing to do with Piers the painter, who left Scotland in 1508.

According to Pitscottie, James V brought foreign painters to Scotland, but neither he nor Queen Mary can be proved to have employed Netherlandish painters. James V, however, acquired Netherlandish pictures.[13] In 1532 an unnamed

---

[8]Apted and Hannabuss, *Painters*, 70-2 (for Piers), 75-7 (for Pratt); Campbell, *Early Flemish Pictures*, xxxi-xxxii and references. For the request to Haliburton, see J B Paul, ed., *Accounts of the Lord High Treasurer of Scotland*, iii (Edinburgh, 1901), 162. For Cornelia Bening, C Thompson and L Campbell, *Hugo van der Goes and the Trinity Panels in Edinburgh* (Edinburgh, 1974) (hereafter Thompson and Campbell, *Hugo van der Goes*), 50 notes 5, 6, and references.

[9]P Rombouts and T van Lerius, *Les Liggeren et autres archives historiques de la gilde anversoise de Saint Luc*, i (Antwerp and The Hague, 1864-76), 59.

[10]J Herkless and R K Hannay, *The Archbishops of St Andrews*, i (Edinburgh, 1907), 215-71.

[11]The Arras drawing of James IV is reproduced in R L Mackie, *King James IV of Scotland, A Brief Survey of his Life and Times* (Edinburgh, 1958) (hereafter Mackie, *James IV*), facing p. 53. The Mytens painting, in a private collection, is reproduced in Mackie, *James IV*, facing p. 84. See further W A Shaw, *Three Inventories ... of Pictures in the Collections of Henry VIII and Edward VI* (London, 1937), 46 (134); O Millar, 'Abraham van der Doort's Catalogue of the Collections of Charles I', *The Walpole Society*, xxxvii (1960), 4.

[12]Royal Collection, Holyroodhouse, reproduced in Mackie, *James IV*, facing p. 101. See further Shaw, *Three Inventories*, 31 (26); Millar, 'Abraham van der Doort', 4, 28; O Millar, *The Tudor, Stuart and Early Georgian Pictures in the Collection of Her Majesty The Queen* (2 vols, London, 1963) (hereafter Millar, *Tudor, Stuart*), 84-5.

[13]R Lindesay of Pitscottie, *The Historie and Cronicles of Scotland*, ed. A J G Mackay, (Scottish Text Society, 3 vols, Edinburgh, 1899-1911), i, 353-4.

painter of Brussels executed at the command of Mary of Hungary portraits of her nieces, the exiled princesses Dorothea and Christina of Denmark, and these were delivered to a Scottish ambassador who had requested them for his master the king. Pitscottie confirms that 'the ambassadouris', Sir John Campbell of Lundie and Sir David Lindsay of the Mount, 'brocht hame thair pictouris into the kingis grace of Scottland and presentit the samin into him'.[14] In 1535, the Treasurer paid £17 for 'certane fyne picturis of Flandris coft fra John Broune to the Kingis grace', bought for James V from John Brown, apparently the Leith shipmaster of that name who frequently transported articles for the royal household from the Low Countries.[15]

James VI employed at least two Netherlandish painters at his court in Scotland. One was Arnold Bronkhorst, who in Scottish sources is referred to as Arnold but who in English sources is called Arthur.[16] His name was clearly Aert, which the Scots translated correctly as Arnold but which the English expanded incorrectly as Arthur. He came to Scotland from England in about 1579 to prospect for gold and is said to have been detained here by the earl of Morton.[17] He was perhaps the unnamed Flemish painter who in May and June 1579 was producing, under difficult circumstances, a full-length portrait of James which was to be sent to Queen Elizabeth of England.[18] In 1580, Bronkhorst painted several portraits for James, who in 1581 appointed him his painter with a yearly pension of £100.[19] Bronkhorst's wife remained in London, where he must have visited her often, for they had children baptized in December 1579, October 1582 and April 1584.[20] His pension was not paid after Martinmas 1583; he returned to London, where he was last recorded in 1586.[21] His widow was still alive in London in 1625.[22] Bronkhorst was replaced by another Netherlander, Adrian Vanson, who

[14]J Finot, *Inventaire sommaire des archives départementales antérieures à 1790, Nord, Archives civiles, Série B*, v (Lille, 1885), 31; Pitscottie, *Historie*, i, 354.

[15]J B Paul, ed., *Accounts of the Lord High Treasurer of Scotland*, vi (Edinburgh, 1905), 250.

[16]Apted and Hannabuss, *Painters*, 31; M Edmond, *Hilliard and Oliver* (London, 1983), 55-7.

[17]G L Meason, ed., *The Discoverie and Historie of the Gold Mynes in Scotland, By Stephen Atkinson: written in the Year M.DC.XIX* (Bannatyne Club, Edinburgh, 1825), 34.

[18]C Sharp, *Memorials of the Rebellion of 1569* (London, 1840), 390 note *.

[19]A MacDonald, 'A short Notice of Arnold Bronckhorst', *Archaeologia Scotica*, iii (1831), 312-13; E Auerbach, *Tudor Artists* (London, 1954), 117, 151-2; D Thomson, *Painting in Scotland 1570-1650* (exhibition catalogue, Scottish National Portrait Gallery, Edinburgh, 1975) (hereafter Thomson, *Painting*), 22.

[20]W A Littledale, ed., *The Registers of St Vedast, Foster Lane, and of St Michael le Quern, London*, i (Harleian Society, Registers, xxix, London, 1902), 11; W Brigg, *The Register Book of the Parish of St Nicholas Acons, London, 1539-1812* (Leeds, 1890), 9.

[21]Ibid.

[22]R E G and E F Kirk, eds, *Returns of Aliens dwelling in the City and Suburbs of London* (Huguenot Society, x, 4 vols, Aberdeen, 1900-8), iii, 289.

had a cousin in London but who probably came from Breda.[23] Vanson had earlier, in 1581 and 1582, painted for the Scottish court.[24] Living in Edinburgh among a small immigrant community of merchants and craftsmen, he seems also to have owned a ship;[25] while his wife Susanna de Colone traded in Edinburgh on her own account.[26] Vanson followed James to London in 1603 but was dead by 1610.[27] His widow was still alive, residing in the parish of St Martin in the Fields in Westminster, when in 1619 their daughter Susan married a prosperous English cleric, Giles King.[28]

Two paintings by Bronkhorst are identifiable, but they were painted in England before and after his period at the Scottish court. The *Portrait of Oliver St John, first Baron St John of Bletso* is signed and dated 1578;[29] a hitherto unpublished *Portrait of a Lady* is stated to be inscribed on the back 'Brounkhorst 1585' (see plate 3).[30] Bronkhorst was probably responsible for the likeness of James VI that was circulating in 1583, whereas later portraits of James were presumably by Vanson.[31]

Much less is known about the patronage of the Scottish nobility. The Lennox Stewarts, while residing in England, employed the Netherlandish painters Hans Eworth and Lieven de Vogelaar, both of whom came from Antwerp. Eworth

---

[23]Public Record Office, Prerogative Court of Canterbury Wills, PROB 11/73, 15, Will of Peter Matheus, London, 17 October 1588 (proved 23 December 1588). The testator owned property in Breda and bequeathed 'to my cosen Adryan van Zont paynter of the Kings Maiestye of Scotland the three pictures of the conterfaytings of my Late ffather and mother and also of me and also the Arte concerning Lymming'. For Vanson's appointment as painter to James VI, see G Donaldson, ed., *Register of the Privy Seal of Scotland*, viii (Edinburgh, 1982), 396 (2287).

[24]Thomson, *Painting*, 25; Apted and Hannabuss, *Painters*, 98-9.

[25]Thomson, *Painting*, 25; for the ship, J Pinkerton, *The Scottish Gallery* (London, 1799), 6, citing a 'privilege' of 1594 then in Pinkerton's possession.

[26]Apted and Hannabuss, *Painters*, 98.

[27]E Croft-Murray, *Decorative Painting in England*, i (London, 1962), 215; Apted and Hannabuss, *Painters*, 98.

[28]Guildhall Library, London, Allegations for Marriage Licences issued by the Bishops of London, MS 10091/7, under 23 November 1619. Giles King, cleric, Great Catworth, made his will on 2 December 1658 (Public Record Office, Prerogative Court of Canterbury Wills, PROB 11/286, 41). This was proved on 10 February 1659 by his relict Susan, who was perhaps the Susanna King buried at Great Catworth on 27 May 1682 (parish register transcript, Society of Genealogists, London).

[29]Thomson, *Painting*, 23.

[30]Private collection: photograph in the Witt Library, Courtauld Institute of Art, London, negative B 65/428.

[31]See the double portrait of James with his mother, dated 1583, at Blair Castle, reproduced in R K Marshall, *Queen of Scots* (Edinburgh 1986), 190; and the two portraits of James dated 1595, both in the Scottish National Portrait Gallery, reproduced in Thomson, *Painting*, 28-9.

monogrammed portraits of Lord Darnley in 1555 and 1563;[32] Lieven de Vogelaar signed the *Memorial of Lord Darnley* in 1568.[33] Eworth may have visited Scotland. His monogrammed portrait of a sitter identified as the earl of Moray is dated 1561 and is clearly the pair to an unsigned, undated portrait of a lady, presumed to be the earl's wife Agnes Keith. As the earl married Agnes Keith in Edinburgh on 8 February 1561/2, and if the sitters are correctly identified, the portraits would seem to have been painted in Scotland in February or March of 1561/2.[34] George, the fifth Lord Seton, sat at least twice to Netherlandish painters: in about 1560, it would appear, to a follower of Guillaume Scrots;[35] and in 1572, with five of his children, to Frans Pourbus the Elder, who by 1572 was established in Antwerp but who spent part of that autumn in Bruges.[36]

More can be discovered about the Scottish clerics, for example Lawrence of Lindores, who had been a penitentiary and papal chaplain in Rome and who became in 1436, by apostolic authority, abbot of Culross. After some resistance from a rival candidate, Robert Waddell (who had been Master of Works at Linlithgow Palace), Lawrence gained possession of the abbey but was ejected by Robert and died in Rome in 1443 or 1444.[37] In November 1441, Lawrence wrote to Bernardo Portinari, manager of the Bruges branch of the Medici Bank, who was to supply him with a 'parchment book of St Mary' and an altar cloth, which was presumably painted.[38] These objects were probably for Culross.

It was Edward Bonkil, provost of the Collegiate Church of the Holy Trinity in Edinburgh, who brought to Scotland the triptych by Hugo van der Goes from which only the wings survives (see plates 4-7). The portrait of Bonkil on the reverse of the right wing was clearly done from life and must have been painted in

---

[32]Millar, *Tudor, Stuart*, 68; R Strong, *Hans Eworth* (exhibition catalogue, Museums and Art Gallery, Leicester, 1965) (hereafter Strong, *Eworth*), 3, 8.

[33]Millar, *Tudor, Stuart*, 75-7.

[34]Strong, *Eworth*, 6. The portraits are stated to have passed by descent from the sitters. The man's portrait is inscribed 'RECT SECVRVS' but the earl of Moray used the motto 'SALVS PER CHRISTVM'. For the date of the earl's marriage, see T Thomson, ed., *A Diurnal of Remarkable Occurrents* (Maitland Club, Edinburgh, 1833), 70.

[35]Thomson, *Painting*, 32-3.

[36]C Thompson and H Bristocke, *National Gallery of Scotland, Shorter Catalogue*, (2nd edn, Edinburgh, 1978), 76; reproduced in R K Marshall, *Queen of Scots* (Edinburgh, 1986), 172; for Pourbus's movements, P Huvenne, *Pierre Pourbus* (exhibition catalogue, Memlingmuseum, Bruges, 1984), 311.

[37]On Lawrence of Lindores, see J Twemlow, ed., *Entries in the Papal Registers relating to Great Britain and Ireland*, ix (London, 1913), 349-50; A I Cameron, *The Apostolic Camera and Scottish Benefices 1418-88* (St Andrews University publications, xxxv, London, 1934), 22; A I Dunlop and D MacLauchlan, eds, *Calendar of Scottish Supplications to Rome*, iv, 1433-47 (Glasgow, 1983), 79, 210, 271. For Waddell at Linlithgow, see G Burnett, ed., *The Exchequer Rolls of Scotland*, iv (Edinburgh, 1880), 652.

[38]Archivio di Stato, Florence, Medici avanti il principato, MAP 47/5. This document was discovered and brought to my attention by Dr Paula V Nuttall, who kindly sent me a transcript and who will publish it in due course.

the Low Countries. It differs markedly in style from the portraits on the interior faces of the wings, where James III and Margaret of Denmark are represented. The head of the queen was apparently done from drawings sent from Scotland, while the head of James III has been overpainted, evidently in an effort to improve the likeness. If that is so, the artist who executed the visible head would have been working in Scotland and almost as soon as the panels arrived in Edinburgh. As I have argued elsewhere, it was evidently Bonkil alone who was responsible for commissioning the triptych; the royal portraits would have been included out of courtesy to the monarch, who was the patron of Bonkil's church. Bonkil came of a family of Edinburgh merchants, several of whom traded with the Low Countries, and was well placed to commission such an altarpiece. Not mentioned in any written source before 1617, the panels were painted in the mid-1470s.[39]

William Scheves, archbishop of St Andrews, is represented in a medal dated 1491 and attributed to the painter Quinten Metsys, who came from Louvain but who became a master of the Antwerp Guild of St Luke in 1491. Scheves visited Louvain in 1491 and matriculated in the Faculty of Theology at Louvain University in February of that year.[40]

Other Scottish clerics passing through the Netherlands in the 1490s took the opportunity to commission works of art. At Bruges in 1494 Robert Ballantyne, abbot of Holyrood, purchased vestments for his abbey,[41] while James Brown, dean of Aberdeen, visiting the Low Countries in 1498 on his way home from Rome, acquired a book of hours.[42]

In the 1500s, George Brown, bishop of Dunkeld, imported from Flanders 'tabernacles' and 'images' of Saints John and Catherine which may have been paintings or sculptures'[43] and two 'tabernacles' commissioned in Flanders were set up at Pluscarden Abbey shortly before October 1508.[44] Bishop Brown of Dunkeld employed his own painter, one William Wallanch or Wallange, recorded in the Dunkeld accounts between 1505 and 1516.[45] He was possibly a Fleming. Willem Wallinc, who came of a family of Bruges painters, became a master of the Bruges guild in October 1506 but was not mentioned again in the Bruges records until the summer of 1516, after which he was regularly documented at Bruges until his

---

[39]Thompson and Campbell, *Hugo van der Goes*; L Campbell, 'Edward Bonkil, a Scottish patron of Hugo van der Goes', *Burlington Magazine,* cxxvi (1984), 265-74.

[40]On the medal, and on Scheves at Louvain, see R F Burckhardt, 'Medaille auf Wilhelm Schevez', *Anzeiger für schweizerische Altertumskunde,* NF xiii (1911), 42-6; A Schillings, ed., *Matricule de l'Université de Louvain,* iii (Commission royale d'histoire, Brussels, 1958), 68.

[41]F C Eeles, 'The Holyrood Ordinale', *Book of the Old Edinburgh Club,* vii (1914), 213.

[42]D McRoberts, 'Dean Brown's Book of Hours', *Innes Review,* xix (1968), 144-67.

[43]R K Hannay, *Rentale Dunkeldense, being Accounts of the Bishopric (1505-17)* (Scottish History Society, 1915) (hereafter Hannay, *Rentale*), 2-4.

[44]S R Macphail, *History of the Religious House of Pluscardyn* (Edinburgh, 1881), 236-7.

[45]Hannay, *Rentale*, 18, 80, 91, 272, etc.; Apted and Hannabuss, *Painters,* 97-8, who suggest that Wallanch may be a corruption of Valance.

death in 1553.[46] The absence of Willem Wallinc from the Bruges records coincides almost - though not absolutely - exactly with the presence of William Wallanch in the diocese of Dunkeld. A later bishop of Dunkeld, George Crichton, sent a representative to Antwerp in 1536 to commission his tomb. The tomb, completed in 1537, was of polished black marble and on it rested a great plaque of brass which the painter Jan Mandijn ornamented with 'painting and images'.[47] Mandijn, known for his imitations of Bosch's pictures, was perhaps an odd choice for this commission. The tomb was set up in the abbey church of Holyrood.[48] It was the same George Crichton who imported from the Netherlands the brass lectern now in St Stephen's church at St Albans.[49]

Scots of less exalted rank also had dealings with Netherlandish painters. In December 1439 William Knox, from Edinburgh, was in possession of 'a gilded panel with images which he had bought at Antwerp from Jan van Battel of Malines'.[50] Jan van Battel was a prominent painter of Malines but the 'gilded panel' supplied to Knox may have been a carving that Jan had polychromed rather than a painting.[51] In 1495, Andrew Haliburton acquired from an unnamed Antwerp painter for 'Jon of Pennycuk' an image of St Thomas of Canterbury. It was either a painting or a polychromed sculpture and 'Jon of Pennycuk' was apparently John Penicuik of Penicuik.[52]

Among the large numbers of painters who worked at Bruges in 1468 on the decorations for the marriage festivities of Charles the Bold and Margaret of York were two Scotsmen. 'Jehan Brou, Escochois' was among the painters 'recently arrived' in early June 1468 and was paid 3 *sols* 6 *deniers* a day; 'Sanders Escochois'

[46]W H J Weale, 'Documents inédits sur les peintres brugeois', *Le Beffroi*, iii (1866-70), 231-45; R A Parmentier, 'Bronnen voor de geschiedenis van het Brugsche schildersmilieu in de XVIe eeuw, xxx. Willem Walin', *Revue belge d'archéologie et d'histoire de l'art*, xvii (1947-8), 119-30.

[47]F J van den Branden, *Geschiedenis der Antwerpsche schilderschool* (Antwerp, 1883), 161.

[48]W Maitland, *The History of Edinburgh from its Foundation to the Present Time* (Edinburgh, 1753), 154-5.

[49]*Angels, Nobles and Unicorns, Art and Patronage in Medieval Scotland* (exhibition catalogue, National Museum of Antiquities of Scotland, Edinburgh, 1982), 115-16.

[50]G Asaert, 'Documenten voor de geschiedenis van de beeldhowkunst te Antwerpen in de XVe eeuw', *Jaarboek van het Koninklijk Museum voor schone kunsten, Antwerpen* (1972), 43-86, 48.

[51]E Neeffs, 'La peinture et la sculpture à Malines', *Messager des sciences historiques* (1872), 283-7; J B Stockmans, 'Lyrana', *Académie royale d'archéologie de Belgique, Bulletin* (1908), 267-310, 275-7.

[52]C Innes, ed., *Ledger of Andrew Halyburton* (Edinburgh, 1867), 9; for Penicuik, see H M Paton and G Donaldson, eds, *Protocol Book of James Young, 1485-1515* (Scottish Record Society, Edinburgh, 1941-52), no. 590.

was paid 8 *sols* a day.[53] Both Jehan Brou and Sanders were presumably already in the Low Countries. Sanders may have been the illuminator Sanders Bening, who became a master of the Ghent guild in 1469, when his cautioners were Joos van Wassenhove and Hugo van der Goes. The names Sanders and Bening sound Scottish and Sanders Bening's daughter Cornelia married Andrew Haliburton, Conservator of the Privileges of the Scots in the Netherlands. At least four painters named Binning worked in Edinburgh in the sixteenth century. Sanders Bening may have been a member of a dynasty of Scottish artists.[54]

Jehan Brou and Sanders Escochois probably went to the Low Countries to learn and doubtless many Scots sought instruction in painting there. Some may have settled permanently as Sanders Escochois may perhaps have done, while others would have returned to Scotland. There is little evidence, but it is known that Adam de Colone, son of James VI's court painter Adrian Vanson, was born in Scotland 'and broght up heir till he approcheit to the yearis of his majoritie, at quhilk tyme for his better inhabling in the practise and knawledge of his fatheris calling' he went 'to the Low Cuntreyis of Flanderis, quhair he remanit some certane yeiris'.[55]

From this scattering of evidence, it is difficult to draw any but the most obvious conclusions: that the Scots looked to the Low Countries for a lead in artistic matters and that some Scottish patrons had the discernment to place commissions with the leading Netherlandish painters. The lack of documentary evidence on painters working in Scotland, and above all the destruction of almost all the paintings produced in Scotland, prevent us from forming any clear idea of the impact of Netherlandish upon Scottish painting.

Additional Note

A painting of William Elphinstone, bishop of Aberdeen and founder of the university of Aberdeen, is in the possession of the university. It dates from the late fifteenth or early sixteenth century and is probably the work of a Netherlands artist. (See L J Macfarlane, *William Elphinstone and the Kingdom of Scotland, 1431-1514*, Aberdeen, 1985, frontispiece.) John Dick and the present writer are engaged in preparing for publication a full study of this important work.

---

[53]L de Laborde, *Les ducs de Bourgogne*, Seconde partie, *Preuves* (3 vols, Paris, 1849-52), ii, 366, 335; for Sanders Escochois, see also Brussels, Archives générales du royaume, Acquits de Lille 923, iij^e paiement, etc.

[54]D McRoberts, 'Notes on Scoto-Flemish artistic contacts', *Innes Review*, x (1959), 91-6; Thompson and Campbell, *Hugo van der Goes*, 50, notes 5, 6. For the Edinburgh painters named Binning, see Apted and Hannabuss, *Painters*, 26-30.

[55]D Masson, ed., *Register of the Privy Council of Scotland*, xiii (Edinburgh, 1896), 698.

1   Jacques Le Boucq, 'Jacques Roy descoce' (James I), from the Recueil d'Arras, Bibliothèque Municipale, Arras, MS 266, fo. 18. (Copyright IRPA-KIK, Brussels)

2   Jacques Le Boucq, 'Legyptienne quy Rendist santè ... au Roy descoce', Recueil d'Arras, fo. 22. (Location and copyright as plate 1)

3   Arnold Bronkhorst, *Portrait of a Lady*, private collection. (Copyright Courtauld Institute of Art, London)

4   Hugo van der Goes, *The Trinity Panels*, National Gallery of Scotland: James III accompanied by his son James, presented by St Andrew. (The Royal Collection: © Her Majesty the Queen)

5   *Trinity Panels*: **Margaret of Denmark presented by St George (?). (Location and copyright as plate 4)**

6   *Trinity Panels*: The Trinity. (Location and copyright as plate 4)

7　　*Trinity Panels*: **Edward Bonkil with two Angels. (Location and copyright as plate 4)**

8

SCOTS IN THE WARS OF THE LOW COUNTRIES, 1572-1648

Hugh Dunthorne

Preserved in the Royal Library in Brussels is a manuscript volume of ballads, written in the early years of the seventeenth century by Willem de Gortter and illustrated with the author's own watercolour drawings. De Gortter was a native of Mechelen in the southern Netherlands and his book seems to have been intended for the city's Chamber of Rhetoric, a characteristic institution of many Low Countries towns at this time, combining the functions of a debating club, a literary circle and a dramatic society. The members of these chambers were often liberal or even radical in their political and religious attitudes; and it was probably in order to recall the time, not many years earlier, when Mechelen itself had been a radical city that de Gortter put his collection of verses together. In the early stages of the Revolt of the Netherlands, Mechelen had been one of the first cities of the south to give its support to William of Orange in resisting the Spanish regime in the Low Countries, and as a result it had been ferociously sacked by the duke of Alva in October 1572. For a dozen years thereafter it held on to a precarious independence, surviving as an embattled city between the opposing armies, until its final and permanent surrender to the Prince of Parma in 1585.[1]

Born in that year, Willem de Gortter evidently came to regard the 1570s and early 1580s as the heroic period of his city's recent history. So it is interesting - especially in the context of the present volume - to find that among the contemporary heroes whose memory he chose to celebrate in his book were several Scottish soldiers. Some of these men can be identified from the coats of arms included in the drawings that decorate the manuscript. The ensigns depicted on folio 10 (plate 1), for example, belong (in the case of the figure on the right) to the company of Captain Thomas Newton, commissioned in November 1577, and (in the case of that on the left) to a company commanded by a member of the Wemyss family. Others are actually named in the text, as with the 'Capiteyn Bleyre en Capiteyn Gordon' who appear on folio 5 (plate 2) and who, according to the couplet at the head of the page, 'served under Stuart's colonelship at the time [before 1585] when Mechelen was a friend to the States'. They are probably to be identified with James Blair and Alexander Gordon, both officers in the regiment of Colonel William Stewart of Houston, who received a commission from the States of Holland in the mid-1570s.[2]

---

[1] G Parker, *The Dutch Revolt* (London, 1977), 59, 141, 196, 215.
[2] W H Finlayson, 'Early paintings of the Scots Brigade', *Scottish Historical Review*, xxviii (1949), 119-20; J Ferguson, ed., *Papers illustrating the history of the Scots Brigade in the*

De Gortter further emphasized the Scots' contribution to the Netherlands cause by drawing attention to particular military engagements in which their role had been prominent. One such was the battle of Rijmenant (a village to the south-east of Mechelen), fought on Lammas day (1 August) 1578, when the valour and fury of the Scots contingent had been crucial in enabling the States General's forces to defeat the reputedly invincible army of the Spanish commander, Don John.[3] It was to this victory - one which might have been decisive if only it had been followed up - that de Gortter was referring in the rhymed captions placed immediately above and below his picture of the Wemyss and Newton standard-bearers:

> Augustij een Bossu (naer dat Spaens Jan 't bestant
> Ghebroken heeft) slaet hij zijn heyr bij Rijmenant.
> [On August 1 (after the Spaniard Don John had broken
> the truce) Bossu routed his army at Rijmenant.]
>
> Schotsche vendricks die te Rymelant dan laghen
> Oock vromelyck hun Lyf teghen Don Jan waghen.
> [Scots ensigns who were then at Rijmenant
> Piously risked their lives against Don John.][4]

I

Like most armies in early modern times, the forces employed by the States General in its so-called Eighty Years' War against the Spanish monarchy were multinational, drawing together companies of French, German and British soldiers as well as those recruited in the Netherlands. It is clear, moreover, that by the time of the battle of Rijmenant the Scots contingent was already a well-established part of this polyglot army. Upholding a tradition of soldiering in the Low Countries that went back at least to the early fifteenth century,[5] the earliest Scots adherents to the Prince of Orange's cause had landed in Holland in 1572 to assist in the defence of Haarlem; and Scots were certainly among those massacred when the town fell to the Spanish army in July 1573. Further contingents were soon arriving, and before the end of the year the first Scots regiment had been brought together under Cap-

---

service of the United Netherlands, 1572-1782 (Scottish History Society, 3 vols, Edinburgh, 1899-1901) (hereafter Ferguson, *Papers*), i, 14, 16n3, 38, 46n1, 47n2, 60, 115-18; F J G ten Raa and F de Bas, *Het Staatsche Leger, 1568-1795* (8 vols, Breda, 1911-64) (hereafter Ten Raa, *Staatsche Leger*), i, 265-6; *Register of the Privy Council of Scotland*, ed. J H Burton and others (Edinburgh, 1877-[in progress]) (hereafter *Privy Council*), first series, ii, 731.

[3] J M B C Kervijn de Lettenhove, ed., *Relations politiques des Pays-Bas et de l'Angleterre sous le règne de Philippe II* (11 vols, Brussels, 1882-1900), x, 684-7; G Gates, *The Defence of the Militarie Profession* (London, 1579), 58-61; C Wilson, *Queen Elizabeth and the Revolt of the Netherlands* (London, 1970), 67-8.

[4] The States commander, Count Bossu, had earlier served under Alva but changed allegiance in 1576.

[5] J Grant, *The Scottish Soldiers of Fortune* (Edinburgh, 1889) (hereafter Grant, *Scottish Soldiers*), 144-5.

tain Andrew Ormiston, a force of ten companies amounting in total to around one thousand men.[6] In 1578 the demands of the campaign against a new Spanish commander, Don John of Austria, led to the formation of a second Scots regiment, initially under William Stewart of Houston - the regiment whose ensigns were to be depicted in De Gortter's manuscript - and this arrangement seems to have been maintained for about six years. But it was not until 1603, during the long siege of Ostend, that the States General established a second Scots regiment on a more permanent basis, and by doing so raised the total Scots force in Dutch service to around 3,000 men.[7]

During the later stages of the Eighty Years' War some minor adjustments were made to the arrangements under which Scots were employed in the army of the States General. In 1628, when the Dutch were enjoying a string of military successes, the Scots companies were reorganized into three regiments. And for a few months in 1629, when the States army grew to unprecedented size, a fourth Scots regiment was temporarily drafted in to reinforce Prince Frederick Henry's siege of 's-Hertogenbosch. But despite such modifications, the number of Scots soldiers in Dutch service during the first half of the seventeenth century generally remained more or less constant at around 3,000, somewhere between 4 per cent and 7 per cent of the total strength of the Dutch army (see Table I).[8]

Not all Scots soldiers serving in the Low Countries during these years, however, did so as members of the three regiments discussed so far. These were *infantry* units; and from 1586, if not before, there was usually at least one company of Scots *cavalry* in Dutch pay alongside them.[9] At the same time there were also Scots soldiers - infantry and cavalry - in the pay of the king of Spain, serving in the famous Army of Flanders. In 1588, for example, the forces assembled by the Prince of Parma for the projected invasion of England included a *tercio* (regiment) of 1,000 Irish and Scots; and a *tercio* of Scots infantry was mustered in Flanders in 1623, under the command of the seventh earl of Argyll.[10] There were in addition a number of individual Scots gentlemen serving from time to time with the Army of Flanders - men such as Sir William Foret, who died in 1600 and was commemorated in the St Walburgaskerk of Bruges by an elaborate tombstone describing him as the 'captain of 150 lances in the service of their

---

[6]Ferguson, *Papers*, i, 3-8; Ten Raa, *Staatsche Leger*, i, 265.

[7]Ferguson, *Papers*, i, 16, 33, 43-8, 64-6, 115-16; Ten Raa, *Staatsche Leger*, i, 265-7, ii, 163.

[8]Ferguson, *Papers*, i, 311, 385-401; Ten Raa, *Staatsche Leger*, iv, 244-6.

[9]Ferguson, *Papers*, i, pp. xii-xiii, 18n1, 58, 90-2, 318; J Mac Lean, *De Huwelijksintekeningen van Schotse Militairen in Nederland, 1574-1665* (Zutphen, 1976) (hereafter Mac Lean, *Schotse Militairen*), 416.

[10]H O'Donnell y Duque de Estrada, 'The Army of Flanders and the invasion of England, 1586-88' in *England, Spain and the Gran Armada*, ed S Adams and M J Rodriguez Salgado (Edinburgh, 1991), 222, 232; Relacion de los oficiales y soldados ... Ano de 1623, British Library, Add. Ms. 14007, f. 385. I am grateful to my colleague Dr Robert Stradling for these references and for help generally with the substance of this paragraph.

Highnesses, the States of Flanders'.[11] Clearly some of these soldiers were good Roman Catholics, fighting to sustain what they believed to be the just cause of the Catholic King. (Argyll, for example, had converted to Catholicism a few years before joining the Army of Flanders - though it is probable that a wish to escape his creditors also prompted his departure for the continent.) But others - and perhaps a majority - were simply opportunists, prepared to defect from one side to the other, either as a protest against some injustice done to them by their superiors or else in response to the enemy's bribery. The 1580s, in particular, saw a succession of towns simply being sold to Parma by their defecting garrisons of English and Scots: Lier in 1582, betrayed by Captain William Sempill; Aalst and Bruges in 1584; Deventer and Geldern in 1597; St Geertruidenberg in 1589.[12] From the 1590s improved techniques of war finance and more regular pay for the troops greatly reduced the incidence of defection. But the problem never disappeared altogether. Hearing in 1618 of Argyll's arrival in Brussels to assume 'the command of a regiment of the King's [James VI's] subjects in the service of the Spaniard', the English ambassador Sir Dudley Carleton observed how 'ever ready' English and Scots troops were 'upon such new occasions to run to the enemy'.[13]

II

That Scots were to be found serving on both sides in the Low Countries wars of the sixteenth and seventeenth centuries is hardly suprising. As Sir Thomas Urquhart remarked in 1652, there was hardly a battle fought in Christendom in those days in which the opposing armies did not *both* number Scots among their forces. The ubiquitous Scottish soldier, Urquhart said, was 'like Ismael, whose hand was against everyman, and everyman's hand against him'.[14] If in the present essay attention is directed mainly towards Scots in the service of the States General, it is firstly because they constituted one of the largest and most enduring British units to be found on the Continent during this period (the three regiments established during the Eighty Years' War continued in Dutch service, almost without interruption, down to 1782); and secondly - perhaps more importantly - because they are one of the best documented contingents. In the General State Archives (Algemeen Rijksarchief) at The Hague there is a mass of more or less official documentation relating to the Scots regiments in Dutch service - accounts and pay lists, commissions, petitions, grievances, recommendations - much of which was collected and edited (mostly in English translation) by James Ferguson in three

---

[11]Grant, *Scottish Soldiers*, 147; Sir T Urquhart, *Works*, ed. T Maitland (Edinburgh, 1834) (hereafter Urquhart, *Works*), 216-18.

[12]Ferguson, *Papers*, i, 7n1, 24, 26, 46n1; G Parker, *The Army of Flanders and the Spanish Road, 1567-1659* (Cambridge, 1972), 241.

[13]Ferguson, *Papers*, i, 223n1; Urquhart, *Works*, 218.

[14]Urquhart, *Works*, 218. For Scots soldiers in service elsewhere in Europe at this time, see P Dukes' contribution to *The Scottish Soldier Abroad, 1247-1967*, ed. G G Simpson (Edinburgh, 1992), 47-54, and the sources there cited.

volumes published by the Scottish History Society between 1899 and 1901. The same sort of material also formed the basis of the account of the Scots regiments given by Colonels Ten Raa and De Bas in their official history of the States army. More recently, the records of Dutch local and church archives have been used by Dr Johannes Mac Lean, a Dutchman of Scots descent, to reconstruct genealogies of the many Scots soldiers who put down roots in the Netherlands and married into the local population.[15]

Inevitably, there are some gaps in the surviving evidence. It appears that no Scot in Dutch service during the Eighty Years' War left the kind of informal, semi-autobiographical account that soldiers (including Scots soldiers serving elsewhere in Europe) were beginning to write in this period: accounts like Robert Monro's narrative of his regiment's service with the Swedish army in the 1620s and 1630s, or the descriptions of the Low Countries wars written by Welsh and English soldiers such as Sir Roger Williams in the later sixteenth century and Henry Hexham in the seventeenth.[16] The closest approach we have to a work of this kind produced by a Scot in the Netherlands is William Lithgow's *Discourse upon the Siege of Breda* (1637), supposedly based on the author's own experience of the action as well as on his contacts among the 'common souldiers, who daily and nightly were incident unto the Tragicall accidents of the subject'.[17] It has to be said, though, that Lithgow was primarily a traveller and travel writer rather than a soldier and that this narrative necessarily covers only a few weeks in a war that lasted many years.

The historical records available for reconstructing Scots' experiences in the Low Countries wars of this period, then, are reasonably plentiful if rather impersonal in character. Yet despite their limitations they provide enough material at least to suggest answers to some of the more obvious problems raised by the subject. It is with these problems that the remainder of this essay will be concerned.

III

To begin with, there is the problem of recruitment. How were Scots recruited for service in the Netherlands? And what motives prompted them to enlist? In the business of raising recruits, the key figure at this time was the company captain, who was responsible not only for leading his troops in battle and distributing their pay, but also for maintaining the numerical strength of his company. This latter duty involved returning home to Scotland at intervals in order to take on fresh manpower - as, for example, Captain Ormiston did in the summer of 1573 and

---

[15]Titles in notes 2 and 9 above.

[16]*Monro his Expedition with the Worthy Scots Regiment call'd Mackays* (London, 1637); Sir R Williams, *A Briefe Discourse of Warre* (London, 1590) and *The Actions of the Lowe Countries* (London, 1618); H Hexham, *A Historicall Relation of the Seige of the Busse* (Delft, 1630), *A Journall of the Taking in of Venlo* (Delft, 1633), and *A True and Brief Relation of the Famous Siege of Breda* (Delft, 1637).

[17]W Lithgow, *A True and Experimentall Discourse upon the Last Siege of Breda* (London, 1637), prologue.

Henry Balfour a couple of years later and again in 1577. Recruiting seems to have been carried out mainly in the Lowland counties, particularly those around the mouth of the Forth; and the men were then shipped from Leith to the ports of Zeeland and South Holland.[18] Apart from issuing royal warrants from time to time permitting the raising of recruits for service abroad, the Scottish government played no part in this process; nor, on the whole, did the States General. It is true that in the summer of 1632 the States decided to offer a special incentive to re-cruiting officers in Britain - eight guilders for every new recruit brought across plus the prospect of a company command. But this was done because the raising of recruits happened on this occasion to coincide not only with the harvest, when men could earn 'a big wage' at home, but also with a high point in the European war, when the Swedish and Russian armies were also actively recruiting in Brit-ain, competing with the Netherlands for Scottish manpower. It is true, further-more, that from time to time the Dutch took into their service existing Scots regi-ments which had previously been in the service of other states in Germany or the Baltic. But again this method seems to have been adopted only in unusual circum-stances, as in the period of rapid expansion of the States' forces during the late 1620s.[19] In normal conditions, special arrangements or inducements were simply not necessary, since the traditional pressures encouraging men to volunteer for the wars were quite strong enough to maintain unit strengths.

What, then, were the considerations that led men to the recruiting officer? In Scotland, as elsewhere in Europe, one major reason for enlisting was to escape hunger and poverty. It was, for example, at a time of 'hunger, derth and scarcitie' in June 1572 that the Privy Council of Scotland first authorized 'hable men and suldartis ... to pas to the Warres in Flanders ... quhair thay may haif sufficient interteinment' - that is, subsistence.[20] Equally, men went off to the wars in order to avoid creditors or escape the law - as in the case of one James Hamilton who 'depairtit furth of this realme to the countrey of Flanderis' in 1596 'for eshewing of punishment' after he had robbed and attempted to murder James Mure.[21] Some-times criminals were forcibly conscripted as a form of punishment - as happened to 150 unruly members of the Graham clan, sentenced in 1605 to be sent off to the Low Countries wars 'in the hope that most of them would die there'. A few years later three poor Edinburgh millers, sentenced to be hanged for 'stealing of some littil quantitie of wheate' intended for the common supply of the city, had their sentence commuted thanks to a petition from Sir William Brog, the long-serving colonel of the first Scots regiment in the Netherlands, on the grounds that 'thair service in the warres ... wald be more steadeble then ony goode that was to follow upoun their executioun'.[22]

---

[18]Ferguson, *Papers*, i, pp. xxv, 6, 10, 13; Mac Lean, *Schotse Militairen*, 417.

[19]Ferguson, *Papers*, i, 115n1, 355-6 and n1.

[20]*Privy Council*, first series, ii, 148.

[21]*Privy Council*, first series, viii, 779.

[22]G Parker, *The Military Revolution* (Cambridge, 1988), 49; *Privy Council*, first series, xiii, 137, 146, 630-1.

There were also more positive reasons for enlisting in the service of the States General. In the official orders of the Scottish Privy Council authorizing the raising of recruits, men were frequently urged to fight 'in the defence of Goddis trew religioun aganis the persecutiouris thairof' - and some undoubtedly did so.[23] Others regarded military experience in the Low Countries as the necessary foundation for building a career as a professional soldier. By the end of the sixteenth century, the reforming commander Maurice of Nassau had established the reputation of the Dutch army as a universal school of war, capable of attracting professionals or would-be professionals from across Europe. And it was a school in which promotion was to be achieved through merit rather than birth. As Sir William Edmond (Brog's predecessor as colonel of the first Scots regiment) liked to point out to new recruits, he himself was not 'a great man borne', merely the son of 'a poore Baker of Edenbourgh ... [who] workes hard for his living'.[24]

Finally, men volunteered out of loyalty to their clan or family. For, like many late medieval and early modern regiments, the Scots contingent in the Netherlands was 'a strongly family affair', the same surnames recurring through its list of officers - Balfours, Mackays, Halketts and so on - as fathers were succeeded by sons and grandsons in an almost continuous line down the two and a half centuries of the regiments' existence.[25] Moreover the sense of dynastic continuity was reinforced by the tendency for Scots soldiers to continue in service well into old age. When Sir William Brog died in 1636 - a few months after sitting for his portrait to the Hague engraver Van den Queboorn (plate 3) - he had served in the forces of the States General for almost fifty years. There were members of the rank and file who had served almost as long.[26]

IV

Once transported to the Netherlands, how were Scots recruits deployed in campaign? And what was their position in relation to their fellow-soldiers and to the Dutch authorities? In its early years the Revolt of the Netherlands was a war of considerable movement, and the experience of the Scots units reflected this. During the 1570s they were to be found fighting in defence of the towns of Holland and Zeeland as well as in Flanders and Brabant, and (in 1579) in an unsuccessful attempt to relieve the besieged Limburg stronghold of Maastricht. As time went on, operations were gradually contained within a more narrowly-defined war zone, extending in a crescent from the Flanders coast through north Brabant to the eastern parts of Gelderland and Overijssel. It was about this time, too, that Scots troops began to be stationed rather more permanently in particular garrison

---

[23]*Privy Council*, first series, ii, 237, 256-7, 638, 643; iii, 23; Ferguson, *Papers*, i, 5-7. Company captains were also required to ensure that their men 'sall na wayis serve with Papistis aganis the Protestantis professouris of the Evangell of Jesus Chryst'.

[24]H Peacham, *The Compleat Gentleman* (London, 1622), 15.

[25]Ferguson, *Papers*, i, pp. xxiv-vi, 67; Wilson, *Queen Elizabeth and the Revolt of the Netherlands*, 29n; Parker, *Military Revolution*, 174n13.

[26]Ten Raa, *Staatsche Leger*, ii, 162, iii, 183; Ferguson, *Papers*, i, 54n3, 337.

towns, most of which lay within a broad defensive band across the centre of the region, from Delft and Dordrecht in south Holland and Bergen-op-Zoom on the coast of Flanders (all of which had garrisons of Scots soldiers by the mid-1580s) over to Nijmegen and Grave near the eastern frontier. There were Scots troops garrisoned in the major strongholds of north Brabant such as Breda (in the 1590s and again after 1637, when the city was recaptured from the Spanish), St Geertruidenberg, Heusden and 's-Hertogenbosch; and they were to be found in strategically important river towns like Rotterdam and Schiedam on the Maas and Gorinchem and Tiel on the Waal, as well as at a few more isolated points further north, including Utrecht and Zwolle (see Table II). Even during this later, more static phase of the conflict, however, Scots companies continued to fight across a wide geographical area - from the siege of Groningen in 1594 to the campaigns in Flanders during the 1640s.[27]

Like all multinational forces, the army of the States General was by its very nature subject to internal conflict. Indeed, William of Orange's first campaign in 1568 had been hampered by the outbreak of 'broyles' among the various national groups under his command - French and Burgundians on one side against Germans and Swiss on the other.[28] In an attempt to forestall friction of this sort, the practice was adopted of maintaining companies and regiments as distinct and separate national units so that potentially hostile groups would be kept at arm's length from one another. Thus in 1628, for instance, the States of Holland insisted that the command of an English cavalry company should be given 'to an Englishman and not to a Scot, to prevent confusion of the two nations'.[29] In camp, too, as surviving plans reveal (plate 4), English and Scots contingents were kept quite separate and usually as far away from each other as possible. And on the whole the system worked. There were relatively few cases of violence between Scots on the one hand and either English, French or Dutch on the other; and when trouble did occur, occasionally involving murder, it tended to be within the Scottish contingent and to reflect old family feuds - Bruces against Hamiltons, for example, culminating in a fatal duel in 1604, or Ramsays against Stuarts.[30]

Responsibility for settling disputes 'among the soldiers of his nation' rested squarely with the company captain or regimental colonel, and it is worth paying attention to the changing position of these officers in the Dutch army's chain of authority. In the early stages of the Eighty Years' War, a colonel or a captain was generally allowed to operate quite independently, responsible to the Prince of Orange (as commander-in-chief) and to the States General (from whom he normally received his commission) but otherwise free to lead his men and to appoint junior-

---

[27]The summary offered in this paragraph is based on Ferguson, *Papers*, i, 3-35, 221-5, 307-17.

[28]T Churchyard, *A Lamentable and Pitifull Description of the Wofull Warres in Flanders* (London, 1578), 39. For a similar instance in 1583, see Ferguson, *Papers*, i, 23.

[29]Ferguson, *Papers*, i, 322n1.

[30]*Privy Council*, first series, x, 476-7; Ferguson, *Papers*, i, pp. xxix, 7-8, 48, 199, 208, 221, 278-9, 298-302.

officers in his unit without interference from any higher authority.[31] By the turn of the century, however, this independence was being gradually undermined. New staff officers were being created - lieutenant-colonel, sergeant-major (to drill and train the men), quartermaster, company chaplain, company surgeon - and increasingly it was the Prince of Orange or the States who made these appointments.[32] Moreover, closer central control over the issuing of commissions was only part of a larger pattern of military reform, initiated by Maurice of Nassau around 1590 and soon transforming the Dutch army into a model force of international reputation. Naturally enough, the prince's reforming initiative was reflected in various ways in the experience and records of the Scots regiments. Companies were reduced in size (from 200 to 150, from 100 to 70) in order to match the resources available to finance them.[33] Wages were paid more regularly and a little more frequently (every forty-second day instead of every forty-eighth!) and there is evidence that pensions were paid to soldiers' widows and other dependents.[34] Minor disputes over pay continued to occur from time to time, of course, but not the full-scale mutinies which had paralysed the States army during the 1580s and in which Scots soldiers had certainly played a part.[35] Partly because it was better paid, the army of Maurice of Nassau was also better disciplined and its relations with the local population gradually became more cordial. One symptom of this was the significant number of Scots who chose to settle permanently in the Netherlands, taking up civilian trades as weavers, tailors, sailors and so on. Another was the proportion (reckoned at 5 per cent or more) who married Dutch women.[36]

From the 1590s onwards, the forces employed by the States General were also technically superior to those that had fought for the Dutch cause in earlier decades. In 1599 the States financed a general re-equipment of the army with weapons of standard size and calibre. Hence the order issued a few years later requiring that Scots recruits were to be

> able-bodied men of arms, properly armed, conform to regulations, also with side-arms, and the musketeers with muskets; the muskets to be of full length and four feet long, shooting balls of twelve in the pound; no boys or elderly men shall pass muster.[37]

Moreover, this was an army closely attuned to the latest developments in the technology of war, whether in the improvement of fortifications or the development of artillery and siege machinery; and in all these areas the Scots' natural bent for

---

[31]J A Dop, *Eliza's Knights: soldiers, poets and Puritans in the Netherlands, 1572-86* (Alblasserdam, 1981), 131.

[32]Ferguson, *Papers*, i, pp. xiv-xvi, xxix, 292-3, 438-9.

[33]Ibid., i, pp. xiv, 84, 93.

[34]Ibid., i, pp. xiv-xv, 74-5, 349.

[35]Ten Raa, *Staatsche Leger*, i, 264n3, 266n5; Ferguson, *Papers*, i, 21, 23, 135.

[36]Ferguson, *Papers*, i, pp. xxvii-xxviii, 236-7, 239, 272; Mac Lean, *Schotse Militairen*, 417.

[37]Parker, *Military Revolution*, 20; Ferguson, *Papers*, i, pp. xvii-xviii and n.

mathematics and engineering made its mark. As early as 1574, one John Cunningham was put in charge of the artillery battery defending the town of Haarlem (and later was appointed adjutant to Count William Louis of Nassau, Prince Maurice's cousin and collaborator); while in 1608 another Scot, James Lawson, was recommended for the post of cannoneer to the city of Breda.[38] More remarkable still was the case of William Douglas - company captain, general engineer to the States of Holland, inventor and mathematician (reputedly the equal of John Napier) - who in the 1620s presented the Dutch authorities with a string of proposals for new weaponry. His ideas included 'a pike which can do the work both of a musketeer and a pikeman', perhaps a blueprint for the later combination of rifle and bayonet. He was paid handsomely for his efforts; and at least one of his inventions, a rapid-firing field gun, was actually manufactured in prototype and demonstrated in the presence of the Prince of Orange and members of the Council of State. It managed to fire five shots in the time normally taken to fire two. But in the end the Council of State decided to be cautious. Captain Douglas's inventions were 'ingenious', they agreed, but not of such importance as to require any immediate change in the standard weaponry used by the army. If the captain was inclined to show his inventions to 'other princes or republics' he might do so - 'but not to such as are enemies of this state'.[39]

V

Statistically, the Scots companies never accounted for much more than 7 per cent of the total strength of the Dutch army during the period considered in this paper. Yet by the beginning of the seventeenth century they had acquired a reputation - and, arguably, a military importance - out of proportion to their actual numbers. Their standing was in part a reflection of experience and expertise gained over a long period of service. As one Scots veteran observed with only slight exaggeration, theirs was 'the first and oldest regiment of foreign nationality in these Netherlands'. Their reputation also reflected the 'many notable and excellent services' performed by Scots companies in action in the Low Countries - services that were chronicled, and sometimes prominently chronicled, in contemporary histories, news-pamphlets and verses.[40] In the fighting that culminated in Prince Maurice's pyrrhic victory at Nieuwpoort in 1600, for instance, it was Scots companies that bore the brunt of the Spanish army's attack, losing more than half their men in the process. No wonder that the prince's younger brother, Frederick Henry, called them 'the bulwark of the Republick; and after his famous siege of Bois-le-Duc in 1629, he shewed them many marks of his favour and esteem'.[41] This was a judgement that even the English were ready to confirm. 'The Scottish,' said one

---

[38]Ferguson, *Papers*, i, 4, 56n2, 241; Ten Raa, *Staatsche Leger*, i, 216.

[39]Ferguson, *Papers*, i, 358-61, 368; Urquhart, *Works*, 218-19; Ten Raa, *Staatsche Leger*, iv, 265.

[40]Ferguson, *Papers*, i, 285, 326n1-327.

[41]*Strictures on Military Discipline with some Account of the Scotch Brigade in Dutch Service* (London, 1774), 73.

contemporary observer, 'are like Beanes and Peas among chaffe. These are sure men, hardy and resolute, and their example holds up the Dutch.'[42]

If the Scots regiments made their mark on the course of the Low Countries wars, their experience of continental campaigning enabled them also to exert considerable influence in Britain and particularly on the civil wars of the mid-seventeenth century. As early as 1579, Queen Elizabeth's secretary, William Cecil, had recognized that Scots involvement in the Revolt of the Netherlands could pose a danger to England. 'The Scottish nation,' he observed, 'is at this day stronger in feats of arms than it was aforetime, by reason of their exercise in civil wars at home and their being abroad in the Low Countries'.[43] And Cecil's warning was borne out sixty years later when the Scottish Covenanters went to war with King Charles I. For it was Scots veterans from the Dutch and Swedish armies who were now recalled to make up the elite of the Covenanters' forces - including their commander, Alexander Leslie, who had served his military apprenticeship under Maurice of Nassau from 1605 to 1608 before transferring his allegiance to Gustavus Adolphus.[44] It was also almost exclusively from the Netherlands that the Covenanting armies imported their arms and ammunition, starting in 1639 with a shipment of 10,000 muskets and 4,000 pikes, precisely the ratio of firearms to pikes that was then standard in the Dutch army.[45]

Along with arms and men brought over from the Netherlands, there also came ideas. Covenanter pamphlets were printed in Holland and then smuggled into Britain, among them a reprint of George Buchanan's radical resistance tract, *De Iure Regni apud Scotos* [The right of government among the Scots].[46] Robert Baillie, a leading propagandist of the Covenanters, cited the Dutch Revolt as a precedent to demonstrate the legitimacy of resisting an unjust and oppressive prince and to show that determined resistance could prosper.[47] And there was even a whiff of Netherlands republicanism blowing across the North Sea. Of the eighth earl of Argyll and his fellow-Covenanters it was reported in 1648 that their intention was 'to transforme the Kingdom of Scotland into a Free State like the Estates of Holland'.[48] Republican aspirations of this kind may not have been typical. What most Covenanters wanted was probably not so much a free state as a

---

[42]Quoted in C Dalton, *Life and Times of Sir Edward Cecil* (2 vols, London, 1885), ii, 17.

[43]Ferguson, *Papers*, i, 21n1.

[44]Furgol, *Covenanting Armies*, 2, 28, 29, 119; Ferguson, *Papers*, i, 325n1; C S Terry, *The Life and Campaigns of Alexander Leslie* (London, 1899), 17-18. Military chaplains in the Netherlands, many of them militant Calvinists, were active in urging Scots veterans to return home to support the cause of the Covenant: K L Sprunger, *Dutch Puritanism: a history of the English and Scottish churches of the Netherlands in the sixteenth and seventeenth centuries* (Leiden, 1982), 389.

[45]Furgol, *Covenanting Armies*, 3, 7.

[46]P Donald, *An Uncounselled King: Charles I and the Scottish Troubles, 1637-41* (Cambridge, 1990), 188.

[47]R Baillie, *Ladensium αυτοκατακρισις, the Canterburians self-conviction* (3rd edn, [London], 1641), 121-2.

[48]C Walker, *Relations and Observations* (London, 1648), 8.

constitutional monarchy in which the king's powers would be reduced to something like those of a Dutch stadholder, the office held by successive princes of Orange. But even this more moderate aim shows clearly enough the influence of the Netherlands on Scottish affairs.[49] And there can be little doubt that Scotland's close military connections with the Low Countries constituted one of the channels through which such influence made itself felt.

Interaction between Dutch and Scots communities was of course not confined to the military and political spheres discussed in this essay. Nor was it limited to the period of the Eighty Years' War. When, at the end of the seventeenth century, Andrew Fletcher of Saltoun urged the establishment of local citizen militias in Scotland, he was proposing a force very different in some respects from the multinational army of mercenaries which operated in the Dutch Republic and which he had seen for himself whilst living as a political exile in Utrecht during the 1680s. Yet Fletcher's suggestions about the *training* of these militias have a distinctly Netherlandish ring to them. Among other things, he recommended that the men should be regularly drilled in 'the use and exercise of arms' and instructed in fortification and gunnery; he advocated the study of classical authorities on the art of war; and he insisted on the adoption of a severe and rigorous code of reward and punishment, calculated to teach virtue as well as to instil military discipline.[50] Reading these recommendations from the 1690s, the historian can hardly avoid a sense of *déjà vu*. One hundred years on, the spirit of Prince Maurice's military reforms was evidently still a force to be reckoned with.

---

[49] In recommending a mixed constitution for Britain, Samuel Rutherford, another leading pamphleteer for the Covenanters, referred specifically to that of the Dutch Republic as a model to be emulated: Rutherford, *Lex, Rex* (London, 1644), 211; D Stevenson, *Revolution and Counter-Revolution in Scotland, 1644-51* (Edinburgh, 1977), 237.

[50] Andrew Fletcher of Saltoun, *Selected Political Writings and Speeches*, ed. D Daiches (Edinburgh, 1979), 20-4.

Table 1: Relative numerical strengths of the Scots Contingent and of the Army of the States General

Year	Scots contingent		Scots as percentage of total strength of army of States General	Total strength of army of States General	Year
1573	1,000	(1 regiment of 10 companies)			
1574	1,500	(1 regiment of 15 companies)			
1579	2,000	(2 regiments of c. 8 companies each)	5.7%	30,000	1568
				34,500	1580
				32,500	1585
1587	1,707	(1 regiment of 12 companies)	5.25%		
1599	1,500	(1 regiment of 13 companies)	4%	36,700	1599
1607	3,600	(2 regiments comprising 24 companies)	6%	60,000	1607
1609	2,220	(2 regiments comprising 28 companies)	7.4%	30,000	1609
1621	2,420	(2 regiments comprising 18 companies, & 1 cavalry company)	4.6%	52,000	1621
1629	4,000 (?)	(4 regiments comprising c. 40 companies)	3.1%	Feb. 71,000 / July 128,000	1629
1636	3,000	(3 regiments of 10 companies each)	4.2%	70,000	1636
1643	3,000	(3 regiments comprising 29 companies)	5%	60,000	1643

Sources: Parker, *Dutch Revolt*, 110; Ten Raa, *Staatsche Leger*, i, 54-8, 82, 265-7, ii, 350-3, 366-7, iii, 290-3; Ferguson, *Papers*, i, 18, 43, 46, 51, 59, 69-72, 74-5, 115-16, 318, 322-30; J I Israel, *The Dutch Republic and the Hispanic World, 1606-61* (Oxford, 1982), 18, 42-3, 176-7, 317.

Note: Given the constantly changing strength of individual companies and the vagaries of early modern record-keeping, all the figures given above should be treated as approximate. Although the size of the Scots contingent in Dutch service did not vary much during the first half of the seventeenth century, the period did see a steady increase in the *total* number of Scots employed in European armies. Between 1624 and 1637 alone, warrants were issued by the Privy Council of Scotland permitting the recruiting of 41,000 Scots for military service on the Continent (E M Furgol, *A Regimental History of the Covenanting Armies, 1639-51*, Edinburgh, 1991, p. 2). The demographic implications for Scotland of this export of manpower must have been considerable.

Table II: Town Garrisons with Scots Soldiers, c. 1585-1648

Principal towns in the Netherlands whose garrisons included Scots soldiers are here listed by province. Dates in brackets indicate the years for which there is documentary evidence of the presence of Scottish officers in the town in question.

BRABANT: Bergen-op-Zoom (1585-8, 1596-7, 1600-48).
             Breda (1591-5, 1598-1602, 1621, 1637-48).
             Heusden (1592-5, 1599-1626, 1636-48).
             Grave (1604-48).
             St Geertruidenberg (1612-48).
             's-Hertogenbosch (1630-51).

HOLLAND: Delft (1586-8, 1592-8, 1604-12, 1622).
             Dordrecht (1586-7, 1590-6, 1600-08, 1623-32, 1646).
             Rotterdam (1588, 1592-1605, 1619-35).
             Schiedam (1588, 1621, 1632-48).
             Gorinchem (1593-1601, 1614-19, 1624, 1632-48).
             Alkmaar (1613-32).

GELDERLAND: Nijmegen (1592-1648).
             Tiel (1597-1629, 1634).
             Zutphen (1604-14, 1624).
             Arnhem (1601, 1608, 1624-33).

UTRECHT: Utrecht (1602-48).

OVERIJSSEL: Zwolle (1588-94, 1606-32).

GRONINGEN: Groningen (1603-14, 1628-33).

Source: Mac Lean, *Schotse Militairen*, 337-43.

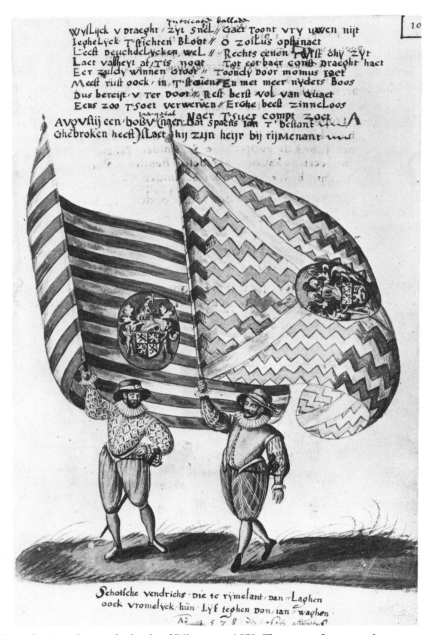

1   Scots ensigns at the battle of Rijmenant, 1578. The coats of arms on the company standards are those of the Wemyss family (left) and Thomas Newton (right). From a manuscript volume of ballads by Willem de Gortter, c. 1610. (Brussels, Bibliothèque Royale, MS. 15662, fo. 10) (Copyright Bibliothèque Royale)

2   Captains Blair and Gordon of the regiment of Colonel William Stewart of Houston, serving in the Netherlands, c. 1580. From a manuscript volume of ballads by Willem de Gortter, c. 1610. (Brussels, Bibliothèque Royale, MS. 15662, fo. 5) (Copyright Bibliothèque Royale)

Heer WILHELM BROG *Ridder*
ende Coronel Generael vande
Scotsche natie A^no 1635.
Crispiaen van queboren sculpset

3   Sir William Brog, Colonel of the first Scots regiment in the Netherlands: engraving by Crispijn van den Queboorn, 1635. (London: British Museum, Department of Prints and Drawings, 1848-8-11-383) (Copyright British Museum). Brog is recorded serving in the Netherlands in 1588 as sergeant-major, in 1590 as captain, in 1600 as lieutenant-colonel, and from 1606 until his death in 1636 as colonel.

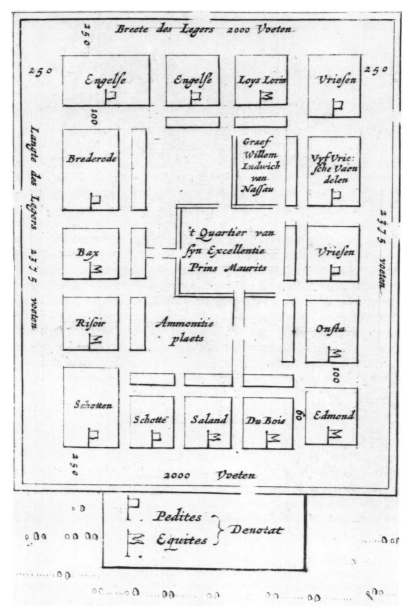

4   **Camp of Prince Maurice** at the siege of Grol, 1597. From Jan Blaeu, *Novum ac magnum theatrum urbium Belgicae Regiae* (2 vols, Amsterdam, 1649), i, [p. 50]. (Copyright British Library). The English infantry are placed at the north-west corner of the camp, the Scots infantry at the south-west corner, and the Scots cavalry (under Sir William Edmond) at the south-east corner.

9

SOME SCOTTISH STUDENTS AND TEACHERS AT THE UNIVERSITY OF LEIDEN IN THE LATE SIXTEENTH AND EARLY SEVENTEENTH CENTURIES

James K Cameron

In the late sixteenth and early seventeenth centuries the Scottish student was as familiar a figure on the continent as he had been in the two previous centuries. He was still to be found in the older universities as far apart as Paris and Vienna, Rostock and Padua. When new academic institutions were founded in the wake of the Reformation, there too the Scottish student and the Scottish teacher made an immediate appearance. Patrick Hamilton, the first Scottish Protestant martyr, who had previously studied at Paris, Louvain and St Andrews, was amongst the first to matriculate at the new university founded by Philip of Hesse at Marburg and the first to defend there a set of academic theses.[1] Hamilton was accompanied by two other Scots. Some years later Peter Young (1544-1628), subsequently one of the tutors of the young King James VI, entered his name on the first page of the Rector's album of Calvin's Academy in Geneva in 1559, where he remained till 1568 along with his uncle Henry Scrymgeour, the distinguished legal scholar and teacher.[2] As Protestant academies were erected in France, there too young Scotsmen were prominent both as students and teachers, among them Walter Donaldson (c. 1570-1630), principal of the Academy at Sedan,[3] Arthur Johnston (c. 1587-1641) at Heidelberg and Sedan and afterwards at La Rochelle,[4] and Mark Duncan (c. 1570-1640)[5] and John Cameron (1579-1625) at Saumur.[6] At the new university of Helmstädt the widely celebrated Aberdeen scholar Duncan Liddel

---

[1]*Catalogus studiosorum scholae Marpurgensis*, ed. Julius Caesar (Marburg, 1875; Kraus reprint, 1980), 2; Gerhard Müller, *Franz Lambert von Avignon und die Reformation in Hessen* (Marburg, 1958), 52.

[2]S Stelling Michaud, *Le Livre du Recteur de L'Académie de Genève (1559-1878)* (Geneva, 1959), i, 49; (1980), vi, 274.

[3]*Dictionary of National Biography* (hereafter *DNB*), xv, 215.

[4]*DNB*, xxx, 58.

[5]*DNB*, xvi, 171.

[6]A H Swine, *John Cameron: Philosoph und Theologue (1579-1625)* (Marburg, 1968); B G Armstrong, *Calvinism and the Amyraut Heresy* (Madison, 1966).

(1561-1613),[7] and, at the new academy at Herborn, Robert Howie (c. 1565-1645),[8] subsequently the first principal of Marischal College, Aberdeen, were distinguished students.

It is not therefore remarkable that almost immediately after the founding of the university of Leiden in 1575, with renowned international scholars amongst its early teachers, it too should draw to itself students from many lands.[9] Indeed Leiden among the new universities came to attract by far the largest number of foreign students, among whom not surprisingly were many Scots. For centuries the two countries, Scotland and the Netherlands, had engaged in mutually profitable trading and in the late sixteenth century they had in common a religious faith secured against a background of political and constitutional struggle.

The late Professor J A van Dorsten wrote that the guiding principle in the founding of the university of Leiden was 'the introduction of a complete humanistic *Academia* in which no faculty was necessarily superior to another'.[10] It became noted for its religious tolerance as well as for the breadth of vision which it exercised in the choice of its professors. It took into its service some of the outstanding intellectual leaders of the day, among them Justus Lipsius,[11] Bonaventura Vulcanius, and J J Scaliger.[12] With the appointment of two peace-loving and renowned theologians, Lucas Trelcatius in 1587 and Franciscus Junius in 1592, the faculty of divinity, which had an insecure beginning, began to develop and lay foundations for securing an international reputation.[13]

We are told that the reasons for the university's remarkable thriving in the sixteenth and seventeenth centuries are to be found in the efforts of a number of devoted individuals, such as the civic leader Janus Dousa, which succeeded in bringing such distinguished scholars as have just been mentioned to Leiden. These scholars in turn drew to the university students from many countries such as Scandinavia and Scotland and thereby enabled some of them for whom it was their first experience of studying abroad 'to get into touch with European scholarship'.[14] From the outset the new university set in Protestant Leiden not surprisingly also maintained a particularly close connection with similarly minded academic institutions in France, Germany, England and Scotland.

---

[7]*DNB*, xxxiii, 221.

[8]J K Cameron, *Letters of John Johnston (c. 1565-1611) and Robert Howie (c. 1565-1645)* (Edinburgh, 1963), xxxiiiff.

[9]*Leiden University in the Seventeenth Century: an exchange of learning*, ed. Th H Lunsingh Scheurleer and G H M Posthumus Meyjes (Leiden 1975), (hereafter *Leiden University*).

[10]J A van Dorsten, *Poets, Patrons and Professors: Sir Philip Sidney, Daniel Rogers and the Leiden Humanists* (Leiden, 1962), 6.

[11]G Oestreich, 'Justus Lipsius als Universalgelehrter zwischen Renaissance und Barock', in *Leiden University*, 177-201.

[12]J H Waszink, 'Classical Philology', ibid., 161-75.

[13]Ibid., 4f., 28ff., 384f.

[14]J J Woltjer in ibid., p. iff., 17.

Scottish students began to arrive at Leiden virtually from the opening of the university and continued to go there throughout the seventeenth century in ever increasing numbers. From May 1582 to May 1642, the names of the some seventy-nine Scots were entered in the *Album Studiosorum*.[15] Of this number eight were designated Masters of Arts, and many of them can be traced in extant Scottish university records. Almost all of the remaining number can be identified as having attended a Scottish university. Distribution among the faculties over this period of sixty years is remarkably even. It is, however, difficult to be accurate in these matters as the register does not always supply as much information as we would like and sometimes students registered initially in one faculty and studied in another. From the outset legal studies and theology were about equally popular, but before long medical matriculations were catching up and there was almost a constant number of registered students in philosophy, letters and history.[16] Further, the statistics provided by those who have made detailed studies do not always agree. In this essay little will be said about Scottish legal and medical students, as both subjects have already received considerable attention.[17] We will concentrate on some of the arts and theology students to whose subsequent careers both on the continent and in Britain Leiden University made a significant contribution, and then turn to consider those Scots who became philosophy teachers at Leiden and thereby had a place in the teaching of that subject in the pre-Cartesian period.

One of the earliest students to matriculate (he did so on 6 April 1588) was James Ramsay, a St Andrews student who had taken his BA in 1571 and his MA in the following year. He matriculated in the Faculty of Law at Leiden but spent the rest of his short life, which will be discussed later, as a teacher of philosophy. In 1593 he received the degree *doctor iuris honoris causa*.[18] In 1589 four students, all MAs, also matriculated in the legal faculty. One was Thomas Seget,

---

[15]*Album Studiosorum Academiae Lugduno-Batavae, MDLXXV-MDCCCLXXV* (The Hague, 1875).

[16]See further Paul Nève, 'Disputations of Scottish students attending universities in the northern Netherlands', *Legal History in the Making: Proceedings of the Ninth British Legal History Conference, Glasgow 1989*, ed. W M Gordon and T D Fergus (London 1991), 95-108. I am indebted to Dr John W Cairns for drawing my attention to this important article. A revised version of Professor R Feenstra's article 'Scottish-Dutch legal relations in the seventeenth and eighteenth centuries', *Scotland and Europe, 1200-1850*, ed. T C Smout (Edinburgh, 1986), has appeared in *Studia historica gandensia*, 27 (1989). Unfortunately the author has not been able to see this revised article nor that of W J Liberton, 'Schotese studenten aan de Universeit te Leiden (1582-1662)', *Mededeelingenblad van Caledonian Society* (1985-6), referred to by Nève.

[17]For biographical details of medical students the most important study is still that of R W Innes Smith, *English-Speaking Students of Medicine at the University of Leyden* (Edinburgh, 1932).

[18]*Album Studiosorum*, 23; *Early Records of the University of St Andrews*, ed. J M Anderson (Edinburgh, 1926), 166, 169, 278; *Album Scholasticum Academiae Lugduno-Batavae MDLXXV-MCMXL* (Leiden, 1941), 122, 191.

who had graduated MA in 1588 from the recently founded university of Edinburgh. He registered on 30 June.[19]

For Thomas Seget (c. 1570-1628), whose age was not recorded in the *Album Studiosorum*, Leiden was to provide an opening into the society of some of the most celebrated literary and scientific scholars of the century. In Leiden he got to know Justus Lipsius from whom he received some years later, on 26 July 1597, a glowing testimonial.[20] Seget's first sojourn in Leiden was relatively brief. He returned to Edinburgh in 1592, where along with his father he entertained Hainzel von Degerstein, a young son of an Augsburg patrician family, who along with his tutor, Caspar Waser (1565-1625), later a distinguished professor of Hebrew at Zürich, was on a grand tour that included Scotland.[21] Subsequently Seget was to visit the Hainzel family in Augsburg. About this time, 1592-3, Seget entered the household of Robert Seton of Seton, later first earl of Winton, as a tutor, a post that he did not retain for long.[22] In 1594 he fell foul of the church for delivering, contrary to the reformed church's law, a funeral oration in Latin at the burial of Sir John Seton. He was disciplined by the presbytery of Haddington and, having confessed his offence and after his confession had been received, he was ordered by the Synod of Lothian to make public confession in the parish church of Haddington.[23] This incident probably led him to write the next year to Justus Lipsius and to take the decision to leave the country and never to return. Much of his subsequent travels can be followed in his remarkable *Album amicorum* now in the Vatican Library.[24]

Seget's career was thoroughly researched by the late Professor Otakar Odlozilík in a learned article in *The Polish Review* in 1966.[25] In the present essay

---

[19]*Album Studiosorum*, 23; *Catalogue of the Graduates in the Faculties of Arts, Divinity and Law of the University of Edinburgh since its Foundation* (Edinburgh, 1859), 9.

[20]Printed in *Justi Lipsii epistolarum selectarum chilias*, cent III (Leiden, 1616), 281. A translation is given in D Irving, *Lives of the Scottish Poets* (Edinburgh, 1804), i, 113-14. It is also clear from Lipsius's entry in Seget's *Album amicorum* (see n. 24) that Lipsius knew Seget well while he was in Leiden.

[21]J K Cameron, 'The British Itinerary of Johan Peter Hainzel von Degerstein by Caspar Waser', *Zwingliana*, xv (1980), 266, 282; see also Johannes Jacobus Heinzellius's entry in Seget's *Album*, dated at Augsburg in 1597. Seget wrote to Waser from Frankfurt am Main on 22 September 1606 and told him of his father's death; see O Odlozilík, 'Thomas Seget: a Scottish friend of Szymon Szymonowicz', *The Polish Review*, xi (1966), 19.

[22]From Seton he wrote to Lipsius on 15 October 1595. This letter is published in *Sylloges epistolarum a viris illustribus scriptarum* (Leiden, 1731), i, 752.

[23]*Records of the Synod of Lothian and Tweeddale, 1589-96, 1640-9*, ed. James Kirk (Edinburgh, 1977), 82; Lipsius's entry in Seget's *Album* is dated 'VI Kal. Sept. MDXCVII'.

[24]An account of the *Album* is given by N Baumgarten, 'Ein schottisches Stammbuch' in *Zeitschrift für vergleichende Literaturgeschichte*, new series, v (Berlin, 1892), 88-95.

[25]Professor Odlozilík for the article cited above in n. 21, 3ff., was unable to obtain information about Seget's early life in Scotland. He considered that the Thomas Seget who graduated at Edinburgh was the same person as the Thomas Seget registered at Leiden, but he did not regard him as the 'hero' of his story. His 'hero' he held to be a younger man

only some of the highlights of a most colourful career are mentioned. They illustrate the way in which his Leiden experience opened up for this young, developing Scottish humanist a remarkable career, one which brought him into contact with some of the greatest *literati* of the day, and to encounter in his journeying a number of his fellow countrymen travelling and studying on the continent, such as John Ruthven, earl of Gowrie, Sir William Keith and Patrick Sands, a fellow student of his Edinburgh days and subsequently a professor at Edinburgh.[26] Among the more distinguished with whom he became closely associated was none other than Galileo Galilei in 1599. Seget was for a time administrator of the library of J V Pinelli. While in Padua, where he spent some time, he was cast into prison and owed his eventual release to the intervention of Sir Henry Wotton. On securing his freedom he returned north of the Alps and for a time lived in Prague, where he is said to have 'co-operated' with John Kepler and corresponded with Galileo.[27] From Bohemia he visited Poland and then moved to Altdorf, a centre of legal studies, before returning to Leiden to matriculate as a law student on 20 September 1625. He died three years later.[28]

Seget is a minor figure among Scottish humanists, and did not contribute significantly to the learning or literature of his day. Nevertheless, his international career has an innate fascination for all interested in the history of the Scottish student on the continent. One who numbered among his friends and associates Justus Lipsius, Sir Henry Wotton, Galileo and Kepler, Erycius Puteanus, Johan Wouverus and Joachim Morsius, was undoubtedly a man of some intellectual stature.

In the first decade of the seventeenth century several Scots who were later to distinguish themselves as philosophers were entered in the Rector's *Album* at Leiden, among them John Murdison (c. 1568-1605), an Edinburgh student, who had studied at Helmstädt in 1588 and 1589, and at Wittenberg in 1591.[29] From 1592 till 1597 he was at the Latin School of Middelburg, studying under Anton Walaeus, and, described as a 'savant' from Scotland, he worked as a private tutor.

---

who, although he was at Leiden while Lipsius was there, did not have his name entered in the *Album Studiosorum*. I have, however, regrettably to disagree with him.

[26]Baumgarten, op. cit., 90ff.; see also Odlozilík, op. cit., 9ff.

[27]Ibid., 10ff.

[28]*Album Studiosorum*, 187. Odlozilík, who has studied a photostatic copy of the relevant manuscript page of the *Album*, considered that Seget had concealed his true age. If Seget graduated at Edinburgh at the age of eighteen in 1588, he would have been fifty-five in 1625. It is just possible that there could have been an error in transcription.

[29]*Catalogue of the Graduates ... of the University of Edinburgh*, 7; matriculated at Helmstädt in 1589 (*Album Academiae Helmstadiensis*, ed. P Zimmermann, Hanover, 1926, i, 76), and at Wittenberg in 1591 (*Album Academiae Vitebergensis ab ... MDII usque ad MDCII*, ed. G Naetebus, Halle, 1894-1905, ii, 383); *Nieuw Nederlandsch Biografisch Woordenboek*, ed. P C Molhuysen and P J Blok (Leiden, 1911-37), ii, 967; Smith, op. cit., 163, who noted a thesis in the British Library, dated Leiden, 1597, dedicated to 'John Murdison, Rector of the Middelburg School'.

On 24 November 1599 he matriculated at Leiden as a law student,[30] and thereafter Leiden became his home. He was appointed a professor of physics and in 1604 took his doctorate in law on 26 November 1599.[31] More will subsequently be said of Murdison.

A little later Gilbert Jack (1578-1628), of whom also more will be said, enrolled as a theology student.[32] Within two years Jack's fellow student at Marischal College, Aberdeen, Thomas Reid (1583-1624) was incorporated in the same faculty.[33] One can imagine the pleasure which these three young men enjoyed in each others' company. Leiden was not the starting point for either Murdison or Jack on their tour of continental universities, but it became their academic home. We have noted that Murdison had studied previously at the Lutheran universities of Helmstädt and Wittenberg. Jack had also been at Helmstädt and at Herborn,[34] to both of which he had undoubtedly been recommended by his Aberdeen professor, Robert Howie. From a contemporary source we learn that Herborn would have been glad to retain Jack as one of its teachers, but he decided to move to Leiden, and although he registered, as has been said, in theology, he was in fact to study medicine, and defended theses for his MD degree there in 1611.[35] Yet he had been engaged in teaching philosophy there from 1604 and was to continue to do so for much of the remainder of his life. He died in 1628.

Thomas Reid probably graduated at Marischal College about 1600.[36] Thereafter he taught briefly at Aberdeen Grammar School, before returning to Marischal to act as a regent for about four years. He may have decided to begin his continental study tour at Leiden in 1605 on hearing that his fellow countryman, Gilbert Jack, was there. We next find him at the university of Rostock, where on 7 December 1608 he was received into the faculty of the philosophical college. There he taught philosophy and humane letters for several years and earned for himself a distinguished reputation.[37]

During his Rostock period Reid presided on several occasions at the defence of theses on metaphysical subjects. He also entered into public debate with Henning Arnisaeus, a professor at Frankfurt. A collection of Reid's theses was published at Rostock on 31 August 1616,[38] by which time he had already left that city for

---

[30] *Album Studiosorum*, 57; his age is given as thirty-one.

[31] *Album Scholasticum*, 108, 193.

[32] He began his academic career at Marischal College, Aberdeen, under Robert Howie (*Fasti Academiae Mariscallanae Aberdonensis*, ed. P J Anderson, 2 vols., Aberdeen, 1889-98, ii, 185); he matriculated at Leiden on 25 May 1603, aged twenty-five (*Album Studiosorum*, 69; *Nieuw ... Woordenboek* (as n. 29, above), i, 1197f., *DNB*, xxix, 85).

[33] *Album Studiosorum*, 77, aged twenty-two; *DNB*, xlvii, 435ff.

[34] *Album ... Helmstadiensis* (as n. 29, above), 136; *Die Matrikel der Hohen Schule und des Pädagogiums zu Herborn*, ed. G Zedler and H Sommer (Wiesbaden, 1908), 7.

[35] *Album Scholasticum*, 78j.

[36] *DNB*, xlvii, 435ff.

[37] *Die Matrikel der Universität Rostock*, ed. A Hofmeister (Rostock, 1889), ii, 294b, 296.

[38] *Bibliographia Aberdonensis*, ed. J F K Johnstone and A W Robertson (2 vols, Aberdeen, 1929-30), i, 172.

Leipzig where he matriculated in the summer of 1613. By September 1614 he was in London, where he attached himself to royal circles. Toward the end of that year he published an elegant memorial on the death of Honoria, daughter of Lord Denny and wife of James Hay, subsequently earl of Carlisle and a favourite of King James. Reid's entry into royal service may have been facilitated by Patrick Young, son of Sir Peter Young, formerly one of the king's tutors. With Patrick Young Reid shared in translating into Latin the king's writings, and held office as the king's Latin Secretary. So far as is known he did not return to his native northern birthplace, but like Duncan Liddel and Thomas Cargill, he did not forget his roots or his *alma mater*. He bequeathed his valuable library, now part of Aberdeen University Library, to Marischal College and the town of Aberdeen.[39]

Leiden can justly claim Thomas Reid as one of her *alumni*, and his interest in metaphysics may have been aroused and encouraged by his former fellow student at Marischal and Leiden, Gilbert Jack. It is also worth noting that Thomas Reid and Thomas Seget were at one time friends. In 1622, when Seget's reputation was again in question, Reid wrote to him and recalled several mutual friends, many of them of his Rostock days, which suggests that Seget may have at one time studied at Rostock.[40]

The Scottish students at Leiden who have been mentioned above have all been humanists and philosophers. It must, however, not be forgotten that after a faltering start Leiden became a centre of theological study of distinction. One of its earliest luminaries was Franciscus Junius the Elder, the great proponent of Irenicism, of whom King James thought so highly, and who died as a result of plague in 1602.[41] In the troubles that beset the church in Scotland after 1603 none was more devastating to the Reformed or Presbyterian section than that associated with the attempts of the Melvillian party to hold in 1605 a General Assembly of the church in Aberdeen. As a result of the ensuing royal displeasure one of the exiled ministers, Robert Dury (1555-1616), became minister of the English Church in Leiden, a post which he held until his death. On 27 March 1610 he was incorporated in the university.[42] This does not mean that he necessarily became a student or teacher but merely that he was considered worthy of being associated with the university. He had studied at St Andrews and had at one time taught at the grammar school of Dunfermline.

More significant than Robert Dury was his more widely known son, John (1596-1680),[43] who was incorporated at Leiden at the age of twelve, some months

---

[39]*DNB*, xlvii, 435ff.

[40]British Library, Add. MSS 38597, fos. 71v.-72r. This reference is taken from Odlozilík, op. cit., 35.

[41]*Leiden University*, 4, 28f.; F W Cuno, *Franciscus Junius der Ältere, 1541-1602* (Amsterdam, 1898).

[42]*DNB*, xvi, 263f.; *Album Studiosorum*, 97.

[43]*DNB*, xvi, 261ff.; *Album Studiosorum*, 102, aged 12; C G F de Jong, *John Forbes (c. 1568-1634)*, (1987), 35f.; J M Batten, *John Dury: advocate of Christian reunion* (Chicago, 1944); G H M Posthumus Meyjes, *Geschiedenis van Het Waalse College te Leiden, 1606-*

subsequent to his father. He was later to study under the exiled Andrew Melville at Sedan. John Dury is remembered for his ceaseless activity and travels in the interests of church union. At Leiden he was enrolled as a student in the faculty of letters, and was also a student at the Walloon College in 1616. His examination for admission to the ministry was held in September 1620 and 1624. After a visit to Oxford he was called to be a minister of the Walloon Church, a position which he held for a brief period. On 27 March 1626 the Classis of Leiden provided him with a testimonial as he was about to leave his charge on health grounds.[44] He had begun to have doubts about his vocation and was advised to pay a return visit to his homeland. He visited Scotland briefly, but was soon back on the continent as minister of the Walloon Church in Cologne. Three years later he was minister to the English Company of Merchants at Elbing in Prussia. By this time Dury had begun to develop his plans for a negotiated union between Lutheran and Reformed Churches. This became an all-consuming interest for the rest of his long life.

For several years Dury travelled throughout Germany attending 'courts and churches, state assemblies and synods in furthering his irenic schemes', before he returned to England, where he accepted 'anglican' ordination and became a royal chaplain. With the support of men of widely differing views such as Archbishops Laud and Ussher and a number of other prominent English divines, he returned to the continent to continue his ecumenical endeavours. He moved from one country to another, including Holland, Sweden and Denmark. In Brunswick he gained the support of the prominent Lutheran irenicist George Calixtus of Helmstädt. In 1640 he was appointed minister to the Merchant Adventurers in Rotterdam, and five years later he was again in England attending the Westminster Assembly of Divines. Returning within five years to the continent he made Amsterdam his headquarters. A brief visit to Geneva in 1654-5, where he was received as a Scottish Presbyterian, had little result. Barred after the Restoration from returning to England, he spent the remainder of his life in endless travels in pursuit of his cherished ideals through Germany, Switzerland, France and Alsace. With old age came disillusionment. Toward the end of his life he wrote, 'The only fruit which I have reaped of all my toils is that I see the miserable condition of Christianity'. He died at Cassel at the age of eighty-four.[45]

Dury was the supreme ecumenical optimist, one born out of due season. It is, perhaps, not too much to say that the experiences of his father and others of his family who had suffered for their faith, together with the spirit of tolerance that was abroad in Leiden during his early years there as a student, nurtured in him that insatiable and noble desire to see Christian brethren, especially Calvinists and Lutherans, dwell in unity and concord one with the other.

In this brief survey of the lives of some of those Scots who studied at Leiden and then went on to follow careers on the continent I have merely made a selec-

---

99 (Leiden, 1975), 160, 191; *Theologische Realenzyklopädie*, ed. G Kraus and G Müller, ix (Berlin, 1982), 242ff.

[44]Posthumus Meyjes, op. cit., 178f.

[45]*DNB*, xvi, 262.

tion. There are many others who did not return to their native country, whose lives on the continent would merit further research. And there are those who, having included Leiden in their continental academic itineraries, returned to their homeland to contribute to the life of the nation and the church. They also form a significant number. Their continental connections would also provide the material for a rewarding study.

As long ago as 1877 Professor John Veitch of the university of Glasgow, in an article in *Mind*, drew attention to the number of Scots who had become professors of philosophy on the continent in the sixteenth and seventeenth centuries. In the following year, J P N Land published his seminal article on the Scottish contribution to education in the academies of the Netherlands.[46] The significant contribution made to philosophical studies by William MacDowell (1590-1666) in the foundation of the university of Groningen in 1614 has been widely recognised.[47] In having a Scot as one of its professors of philosophy that new university was but following the example already set by Leiden, where no fewer than five Scots taught philosophy in the seventeenth century. Some of them have already been briefly mentioned.

The first Scot to teach philosophy was, as has been noticed, James Ramsay.[48] At the time of his incorporation his studies seem to have been combined with a teaching post in the States' College, founded in 1591-2, after the manner of the *Collegium Sapientiae* at Heidelberg and intended for the support of those students who were seeking to become ministers. In 1593 Ramsay became sub-regent of the college but died later that year. His potential as a philosopher had been recognised on his arrival in Leiden, for as early as the summer of 1588 he was authorised to give a course on Aristotle's Logic on a provisional basis. Then having been favourably judged he was appointed an 'extraordinary professor of logic', a post which he occupied till the end of his short life. It is known that he gave 'repetitions' on logic and on physics three times a week and that he also gave daily lectures on logic. Little, however, remains of his writings on which to base a judgment of his abilities. It is, nevertheless, worth noting that Daniel Colonius, subsequently regent of the States College, defended on 10 April 1593 theses entitled *De natura logices*, drawn up by Ramsay.[49]

The next Scot to teach philosophy was John MacCulloch or McKullo from Edinburgh, where he had received his earlier education, and graduated MA in

---

[46]For details see P A G Dibon, *L'Enseignement Philosophique dans les Universités Néerlandaises à l'Epoque Pré-Cartésienne, 1575-1650* (Leiden, 1954), 31f.

[47]Ibid., 167-75, 250.

[48]See above, n. 18.

[49]Dibon, op. cit., 20, 26f.; Posthumus Meyjes, op. cit., 51, 54.; *Leiden University*, 134n. 111.

1592.[50] On 20 November 1597 he was appointed on the recommendation of Prince Maurice (which suggests that he may have been acting as a family tutor) to a post as teacher in philosophy at Leiden, but did not, it appears, hold it for long.[51] In August 1599 he enrolled at Basle along with his elder brother James, who had graduated in arts at Edinburgh in 1588 in the company of Thomas Seget.[52] In January 1602 James was at Leiden, where he matriculated as a medical student, giving his age as twenty-eight.[53] Meantime John had moved to Montpellier. In his entry in the Stammbuch of George Strachan, signed in 1600, he described himself as 'Med.Doctor et Philosophiae Professor in celebri Academia Monspeliensi'.[54] These two brothers, along with their fellow Edinburgh graduate, Thomas Seget, had interesting careers. It seems that both brothers had originally intended entering the ministry. John, who had studied theology at Basle, did in fact enter the ministry of the church. He was minister at Broughton in 1594 but resigned a year later because, as he stated to the Synod of Lothian and Tweeddale, 'he can find na sufficient provisioun'. He requested 'a testimonie of the soundnes of his doctrine and honestie of his lyf',[55] which almost certainly indicates that he intended travelling abroad. After leaving Montpellier he became physician to the Emperor Rudolf, at whose court he probably remained until the death of the Emperor in 1612. Two years later Cosmo II, ruler of Tuscany, invited the two brothers, James and John, to teach at the university of Pisa, where Thomas Dempster, a fellow Scotsman, was professor of civil law. James taught medicine. John is described as professor of 'Chemistry and Physick'. Their appointments, however, were brief. After three years they were asked to leave. The brothers may thereafter have spent some time travelling in Italy. John published a medical treatise at Florence in 1616 and James did likewise the following year. He also contributed to the contemporary art of neo-Latin verse composition, and one of his poems appears in the *Delitiae Poetarum Scotorum*. The brothers returned to Great Britain and became royal physicians. John died in London in 1622 at the age of forty-six and is buried at St Margaret's, Westminster. By this time James was also dead.[56]

---

[50]John Mccullo was a member of the graduating class at Edinburgh in 1592. After his name is added by a later hand 'minister verbi' (*Catalogue of the Graduates ... of the University of Edinburgh*), 10.

[51]Dibon, op. cit., 29; his name does not appear in the Leiden *Album Studiosorum*; Smith, op. cit., 149; F Sassen, *Het oudste wijsgerig onderwijs te Leiden, 1575-1619*, Mededeelingen der Nederlandsche Akademie van Wetenschappen, Afd. Letterkunde, NS 4 (Amsterdam, 1941), 20.

[52]*Die Matrikel der Universität Basel*, ed. H G Wackernagel (Basle, 1956), ii, 466; *Catalogue of Graduates ... of the University of Edinburgh*, 9.

[53]*Album Studiosorum*, 64; Smith, op. cit., 149.

[54]Ibid.; J F K Johnstone, *The Alba amicorum of George Strachan, George Craig and Thomas Cumming* (Aberdeen, 1924), 6.

[55]James had also the words 'minister verbi' written after his name (*Catalogue of the Graduates ... of the University of Edinburgh*, 9f; *Records of the Synod of Lothian and Tweeddale*, ed. James Kirk, Edinburgh, 1977, 70, 88).

[56]Smith, op. cit., 149f.

Of much greater significance for Leiden were the careers of John Murdison and Gilbert Jack. It has already been noted that Murdison was incorporated on 24 November 1599 as a law student, at the age of thirty-one. Two days after his name was entered into the Rector's *Album*, he was accorded the right to teach physics, and when Gerard Vossius, the professor of physics, left in February 1600 to become rector of the Latin School at Middelburg, Murdison was confirmed in his appointment as professor of physics. In 1603 one of his colleagues took charge of the teaching of physics, and Murdison, until his death two years later, confined his teaching to logic, aided by his compatriot Gilbert Jack.[57]

Jack had been incorporated on 25 May 1603, as a student in theology, at the age of twenty-five.[58] On the following 28 June he publicly defended theological theses *De Libero Arbitrio* under the orthodox Calvinist Franciscus Gomarus. For a brief period much of the teaching in philosophy was in the hands of these two Scots. They appear to have worked in harmony and both were staunch defenders of Aristotelianism. P A G Dibon, in his important study, *L'Enseignement Philosophique dans les Universités Néerlandaises a l'Epoque Pré-Cartésienne, 1575-1650* (1954), ranked Jack alongside F P Burgersdijk, his celebrated pupil, and A Heereboord as the most representative professors of Aristotelianism in the Netherlands in the pre-Cartesian period.[59] It has also been authoritatively stated that Jack's widely celebrated *Institutiones Physicae*,[60] first published in 1614, 'represents the first tentative attempt at the systematisation of a philosophy of nature',[61] and that 'it amounts in reality to a rendering in his own words of the doctrine of Aristotle'. It has been remarked, too, that 'there is not a trace of empirical physics in his work'.[62] It is interesting to note that he rejected the system of Copernicus because in his opinion the rotation of the earth was contrary to 'truth'. And while he regarded the contemporary Danish scholar, Tycho Brahe, 'as the greatest astronomer since Ptolemy' he did not accept his teaching.[63] Shortly after Murdison's death in 1605 Jack was appointed professor of logic, and also studied medicine. Six years later he defended theses entitled *De Epilepsia* for the MD degree, which he dedicated to Sir Robert Henderson.[64] Jack was appointed a 'Professor Ordinarius' in 1612 and also appears to have taught physics along with logic, prior to his transference to the chair of physics in 1617.

---

[57]See above, n. 29; *Album Scholasticum*, 108, 193; Dibon, op. cit., 30f.

[58]See above, n. 32; Sassen, op. cit., 25-9, 33-6, 41; Johnstone, *Bibliographia Aberdonensis*, i, 116.

[59]Dibon, op. cit., 31.

[60]First published at Leiden in 1614; editions appeared in 1615, 1624, 1644, and 1646; Dibon, op. cit., 74n., 212; Johnstone, *Bibliographia Aberdonensis*, i, 164, 166f., 218, 328; *Leiden University*, 232, n.15.

[61]Dibon, op. cit., 59.

[62]*Leiden University*, 309.

[63]Ibid.

[64]Johnstone, *Bibliographia Aberdonensis*, i, 150.

At Leiden Jack was from the outset of his career a staunch advocate of the teaching of philosophy, and, although he was employed to teach physics, as early as 1604 he sought to be allowed to give formal lectures on metaphysics, a subject which in Reformed theological and some renaissance circles was considered both unnecessary and undesirable. The students had for some time wanted to have the subject taught and the university authorities did give permission for the subject provided it was not separated from logic and that the teaching of it was entrusted to Murdison.[65] For this study Murdison provided a systematic analysis of the first twelve books of Aristotle's *Metaphysics*.[66] After his death, Jack again requested that the subject be continued, but he repeatedly met resistance from the theologians, who feared that the lines of demarcation between their respective subjects might be confused. Jack's persistence led to difficulties, but he was allowed to teach the subject privately.[67] His *Primae Philosophiae Institutiones*, first published in 1616, show that he had been much influenced by the Spanish philosopher Suarez, although he did not follow him slavishly. A second edition was published in Leiden in 1640 and one at Cambridge in 1649.[68]

During the tenure of their posts both Murdison and Jack took their full share in university teaching. Apart from their formal lectures, both presided at 'undergraduate' disputations *exercitii causa* and the more formal *Disputationes pro gradu*, in their own subjects and in miscellaneous subjects.[69] As professors they were responsible for composing the theses and Dibon informs us that the philosophical theses *De Natura Logices*, defended under Murdison, provide a veritable repertory of sources ancient, medieval, and modern.[70]

Jack, it would appear, was very much at home in Leiden, where his systematic exposition of Aristotelian thought was often, we are told, followed by others late into the century.[71] In 1621 he turned down an offer of the Whyte's professorship of moral philosophy at Oxford.[72] Married to a Dutch lady and with a large family to support (at his death they had ten children), he requested the University Curators, as he had taken his doctorate in medicine, to be allowed to give courses in medicine and that he might be allowed to practise that art, as he wished to make better provision for his family. The authorities did not permit him to do either but did have regard to his needs and consequently agreed to increase his stipend.[73] He did not, however, cease to have an interest in medicine. In 1624 he published *In-*

---

[65]Dibon, op. cit., 67.

[66]Ibid., 47f.

[67]Ibid., 69.

[68]Johnstone, *Bibliographia Aberdonensis*, i, 171, 240, 348; Dibon, op. cit., 69ff.

[69]For details see Dibon, op. cit., 38f., 41ff., 57f. Bibliographical details of a number of theses presided over by Jack are given by Johnstone.

[70]Dibon, op. cit., 56.

[71]Ibid., 255ff.

[72]*DNB*, xxix, 85.

[73]Dibon, op. cit., 77n, 225; Johnstone, *Bibliographia Aberdonensis*, i, 218, 252, 363.

stitutiones Medicae, which were reprinted in 1631 and 1653. This latter third edition had been revised by its author before his death.

Liminary verses along with other sources testify to Jack's friendship with Leiden's leading scholars and humanists, such as Heinsius, Barlaeus, and Vossius.[74] In the Calvinist theological controversy that led to the Synod of Dort in 1618-19 Jack incurred the displeasure of the orthodox Gomarist ministers and was dismissed from his post, as were other notable humanist scholars such as Caspar Barlaeus. But in the following year Jack was again teaching and by 1623 he had been fully restored to his chair, which he retained until his death five years later.[75]

It falls outwith the scope set for this paper to consider the contribution of two other Scottish Aristotelians at the university of Leiden, Adam Stuart, who taught there from 1644 to 1654 and his son David, who taught from 1661 to 1669.[76] They are mentioned here merely to indicate that the philosophical stance maintained by their Scottish predecessors was upheld at Leiden for the greater part of the century. There is general agreement that of all the Scottish teachers of philosophy in the Netherlands Gilbert Jack was 'the most notable'. Dibon maintains that his thinking was followed often to the letter by others later in the century.

In this essay only the surface has been scratched of one aspect of a much wider subject, the Scottish student in the Netherlands in the sixteenth and seventeenth centuries. The university of Leiden during this period developed with astonishing rapidity into one of the foremost academic centres of the continent, more than fulfilling the highest hopes and ideals of its illustrious founders. As a truly international institution it drew its professors and students from far and wide. Its connections with similarly minded universities in Germany, Scandinavia, France, Switzerland, England and Scotland were particularly important for it. It is not surprising that so significant a proportion of both its professors and its students were foreigners.

We have here concentrated on only some of the Scots, but the total picture is much larger. Much research has still to be done. At this stage the temptation to exaggerate their importance must be resisted. Students and professors from other

---

[74]Verses by Heinsius, 'Ad Gilbertum Iacchaeum, philosophiae professorem; cum supremum in medicina gradum confecturus esset' are printed in an edition of Heinsius' poems published at Leiden in 1621; verses by Heinsius and Barlaeus are also printed in Jack's *Institutiones Physicae* and in theses presided over by Jack; verses by Vossius are in Jack's *Institutiones Medicae*; verses by Caspar Barlaeus on Jack's death are printed in his *Poemata*; the funeral address by Adolf Vorstius, professor of medicine, published at Leiden in 1628, also contains verses by Heinsius, Barlaeus, and others. Johnstone, *Bibliographia Aberdonensis*, i, 120, 164, 198, 218, 242, 363, 370; *Leiden University*, 309; Dibon, op. cit., 31.

[75]*Leiden University*, 309.

[76]Ibid., 16, 313, 464, 477; *Album Scholasticum*, 148f; Dibon, op. cit., 5, 31, 122, 185; Edward G Ruestow, *Physics at Seventeenth- and Eighteenth-Century Leiden: philosophy and the new science in the university* (The Hague, 1973), 43-8, 148f.

countries made more significant contributions. And, as has been noted, emphasis must also be placed on what Leiden gave to the visitors it welcomed, not just in providing them with opportunities to advance their education, but also in opening up to them the gates to further participation in the academic and cultural life of the entire continent. What has been presented here is in large measure an interim report on one aspect of the history of that great sixteenth- and early seventeenth-century phenomenon, the *Respublica Literarum*.

10

IMPORTING OUR LAWYERS FROM HOLLAND: NETHERLANDS INFLUENCES ON SCOTS LAW AND LAWYERS IN THE EIGHTEENTH CENTURY

John W Cairns

Perhaps the most significant cultural figure in Edinburgh life in the first half of the eighteenth century was Sir John Clerk of Penicuik, baron of the new Exchequer court established after the Union.[1] It is notable that a lawyer should have had this role, just as it is generally remarkable how many of the *literati* of the Scottish Enlightenment were lawyers: Lord Kames, Lord Monboddo and John Millar are only the most obvious and brightest stars in this firmament.[2] Clerk spent two years as a student in the university of Glasgow studying logic and metaphysics - years that he was to regret as wasted because of the nature of these disciplines as taught at Glasgow. In October 1694, however, he sailed for the Netherlands, there to pursue the study of law at the university of Leiden. He studied civil (Roman) law for two years with Philippus Reinhardus Vitriarius, and for one further year with Johannes Voet.[3] Vitriarius was originally German, and a distinguished

NOTE: A first version of this essay was read as a paper at the Saltire Society's Conference, 'Scotland in Europe: The Cultural Factor', held in Edinburgh from 31 July to 2 August 1992. I am grateful for the criticism and comments of participants at that event, as at the Mackie Symposium. I benefited from helpful discussions with Professor R Feenstra and Dr M Ahsmann of Leiden. The latter kindly commented on an earlier draft. I am delighted to acknowledge permission of the Trustees of the National Library of Scotland, Angus Stewart, QC, Keeper of the Advocates' Library, and the Librarians of the universities of Aberdeen and Edinburgh to cite and in some instances to quote from manuscript material in their care.

[1] See generally Iain Gordon Brown, 'Sir John Clerk of Penicuik 1676-1755: aspects of a virtuoso life' (Ph D, University of Cambridge, 1980). I am grateful to Dr Brown for permission to consult his unpublished thesis.

[2] Ian Simpson Ross, *Lord Kames and the Scotland of his Day* (Oxford, 1972); E L Cloyd, *James Burnet: Lord Monboddo* (Oxford, 1972); William C Lehmann, *John Millar of Glasgow, 1735-1801: his life and thought and his contributions to sociological analysis* (Cambridge, 1960).

[3] John M Gray, ed., *Memoirs of the Life of Sir John Clerk of Penicuik, Baronet, Baron of the Exchequer, Extracted by himself from his own Journals 1676-1755* (Scottish History Society, Edinburgh, 1892), 12-13, 15 (hereafter Clerk, *Memoirs*). Clerk's studies are now the subject of an important paper reprinting his correspondence with his father: Kees van Strien and Margreet Ahsmann, 'Scottish law students in Leiden at the end of the seventeenth century: the correspondence of John Clerk, 1694-97', *Lias*, xix (1992), 271-330, continued in ibid., xx (1993), 1-65 (hereafter van Strien and Ahsmann, 'Clerk').

scholar of German public law. He is of note for attempting to relate civil law to its sources in natural law, and for writing an elementary work on natural law according to the method of Hugo Grotius. He was interested in the philosophical and political origins of law. Thus, his course on civil law, published in Leiden in 1697 as *Universum jus civile privatum ad methodum institutionum Justiniani compositum a Philippo Reinhardo Vitriario jurisconsulto et antecessore Lugdunensi*, was subtitled as a work *in quo praeter principia, et controversias juris civilis, indicantur fontes juris naturae et gentium, unde illa deducta esse videntur.*[4] As well as civil law Clerk initially studied with Vitriarius the law of nature and nations of Grotius, until this met with the vehement disapproval of his father.[5] Voet is the more famous man for his scholarly *Commentarius ad Pandectas*, first published in two volumes in Leiden in 1698 and 1700; he was best known to generations of students, however, for his *Compendium juris juxta seriem Pandectarum* published in Leiden in 1682.[6] The young Clerk acutely remarked of Voet: 'This man I found very distinct, for he kept close to his own Compend on the Instituts and Pandects, but he was far from being such a Corpus Juris as Professor Vitriarius was'.[7] The letters recently published by van Strien and Ahsmann show that Clerk and his father disagreed over whom he should study with - his father preferring Voet and Noodt to Vitriarius.[8] Modern scholars would certainly regard Noodt and Voet as the more significant men.[9]

As well as classes with law professors, Clerk attended courses taught by J Perizonius and J Gronovius whom he described as famous professors of 'eloquence' and whose teaching he described as covering history, Tacitus and Suetonius.[10] These would have been courses on Roman and Greek antiquities covering history, political institutions and legal institutions as discovered from classical authors.

---

[4] A thorough study of Vitriarius is wanting, but see R Feenstra and C J D Waal, *Seventeenth-Century Leyden Law Professors and their Influence on the Development of the Civil Law: a study of Bronchorst, Vinnius and Voet* (Amsterdam and London, 1975), 11, 43-4 n.193 (hereafter Feenstra and Waal, *Law Professors*). For a list of his publications, see M J A M Ahsmann and R Feenstra, *Bibliographie van hoogleraren in de rechten aan de Leidse Universiteit tot 1811* (Amsterdam, Oxford and New York, 1984), nos 988-1014 (hereafter Ahsmann and Feenstra, *Bibliographie Leiden*).

[5] Van Strien and Ahsmann, 'Clerk', 292.

[6] Feenstra and Waal, *Law Professors*, 35-44. For a list of his publications see Ahsmann and Feenstra, *Bibliographie Leiden*, nos 1015-1102.

[7] Clerk, *Memoirs*, 15; the letters in van Strien and Ahsmann, 'Clerk', suggest that Clerk studied criminal law with Voet.

[8] Van Strien and Ahsmann, 'Clerk', 292-3.

[9] G C J J van den Bergh, *The Life and Work of Gerard Noodt (1647-1725): Dutch legal scholarship between Humanism and Enlightenment* (Oxford, 1988) (hereafter van den Bergh, *Gerard Noodt*).

[10] Clerk, *Memoirs*, 15-16.

Both these men were noted classical philologists.[11] Clerk attended a class on church history with F Spanhemius,[12] and one on theology with Johannes van Marck.[13] These were also two very distinguished scholars in their field.[14] The energetic Clerk also studied mathematics, philosophy, and music: he was evidently more interested in mathematics and music than civil law, and he went on to become a moderately distinguished composer, whose work currently enjoys a revival, given the contemporary vogue for baroque music.[15] He also learned to draw with Francis van Mieris and studied Dutch, French and Italian.[16]

This was an education in law inspired by the French humanism of the sixteenth century. Its main focus was on the texts of the *Corpus iuris civilis* - the texts of Roman law gathered together in the early sixth century and consisting of the *Institutes*, an elementary text book, the *Digest* or *Pandects*, a vast collection of writings of Roman lawyers, the *Code*, a collection of imperial legislation, and the *Novels*, a collection of later legislation. The type of history and philology taught by Perizonius and Gronovius aided and deepened comprehension of the Roman legal sources. Studies of eloquence were obviously important for a lawyer. Philosophy could explain the moral foundation of law: Vitriarius emphasised the foundation of civil law in natural law. Mathematics dealt with logic, reasoning, and structure, all of which were important in the organization and conceptualization of law.

This was a type of legal education - polite, gentlemanly, scholarly, the education of a legal *virtuoso* - unavailable in Scotland. It did not focus on narrow, technical skills. It was an education suited to an aristocrat, and it is worth noting that Archibald Campbell, first earl of Ilay and third duke of Argyll, had an education in Utrecht similar to that of Clerk at much the same time; he valued it sufficiently to ensure that his nephews, the earl of Bute and James Stuart Mackenzie also studied law in the Netherlands.[17] Van Strien and Ahsman conclude that Scots rarely attended the free public prelections, but generally went to private *collegia*. Their studies initially emphasised the *Institutes* and natural law, but, after six months to a year, they combined these with study of the *Digest*. They also studied

[11]See, e.g., H J de Jonge, 'The Study of the New Testament', in *Leiden University in the Seventeenth Century: an exchange of learning*, ed. Th H Lunsingh Sheurleer and G H M Posthumus Meyjes (Leiden, 1975), 65-109 at 68-9 (hereafter de Jonge, 'New Testament'.)
[12]Clerk, *Memoirs*, 16.
[13]Van Strien and Ahsmann, 'Clerk', 301.
[14]On Spanheim, see de Jonge, 'New Testament', 86; on Johannes van Marck, see *Nieuw Nederlandsch Biografisch Woordenboek*, ed. P C Mulhuysen and Fr K H Kossmann (Leiden, 1933), ix, cols 648-50.
[15]Clerk, *Memoirs*, 14-15; David Johnson, *Music and Society in Lowland Scotland in the Eighteenth Century* (London, 1972), 59-60.
[16]Clerk, *Memoirs*, 16-17.
[17]John W Cairns, 'William Crosse, Regius Professor of Civil Law in the University of Glasgow, 1746-49: a failure of enlightened patronage', *History of Universities*, xii (1993), 159-96 at 161.

feudal law, and sometimes criminal and even canon law.[18] The broader studies were also important: Clerk may not have studied natural sciences (though he contracted a friendship with the great Boerhaave),[19] but others did. John Spotswood, for example, studied chemistry, while John Erskine attended dissections in the anatomy theatre in Utrecht and took a course in natural philosophy.[20] Scots law students took as much advantage as they could of their attendance at Dutch universities.

Exactly how many Scots sought this type of education in the Netherlands will never be known. The matriculation record for Utrecht in particular is very incomplete. What is certain is that large numbers went to the Netherlands to study law, especially between 1650 and 1750, with a peak between 1675 and 1725.[21] This crucial period can fairly be represented as that when the Faculty of Advocates came of age.[22] Around 40 per cent of the advocates admitted between 1661 and 1750 can definitely be traced as having studied law in the Netherlands:[23] given the problems with the records of matriculations, this undoubtedly under-represents the numbers who did so, especially in the crucial period from 1675 to 1725. These fifty years were when legal education was finally established in the universities of Edinburgh and Glasgow.[24] This suggests that Dutch models of legal education would be influential in the new schools of law. This paper will map out a preliminary approach to dealing with this, and will explore some of its potentially wider ramifications for the Scottish Enlightenment.

---

[18]Van Strien and Ahsmann, 'Clerk', 300-2.

[19]Clerk, *Memoirs*, 17-18.

[20]National Library of Scotland (hereafter NLS), MS 2934, f. 127v; Walter MacLeod, ed., *Journal of the Hon. John Erskine of Carnock 1683-87* (Scottish History Society, Edinburgh, 1893), 166-7, 176 (hereafter Erskine, *Journal*).

[21]See, e.g., Paul Nève, 'Disputations of Scots Students Attending Universities in the Northern Netherlands', in *Legal History in the Making*, ed. W M Gordon and T D Fergus (London and Rio Grande, 1991), 95-108 at 96, 98 (hereafter Nève, 'Disputations'); R Feenstra, 'Scottish-Dutch Legal Relations in the Seventeenth and Eighteenth Centuries', in *Scotland and Europe 1200-1850*, ed. T C Smout (Edinburgh, 1986), 128-42 at 132 (hereafter Feenstra, 'Scottish-Dutch Legal Relations'). Van Strien and Ahsmann, 'Clerk', 279-81, bring forward evidence to suggest that at the very period in the 1690s when matriculations in Leiden were considerably greater than in Utrecht, far more Scots were studying in the latter university.

[22]John W Cairns, 'Sir George Mackenzie, the Faculty of Advocates, and the Advocates' Library', in Sir George Mackenzie, *Oratio inauguralis in aperienda jurisconsultorum bibliotheca* (Edinburgh, 1989), 18-35 (hereafter Cairns, 'Mackenzie').

[23]Feenstra, 'Scottish-Dutch Legal Relations', 133.

[24]Sir Alexander Grant, *The Story of the University of Edinburgh during its First Three Hundred Years* (2 vols, London, 1884), i, 232-3, 284-8 (hereafter Grant, *University of Edinburgh*); John W Cairns, 'The Origins of the Glasgow Law School: the professors of civil law, 1714-61', in *The Life of the Law*, ed. Peter Birks (London, 1993), 151-94 (hereafter Cairns, 'Origins of the Glasgow Law School').

A widely read gazetteer of the newly united Britain in the first half of the eighteenth century was John Chamberlayne's *Magnae Britanniae Notitia: or, the present state of Great Britain*: between 1708 and 1755 this work published in London went through seventeen editions. It provides valuable - if sometimes already for its time out-of-date - information about geography, commerce, and government, indicating what was thought to be significant about Scottish and English institutions from both an insider's and an outsider's point of view. In the account of the Faculty of Advocates in Scotland, there is a prominent, detailed and accurate description of the examination and admission of an advocate. The intrant was first examined in private *viva voce* by the seven private examinators on civil (Roman) law. If found sufficiently qualified he was then allocated a title of Roman law on which he had to print theses in Latin for debate. Appended to the theses were *corollaria* or *annexa* - further unrelated theses for debate. These theses were then defended in public and a number of public examinators were elected each year to impugn them. Following a successful defence, the intrant had to write a speech in Latin on one of the laws or fragments of the title on which his theses had been printed. This he delivered before the Lords of Council and Session. He then took oaths of loyalty to the government and an oath *de fideli administratione* of his public office of advocate and was duly admitted. It was also possible to be admitted by an examination in Scots law, but the work only briefly alluded to this.[25]

This mode of admitting members to the faculty was rich in symbolism and allusion. It emphasised that the faculty was above all a learned corporation, which valued scholarly academic knowledge. These ceremonies of admission deliberately followed those for a university degree in law. In regulating the public examination or trial in early 1693 the faculty had ruled that it would 'both add to the honor of the society and to the regulation of the candidat if the said publict tryall shall proceid in the same way and method as is practised abroad'.[26] Although civil law was central to the Scottish legal tradition and had influenced Scots law, these examinations were not intended to show knowledge adequate for practice but to demonstrate academic scholarship.[27] They demonstrated that among the lawyers of Scotland the advocates were an élite group, set apart by learning as well as status. It is instructive in this respect to look at the opinions of John Spotswood who was to become an influential private teacher of law in Edinburgh in the first

---

[25]John Chamberlayne, *Magnae Britanniae Notitia: or, the present state of Great Britain* (London, 1708), 500, and (London, 1755), part II, book II, 105 (hereafter Chamberlayne, *Magnae Britanniae Notitia*). This description remained identical through all editions. See further John W Cairns, 'The Formation of the Scottish Legal Mind in the Eighteenth Century: Themes of Humanism and Enlightenment in the Admission of Advocates' in *The Legal Mind*, ed. Neil MacCormick and Peter Birks (Oxford, 1986), 253-77 (hereafter Cairns, 'Admission of Advocates').

[26]John Macpherson Pinkerton, ed., *The Minute Book of the Faculty of Advocates, Volume 1, 1661-1712* (Stair Society, Edinburgh, 1976), 121 (3 Jan. 1693) (hereafter *Advocates' Minutes*, i).

[27]Cairns, 'Admission of Advocates', 255-61.

quarter of the eighteenth century.[28] At the age of nineteen he was apprenticed in 1686 to James Hay of Carriber, Writer to the Signet, with whom he stayed until 1692.[29] Scots Calvinists of the later seventeenth century believed it important to lead an examined life. Spotswood was no exception. One autumn during these six years, possibly early in them, Spotswood set out his aims and intentions for the approaching winter. Worrying that the study of Scots law might divert him from learning the styles of Scots law with Hay, he wrote: 'The study of the Scotch law may very fitly be carried along with that of the civil if ever I read it and if it shall be God's will that I do not reach the degree and dignity of an advocat what is more necessary in the first place to be known by a writer or Agent than the Scotch styles and formes of processes...'[30]

Spotswood's remark hints at the division that there was perceived to be between the education of an advocate and that of a writer. Writers needed to know the style of the deeds they drafted and have a grasp of the process by which causes were agented through the courts. The work of one possessing the 'degree and dignity' of an advocate was more profoundly intellectual: law was a system of rules to be grasped by the intellect. The primary focus of scholarly knowledge was Roman law. This view of the roles and education of advocates and writers presupposed different systems of education for their respective professions. Advocates required a period of study of law in a university to follow courses in Roman law and related disciplines; writers were trained through a system of apprenticeship.

It would be easy to exaggerate the contrast between the two branches of the legal profession. It is clear that many writers followed a university education in law, although unnecessary; it is likewise clear that a number of advocates - such as Spotswood - had an initial training in the office of a writer, though it is worth noting that Lord Kames was later to consider this the worst way to train an advocate.[31] This said, it must still be stressed that the advocates valued education in a university in Roman law in a way that the writers did not.

The Faculty of Advocates emerged out of the group of men appointed in the sixteenth century to plead before the Lords of Council and Session reconstituted as the College of Justice in 1532.[32] If much about the early advocates is obscure, one thing is certain - from the beginning education in Roman and canon law was valued. Thus, of the approximately 60 successful intrants between 1575 and 1608, two-thirds based their claim for admission as an advocate on academic study of the Roman and canon laws in a university, most frequently in France; others were

---

[28]John W Cairns, 'John Spotswood, Professor of Law: A Preliminary Sketch', in *Miscellany Three*, ed. W M Gordon, (Stair Society, Edinburgh, 1992), 131-59 (hereafter Cairns, 'Spotswood').

[29]NLS, Ch. 1566; NLS, MS 2934, f. 127v.

[30]Ibid., f. 177r.

[31]G Scott and F A Pottle, eds, *Private Papers of James Boswell from Malahide Castle* (18 vols, New York, 1928-34), xv, 269; see also Erskine, *Journal*, xix-xx.

[32]R K Hannay, *The College of Justice: essays on the institution and development of the Court of Session* (Edinburgh, 1933), 135-64 (hereafter Hannay, *College of Justice*).

admitted on the basis of their long experience on 'practick', typically gained as a servitor to an advocate.[33] There were therefore two modes of admission as an advocate - one by academic study (though usually linked in the sixteenth century with attendance at the courts), the other by a virtual apprenticeship. These two ways of joining the faculty continued into the seventeenth century, while developing in a way that it is not necessary to explore here.[34] The Restoration period, however, saw a number of significant changes, marking the faculty's struggle for greater independence from the Lords of Session. First, the faculty secured the right to examine and to recommend for admission all intrants who sought entry on the basis of academic knowledge, ultimately developing the system of trials outlined above. For a while the lords retained the right to admit others 'extraordinarily' without remitting them to the dean and faculty for examination on civil law; in 1688, however, the faculty persuaded the lords to examine such intrants on their knowledge of the styles, form of process, and principles of Scots law. Finally the lords by an act of sederunt in 1692 changed this so that those entering extraordinarily would be remitted to the dean and faculty for examination of the 'practick', styles and form of process of Scots law.[35]

These crucial developments, whereby the faculty gained considerable control over who entered their ranks, occurred in the same era as the founding of their great library around 1680.[36] It was a period when the faculty felt strong enough openly to defy the lords on a number of occasions, if not always successfully.[37] The faculty had matured into a corporation of learned lawyers secure in and conscious of their status. One vital aspect of this was their social background. The researches of the late Dr Ian Rae have shown that the social composition of the faculty started to change significantly at this time: 'Men from the upper classes of peers and landed gentry, who are relatively modestly represented at the beginning of the period [the 1620s], became the most significant group after the Restoration'.[38] This change explains why the advocates became so concerned after 1660 to stress that the law that they practised was a liberal science rather than a mechanical art. Liberal sciences were taught in universities; mechanical arts were learned by tradesmen though apprenticeships - a mode of teaching not socially suitable for a gentleman. The way to ensure that men of proper education and background came to the faculty was to promote examinations that required an

---

[33]Ibid., 145-7; John W Cairns, 'The law, the advocates and the universities in late sixteenth-century Scotland', *Scottish Historical Review*, lxxiii (1994), 171-90.

[34]Hannay, *College of Justice*, 149-53.

[35]Cairns, 'Admission of Advocates', 255-7.

[36]Thomas I Rae, 'The Origins of the Advocates' Library', in *For the Encouragement of Learning*, eds Patrick Cadell and Ann Matheson (Edinburgh, 1989), 1-22 (hereafter Rae, 'Origins'); Cairns, 'Mackenzie'.

[37]John M Simpson, 'The Advocates as Scottish Trade Union Pioneers' in *The Scottish Tradition: essays in honour of Ronald Gordon Cant*, ed. G W S Barrow (Edinburgh, 1974), 164-77.

[38]Rae, 'Origins', 4.

extensive academic training in civil law, and to discourage entry by examination in Scots law through requiring doubled entry dues and through stigmatising it as less 'honourable'.[39]

The faculty were very successful in this policy. Dr John Shaw has pointed out that of the 295 advocates who were admitted between 1707 and 1750, we know the nature of the trials of 260 of them: they were all on civil law.[40] It seems likely that the remaining 35 were also all admitted by trial on civil law, since in argument before the House of Lords in the case of *Catanach et al.* v. *Gordon* in 1745, counsel for Gordon stated that, since the Union, no advocate had been admitted but upon trial in civil law.[41] In this respect it is likewise telling that in reforming the requirements for admission in 1750, the faculty acted as if entry by trial in Scots law had fallen into desuetude, and merely added a new compulsory examination in Scots law to the existing trials in civil law.[42] If in the early nineteenth century the rigour of the faculty's examinations became questionable,[43] certainly in the first half of the eighteenth century intrants thought it necessary to prepare thoroughly for them, so that Hercules Lindesay, a future professor of civil law in Glasgow, and no doubt others, could eke out a living by specially tutoring intrants for their trials in civil law.[44] Given that before 1699 there were no classes in civil law taught in Scotland, except occasionally in King's College, Aberdeen,[45] these examinations encouraged those intending admission to the faculty to travel abroad to study.

In going abroad to study law between 1675 and 1725, Scots were continuing a long tradition. This raises the question of why they went to the Netherlands. Scots had studied generally in France, especially in Paris, in the late medieval period. Politics, however, affected where they tended to go. Thus, when Paris became difficult for Scots between 1408 and 1417, they moved to Cologne and then, after its foundation in 1425, to Leuven in the southern Low Countries, until the revolt in the Netherlands in the 1550s caused them to look elsewhere. Through the

---

[39]Hannay, *College of Justice*, 155-8; William Forbes, *A Journal of the Session* (Edinburgh, 1714), viii; John Spottiswoode, *The Form of Process, Before the Lords of Council and Session* (Edinburgh, 1711), xxxix.

[40]John Stuart Shaw, *The Management of Scottish Society, 1707-1764: power, nobles, lawyers, Edinburgh agents and English influences* (Edinburgh, 1983), 27.

[41]See copy of Lord Chancellor Hardwicke's notes on arguments of counsel in Aberdeen University Library, MS M. 387/8/2; on the background to this case see Roger L Emerson, *Professors, Patronage and Politics: the Aberdeen universities in the eighteenth century* (Aberdeen, 1992), 66-9.

[42]Cairns, 'Admission of Advocates', 264-5.

[43]Ibid., 275.

[44]Cairns, 'Origins of the Glasgow Law School', 184.

[45]Cairns, 'Spotswood'. On Aberdeen, see John W Cairns, 'Lawyers, law professors, and localities; the universities of Aberdeen, 1680-1750', *Northern Ireland Legal Quarterly*, xlvi (1995) (forthcoming).

sixteenth century many continued to study in French universities.[46] Others went to the German lands (one thinks of Sir John Skene at Wittenberg),[47] or, after its foundation in 1575, to Leiden.[48] It has been suggested that the similar Calvinist theology of the Dutch and the Scots reformed churches encouraged Scots to study in the Netherlands.[49] No doubt this was one encouraging factor. And the attitude and atmosphere of the universities were generally liberal and tolerant, so that oaths troubling to a Calvinist, presbyterian conscience were not demanded. Thus, John Erskine noted in his *Journal* for 7 April 1685: 'I was this day matriculate. The Rector enquired if I would take the colledge oath, but did not propose it by way of an oath, having only desired my promise that I should do or not do such things as he spoke of '.[50] This said, many Scots continued to study law in France through much of the seventeenth century in numbers that will probably remain unknown. Obvious examples of convincedly protestant Scots who studied in France are Sir George Mackenzie at Bourges and Sir John Lauder of Fountainhall at Orléans and Poitiers.[51] The wars of William of Orange with France in the 1690s, however, meant that that country was closed to Scots for study.[52] This no doubt in part explains the large number of Scottish students in the Netherlands at that period. The pattern of study for medical and other students at this time was much the same as for law students.[53] From the second half of the century the Netherlands moreover had become the preferred country of exile for Scots refugees, while Scottish trading links with the northern Netherlands were close and plentiful at this time. The importance of this lay not only in ensuring Scots' familiarity with the Netherlands and their universities, but also in making it easy to organize the complex financing of studies through a well-organized system of

---

[46]Nève, 'Disputations', 95-6; Feenstra, 'Scottish-Dutch Legal Relations', 129; John Durkan, 'The French connection in the Sixteenth and Early Seventeenth Centuries', in *Scotland and Europe 1200-1850*, ed. T C Smout (Edinburgh, 1986), 19-44.

[47]On Skene, see John W Cairns, T David Fergus and Hector L MacQueen, 'Legal Humanism and the History of Scots Law: John Skene and Thomas Craig', in *Humanism in Renaissance Scotland*, ed. John MacQueen (Edinburgh, 1990), 48-74 at 52.

[48]Nève, 'Disputations', 96. See also above, pp. 122-35.

[49]See, e.g., Alexander Murdoch, 'The Advocates, the Law and the Nation in Early Modern Scotland', in *Lawyers in Early Modern Europe and America*, ed. Wilfred Prest (London, 1981), 147-63 at 150.

[50]Erskine, *Journal*, 111.

[51]Cairns, 'Mackenzie', 18; Donald Crawford, ed., *Journals of Sir John Lauder Lord Fountainhall with his Observations on Public Affairs and other Memoranda 1665-76* (Scottish History Society, Edinburgh, 1900), 14, 112-14. Mackenzie's petition for admission as an advocate (NLS, Advocates' MS 25.2.5 (i), f. 290r) claimed that he had studied in both France and the Netherlands; a letter published by van Strien and Ahsmann, 'Clerk', 44, suggests that it was at Bourges only.

[52]See, e.g., T C Smout, *Scottish Trade on the Eve of Union 1660-1707* (Edinburgh and London, 1963), 64-5, 245; William Ferguson, *Scotland's Relations with England: a survey to 1707* (Edinburgh, 1977), 176.

[53]See the tables in Nève, 'Disputations', 96, 98.

bills of exchange and letters of credit passing between Scotland and the Netherlands. The trading links and the presence of numerous Scots merchants in the Netherlands made this possible.[54]

At the same time, the Dutch universities were at their intellectual peak in the early modern period between 1675 and 1725. There were scholars of European pre-eminence in all disciplines.[55] In medical studies in particular, Leiden probably led Europe at this time; Clerk's friend Boerhaave was to reach special fame and influence, and the Dutch medical faculties were to have a determining influence on the development of medical education in Edinburgh.[56] As with medicine so with law. Over the crucial fifty year period when Scots law students flocked to the Netherlands, the professors of law in Leiden were Antonius Matthaeus III (professor at Leiden, 1672-1710), Johannes Voet (professor, 1680-1713), Philippus Reinhardus Vitriarius (professor, 1682-1719) and Gerard Noodt (professor 1686-1725). These were four very distinguished men. Apart from Vitriarius, all had also taught at other universities in the Netherlands.[57] Among their immediate successors were also men of the first rank such as Antonius Schulting and Johannes Westenberg.[58] Over much the same period, Utrecht, the other university favoured by Scots law students, had as professors Voet and Noodt (before they were called to Leiden), Lucas van de Poll, Johannes van Muyden, and Cornelius van Eck.[59] If not as distinguished as their Leiden colleagues, van Muyden and van Eck were popular teachers and writers of successful *compendia* for students.[60] If Franeker was less popular with Scots, some certainly went there attracted by the

---

[54]For a recent overview, see T C Smout, 'Scottish-Dutch Contact 1600-1800', in *Dutch Art and Scotland: a reflection of taste*, ed. Julia Lloyd Williams (Edinburgh,1992), 21-32 at 21-5.

[55]See, e.g., *Leiden University in the Seventeenth Century: an exchange of learning*, ed. Th H Lusingh Schleurleer and G H M Posthumus Meyjes (Leiden, 1975); G W Kernkamp et al., *De Utrechtse Universiteit 1636-1936* (2 vols, Utrecht, 1936); *Universiteit te Franeker 1585-1811: bijdragen tot de geschiedenis van de Friese hogeschool*, ed. G Th Jensma, F R H Smit and F Westra (Leeuwarden, 1985).

[56]G A Lindeboom, *Herman Boerhaave: the man and his work* (London, 1968); E Ashworth Underwood, *Boerhaave's Men at Leyden and After* (Edinburgh, 1977).

[57]Feenstra and Waal, *Law Professors*, 11, 36 n.146, 43-4 n.193; van den Bergh, *Gerard Noodt*.

[58]Feenstra and Waal, *Law Professors*, 12 n.12; R Feenstra, 'Ein später Vertreter der niederländischen Schule: Johann Ortwin Westenberg (1667-1737)', in *Festschrift für Heinz Hübner zum 70. Geburtstag am 7. November 1984*, ed. G Baumgärtel et al. (Berlin and New York, 1984), 47-62.

[59]See Rob Welten, 'Utrechts Hoogleraren in de Rechten (1636-1815): enkele aspecten van de geschiedenis van de rechtenfaculteit te Utrecht', *Tijdschrift voor Rechtsgeschiedenis* (hereafter *TvR*), lv (1987), 67-101 at 87-8.

[60]G C J J van den Bergh, 'Cornelius van Eck 1662-1732: een dichter-jurist', in *Rechtsgeleerd Utrecht: levensschetsen van elf hoogleraren uit driehonderdvijftig jaar Faculteit der Rechtsgeleerdheid in Utrecht*, ed. G C J J van den Bergh, J E Spruit and M van de Vrugt (Zutphen, 1986), 37-54.

fame of Ulrik Huber, whose works gained a wide circulation and popularity in Scotland.[61] A little later, Jean Barbeyrac's fame as a scholar of natural law and expounder of Grotius and Pufendorf attracted Scots students to Groningen where he taught from 1717 to 1744, even if that town could be disparagingly described by one Scot as 'the most fit place for study in the World' because there was 'no manner of diversion'.[62]

Some of these professors - such as Voet, van Eck and van Muyden - were simply successful and able expounders of Roman law; others - such as Noodt and Schulting - were noted for their philological skills and historical concerns; and yet others - such as Huber - for their interest in political theory. Some were interested in all of these. Furthermore, it is of crucial importance that most were interested in natural law, teaching it either from Grotius or Pufendorf.[63] From Noodt, for example, Scots would have learned views favouring religious toleration, constitutionalism, political liberty, and commerce: what one might call proto-Enlightenment values.[64] In general, Scots who studied law in the Netherlands would have learned it as a polite, enlightened science, related to the study of philosophy, philology and history. This was a legal education suitable for gentlemen.

At the same time as the Faculty of Advocates remodelled their examinations, created their library, and gained greater independence from the Lords of Session, they started to campaign for the creation of chairs of law in the Scottish universities. The type of legal education they wished to develop in Scotland was one modelled on the humanistic legal studies found in the Netherlands. The faculty commented in 1695: 'The professione [i.e. professorship] of the laws carys necessarly with it all the belles Letres and the knowledge of ancient and modern history...'[65] They evidently were thinking of chairs in civil law, and indeed at one time suggested it might be possible to attract 'eminent professors from abroad':[66] it is always possible that they had the Netherlands in mind. The university of Edin-

---

[61]Theo Johannes Veen, *Recht en Nut: Studiën over en naar aanleiding van Ulrik Huber (1636-1694)* (Zwolle, 1976); idem, 'De lege regia: opmerkingen over de independentie van geschiedbeschouwing, politieke theorie en interpretatie van Romeins recht bij Ulrik Huber', in *Universiteit te Franeker: bijdragen tot de geschiedenis van de Friese hogeschool*, ed. G Th Jensma, F R H Smit and F Westra (Leeuwarden, 1985), 321-34; idem, 'Interpretations of Inst. 1.2.6, D.1.4.1 and D.1.3.31: Huber's historical, juridical and political-theoretical reflections on the *lex regia*', *TvR*, liii (1985), 357-77. On Huber in Scotland, see Alan Watson, *Joseph Story and the Comity of Errors* (Athens, Ga., 1992), 81-4.

[62]Thomas Dundas to Charles Mackie, 10 Jan. 1728, Edinburgh University Library (hereafter EUL), MS La. II. 91.

[63]C J H Jansen, 'Over de 18e eeuwse docenten natuurrecht aan Nederlandse universiteiten en de door hen gebruikte leerboeken', *TvR*, lv (1987), 103-15.

[64]Van den Bergh, *Gerard Noodt*, 321-33 and passim.

[65]*Advocates' Minutes*, i, 160. See generally Cairns, 'Mackenzie', 23, 33 n.43; idem, 'Spotswood', 145-6.

[66]*Advocates' Minutes*, i, 160.

burgh also became interested in the 1690s in establishing a chair in law.[67] The university and the faculty, however, did not succeed in raising the money to endow a chair. No one else seemed willing to fund one, until in 1698 Alexander Cunningham, a noted classicist, was given by Parliament a salary as professor of civil law 'in this Kingdome': this was renewed in 1704 for a further five years.[68] Cunningham did not teach, however, and this grant was probably simply a means of providing a pension for a protégé of the duke of Queensberry.[69] Private enterprise filled the gap.

Between 1699 and 1710 three advocates teaching in Edinburgh can be traced: Alexander Drummond, John Spotswood and John Cuninghame.[70] Spotswood and Cuninghame were the most important of these three; and both of them had studied law in Leiden.[71] Drummond initially offered classes on both Scots law and Roman law, but in fact appears only ever to have taught the latter, claiming to teach a course on Justinian's *Institutes* 'as they are taught abro[a]d by Explanation and Examination'.[72] These were obviously classes on the model of the *collegia explicatoria* and *collegia examinatoria* found in the Dutch law faculties.[73] Drummond taught between 1699 and probably 1706. Cuninghame, from 1705 until his death in 1710, gave courses on Scots law (using Mackenzie's *Institutions of the Law of Scotland*) and on Justinian's *Institutes* and *Digest*. Spotswood started to teach in 1702, giving classes in Justinian's *Institutes* and various classes on Scots law. He stopped teaching in 1706. Cuninghame was the most successful of these three and captured the market, driving Drummond and Spotswood out of business. Thus, when he died in 1710, there was a tremendous scramble to take over his students.[74] These three first teachers modelled their classes or 'colleges' on the *collegia privata* given by professors in the Netherlands.[75]

---

[67]A Bower, *The History of the University of Edinburgh; chiefly compiled from original papers and records, never before published* (2 vols, Edinburgh, 1817), i, 328-34, 344-6 (hereafter Bower, *University of Edinburgh*).

[68]*Acts of the Parliaments of Scotland*, ed. Thomas Thomson and Cosmo Innes (12 vols, Edinburgh, 1814-75), x, 176 (Act 1698 c. 37), appendix, 27-8, and xi, 203 (Act 1704 c. 9).

[69]See W A Kelly, 'Lord George Douglas (1667/1668?-1693?) and his library', in *Miscellany Three*, ed. W M Gordon (Stair Society, Edinburgh, 1992), 160-72; Feenstra, 'Scottish-Dutch Relations', 134-6.

[70]Cairns, 'Spotswood', 133-4.

[71]*Album studiosorum academiae Lugduno-Batavae MDLXXV-MDCCCLXXV* (The Hague, 1875), cols 700, 724 (hereafter *Album Leiden*).

[72]Cairns, 'Spotswood', 133 and n. 15; *Edinburgh Gazette*, 11/14 Sept. 1699.

[73]See van Strien and Ahsmann, 'Clerk', 288.

[74]Cairns, 'Spotswood', passim.

[75]See van Strien and Ahsmann, 'Clerk', 288-9; on the terminology, see Margaretha J A M Ahsmann, *Collegia en Colleges: juridisch onderwijs aan de Leidse Universiteit 1575-1630 in het bijzonder het disputeren* (Groningen, 1990), 324-36; idem, 'Collegia Publica et Privata: eine Erscheinung deutscher Herkunft an den niederländischen juristischen Fakultäten um 1600?' in *Die rechtswissenschaftlichen Beziehungen zwischen den Niederlanden und*

If Cuninghame was the most successful of these early private teachers, we know most about Spotswood.[76] He taught Justinian's *Institutes* from the *Compendium institutionum Justiniani sive elementa juris civilis*, a popular textbook by J F Böckelmann, a German who taught at Leiden from 1670 to 1681. Böckelmann had revolutionized the teaching of Roman law in the Netherlands by introducing the *methodus compendiaria*, whereby Roman law was taught from a compend rather than from the original texts. Spotswood tried to develop on his own the type of curriculum available at Leiden, and he expressed the humanistic view that to be an educated lawyer it was necessary 'to attain the Knowledge of the Laws, Civil, Feudal, Canon, and Municipal, beside the full Knowledge of History, Politicks, Philology, and Classical learning'. He expected his students to be proficient in languages and to be 'skillfull in *Grammar*, *Rhetorick*, and *Logick*', and, at one stage, he provided for them two teachers of history and philology, because, as lawyers, they required 'to be made Partakers of the *Grecian* and *Roman* Wit and *Prudence*'. Like his teacher Vitriarius, he paid attention to Grotian natural law as the foundation of civil law. This type of education proved popular, as, until Cuninghame started to monopolise legal education, Spotswood could attract as many as 37 students in a year over various courses: this was a substantial number, and his students included some future men of distinction.

These three early private teachers showed that there was a demand for formal legal education in Scotland. Though this demand seems to have been primarily for classes in civil law and secondarily for classes in Scots law, the first chair in law to be created in the modern period in Scotland was the regius chair of public law and the law of nature and nations in the university of Edinburgh.[77] The title of this chair indicates that its province was to be the Grotian law of nature and nations made familiar to Scots by *collegia Grotiana* in the Netherlands; by this time, natural law theory had become central to Scottish ethical thought, whether it was of the school of Grotius or of Pufendorf.[78] This chair was funded by the conversion of a large number of bursaries in divinity for its support. While it has been suggested that this chair was created purely for the benefit of its first holder, Charles Areskine, a regent in philosophy in Edinburgh,[79] this seems unlikely.[80] The reason why this was the first chair in law rather than one in civil law was presumably the recent renewal of Alexander Cunningham's parliamentary privilege as professor of civil law. Areskine was given leave to study law in the Nether-

---

Deutschland in historischer Sicht, ed. Robert Feenstra and Chris Coppens (Nijmegen, 1991), 1-20.

[76]The information and analysis in this paragraph is derived from Cairns, 'Spotswood'.

[77]Grant, *University of Edinburgh*, i, 232-3.

[78]Roger L Emerson, 'Science and Moral Philosophy in the Scottish Enlightenment', in *Studies in the Philosophy of the Scottish Enlightenment*, ed. M A Stewart (Oxford, 1990), 11-36.

[79]See, e.g., Bower, *University of Edinburgh*, ii, 65-6.

[80]See William Scott to James Anderson, 7 Dec. 1714, NLS, Adv. MS 29.1.2 (iv), ff. 180-1.

lands, which he did, returning to be admitted as an advocate in 1711 and advertising classes later in the same year.[81]

The competition for Cuninghame's classes after his death went on for a number of years. Private teachers offered classes not only in Roman law and Scots law, but also in relevant classical literature.[82] But in October 1710, James Craig, evidently one of the more successful competitors, was appointed professor of civil law in the university of Edinburgh by the town council as patrons. They dealt with the difficult issue of endowing the chair by not awarding him a salary. One was granted a few years later out of the revenues of the beer tax in Edinburgh.[83] Although Craig's appointment did not get rid of all the competition for a while, by the end of the decade he seems to have been the only person teaching civil law in Edinburgh. While Craig's education in law is obscure, it is possible that he studied law in the university of Utrecht.[84] He probably taught his course on the *Digest* using van Eck's *Principia iuris civilis.*[85] This class was thus modelled on a *collegium privatum* as taught by a Dutch professor, but Craig also gave - at least at one time - regular free public *praelectiones*, which anyone might attend, though he later described his regular classes as prelections.[86] The establishment of this chair in 1710 was explained as justified by the success of private teaching.[87] That it came in 1710 was no doubt because Alexander Cunningham's parliamentary privilege had expired the previous year.

Late in 1713, in emulation of this development in Edinburgh, the faculty of the university of Glasgow secured the establishment of a chair of civil law with an allocated salary. Little is known of how the first professor, William Forbes, taught civil law, but it is likely that he taught it on the model of Dutch *collegia* using a textbook, such as Voet's *Compendium juris civilis juxta seriem pandectarum.* From the chair of moral philosophy, Glasgow developed a very strong tradition in the teaching of natural law; while, at least at one stage, law students could attend classes in universal history and the classics which were relevant for them.[88]

The next step in the development of legal education in the university of Edinburgh was the appointment of Charles Mackie as professor of universal history in

---

[81]EUL, MS Dc.6.108; *The Faculty of Advocates in Scotland, 1532-1943, with Genealogical Notes*, ed. Sir Francis J Grant (Scottish Record Society, Edinburgh, 1944), 66 (hereafter Grant, *Advocates*); *Scots Courant*, 12/14 Nov. 1711.

[82]See Cairns, 'Spotswood', 154, n. 189.

[83]*Extracts from the Records of the Burgh of Edinburgh 1701 to 1718*, ed. Helen Armet (Edinburgh, 1967), 201-2 (hereafter *Edinburgh Records*); Grant, *University of Edinburgh*, i, 284-5.

[84]The argument for this is involved, and I shall deal with it elsewhere.

[85]Grant, *University of Edinburgh*, i, 285 n.1, ii, 364.

[86]See, e.g., *Scots Courant*, 10/12 May 1710, 11/13 Sept. 1710, 17/20 Nov. 1710, 21/23 Mar. 1711.

[87]*Edinburgh Records*, 202.

[88]Cairns, 'Origins of the Glasgow Law School', 152-83; John W Cairns, 'The Influence of Smith's Jurisprudence on Legal Education in Scotland', in *Adam Smith Reviewed*, ed. Peter Jones and Andrew S Skinner (Edinburgh, 1992), 168-89.

1719. Initially, he had no permanently endowed salary, but eventually had one allocated out of the beer duties. Mackie had studied at Edinburgh, Groningen, and Leiden; in the last university he had matriculated in the faculty of law. Mackie developed courses in Greek and Roman antiquities for law students, and significant numbers of them may be traced in his class lists. These were classes comparable to those of Perizonius and Gronovius in Leiden. This important need for students of civil law was thereby met.[89]

The final stage in the provision of a full curriculum in legal studies in Edinburgh came with the appointment of Alexander Bayne as professor of Scots law in 1722, with a salary allocated from the tax on beer.[90] Bayne had studied Scots law and Roman law with Spotswood, before going on to study law in Leiden.[91] Bayne was admitted to Lincoln's Inn in London, and lived there for a number of years as secretary to the earl of Wemyss, before returning to be admitted as an advocate in 1714.[92] He taught Scots law using Mackenzie's *Institutions*, and went on to develop a separate course in criminal law.[93] Again, this was modelled on the *collegium privatum* as found in the Netherlands, even though he referred to the classes as prelections; and Bayne also provided an examinatory college.[94] Thus, while teaching Scots law, Bayne also followed Dutch models.

By the 1720s, legal education was being offered in the universities of Edinburgh and Glasgow in civil law and Scots law on the Dutch model, along with related studies of natural law, universal history, and Greek and Roman antiquities. These classes were modelled on Dutch *collegia privata* and were not 'public' other than in the sense that anyone could attend who paid the fee. They could be described as private colleges by the professors themselves (as by Charles Areskine in 1711), and by outsiders describing the universities.[95] It is particularly telling that Dutch textbooks were very much the basis of instruction in civil law. We have already noted Spotswood's and Craig's choice of textbooks; one of the private teachers in Edinburgh (probably Robert Craigie) taught from Voet's *Compendium*

---

[89] L W Sharp, 'Charles Mackie, the first Professor of History at Edinburgh University', *Scottish Historical Review*, xli (1962), 23-45.

[90] Grant, *University of Edinburgh*, i, 285, 288; W Menzies, 'Alexander Bayne of Rires, Advocate', *Juridical Review*, xxxvi (1924), 60-70.

[91] Cairns, 'Spotswood', 148; *Album Leiden*, col. 792.

[92] *The Records of the Honourable Society of Lincoln's Inn*, vol. 1 (Admissions 1420-1796) ([London], 1896), 367; Sir William Fraser, *Memorials of the Family of Wemyss of Wemyss* (3 vols, Edinburgh, 1888), iii, 180-92; Grant, *Advocates*, 11.

[93] John W Cairns, 'John Millar's Lectures on Scots Criminal Law', *Oxford Journal of Legal Studies*, viii (1988), 364-400 at 383-6.

[94] See *Alexander Bayne, Professor of the Municipal Law, To the Gentlemen who have attended his College of Prelections*, single sheet, NLS, Pressmark S.302.b.1 (no. 53).

[95] *Scots Courant*, 12/14 Nov. 1711: 'private Lecture[s] on the Laws of Nature and Nations'; Chamberlayne, *Magnae Britanniae Notitia* (London, 1737), separately paginated list of Scottish office holders, 21: 'private Lessons'.

of the *Digest* (as perhaps did Forbes).[96] As yet, some students at least did not find this sufficient, and a number of Spotswood's and Cuninghame's pupils (such as Bayne) continued to go to the Netherlands on a *peregrinatio academica* to take classes from the great Dutch professors and to see some of the world.

The Netherlands presented Scots with polite, enlightened legal education of a type suited for the learned gentlemen that the Faculty of Advocates considered themselves to be. It was a legal education not focused on narrowly technical rules, procedures, and styles, but one that emphasised the liberal connections of law with history, philosophy and even the natural sciences. While it is impossible to quantify or to be precise about the effects of this education on Scots lawyers, it is fair to conclude that it made a contribution to the mental world of the Scots advocates which made them open and receptive to the ideas and concerns of the European Enlightenment. Likewise, it was a model of legal education derived from that found in the Netherlands that was developed in Scotland first by private teachers and then by the universities of Edinburgh and Glasgow - a model that was eventually to produce an Enlightened law professor of the prominence and importance of John Millar in Glasgow.[97]

It is instructive in this respect to look at the first professors as a group. They tended to have significant scientific concerns. Spotswood retained all his life a strong interest in chemistry and mathematics.[98] Bayne was an amateur astronomer who had observations published in the *Philosophical Transactions of the Royal Society of London*. He may have had interests in chemistry.[99] Charles Areskine's library catalogue suggests he had a major interest in the natural sciences.[100] Bayne was a talented musician, whose first published work, after his advocates' theses, was on musical theory and practice, and who helped establish the harpsichord maker Thomas Fenton in Edinburgh.[101] He was described as 'the particular friend' of Richard Steele, and hence friendly also with Joseph Addison and with their

---

[96]See NLS, Adv. MSS 81.8.1-2; EUL MSS Gen.1855-6. Internal evidence shows that these lectures undoubtedly were given in Edinburgh. The dates of the lectures correspond more closely (if not exactly) with the dates advertised by Craigie in the *Scots Courant* for his classes than with those of any other teacher. On Forbes, see Cairns, 'Origins of the Glasgow Law School', 176.

[97]See, e.g., John W Cairns, '"Famous as a School for Law, as Edinburgh ... for Medicine": Legal Education in Glasgow, 1761-1801', in *The Glasgow Enlightenment*, ed. Andrew Hook and Richard B Sher (East Linton, 1995), 133-59.

[98]Cairns, 'Spotswood', 135-6.

[99]Roger L Emerson, 'Society, Science and Morals in Scotland, 1700-40', paper delivered at Swedish Colloquium for Advanced Study in the Social Sciences, Uppsala, Sweden, 5-7 October 1990 (I am grateful to Professor Emerson for permission to cite his unpublished paper).

[100]NLS MS 3283. See also Emerson, 'Society, Science and Morals in Scotland, 1700-40'.

[101]A[lexander] B[ayne], *An Introduction to the Knowledge and Practice of the Thoro' Bass* (Edinburgh, 1717); *Scots Courant*, 8/10 Dec. 1718, 21/23 Jan. 1719.

friends in London.[102] It has been plausibly conjectured that he was sometimes the 'A B' occasionally referred to in the *Spectator* and the *Tatler*.[103] Indicative of the circles within which Bayne moved is the marriage of his daughter to the great portrait painter Allan Ramsay.[104]

These connections and interests all help to indicate that these early professors who established the pattern of legal education in Scotland were concerned with law as a polite discipline closely linked to the moral and natural sciences. The library catalogues of Areskine, Bayne and Spotswood demonstrate their breadth and depth of interests.[105] They - and the others - all believed law to be a *rational* discipline, capable of being set out in a scientific form deduced from natural first principles. In this, of course, they can be seen as following on from Stair who had been much influenced by Grotius;[106] what had also determined their intellectual outlook was their experience of legal education in the Netherlands.

After 1750 Scots evidently found study in the Netherlands less valuable; legal education was now firmly established in Scotland, and, as the Scottish Enlightenment developed, was to go through a golden age in the university of Glasgow after 1760. At the same time, the Dutch law faculties were losing some of their lustre. Knowledge and politeness could be found at home in a particular Scottish form. Yet, this had built on a Netherlands' model: '[W]e... import our lawyers from Holland,' said Reuben Butler to Bartoline Saddletree in *The Heart of Midlothian*.[107] (It is presumably significant that Saddletree bears a form of the name of the great medieval Roman lawyer, Bartolus.) Scotland also imported a method of legal education which was eventually naturalized in the later eighteenth century. Paulus Pleydell - who possesses the name of one of the greatest of Roman lawyers - is de-

---

[102]*The Tatler*, ed. Donald F Bond (3 vols, Oxford, 1982), ii, 32 n.1 (hereafter *Tatler*); see also his letters in John Duncombe, ed., *Letters by Several Eminent Persons Deceased, Including the Correspondence of John Hughes, Esq. ... and Several of his Friends* (2 vols, London, 1770), i, 56-9, 69-72, 94-102, 205-7, 210-13, 223-7.

[103]*Tatler*, i, 271-2 (no. 38, 7 July 1709), ii, 32 (no. 84, 22 Oct. 1709), ii, 326 (no. 145, 14 Mar. 1710), iii, 186 (no. 228, 23 Sept. 1710); *The Spectator*, ed. Donald F Bond (5 vols, Oxford, 1965), i, 392 (no. 92, 15 June 1711) (there are other instances). I am grateful to Roger Emerson for bringing this to my attention.

[104]Alastair Smart, *Allan Ramsay: painter, essayist and man of the Enlightenment* (New Haven and London, 1992), 26, 72.

[105]NLS MS 3283; *A Catalogue of Curious and Valuable Books, Being the Library of Mr John Spotiswood of that Ilk Advocate, lately deceas'd* (Edinburgh, 1728); *A Catalogue of Curious and Valuable Books, Being Chiefly the Library of the late Mr Alexander Bane Professor of Scots Law in the University of Edinburgh* (Edinburgh, 1749) (NLS Mf. 816(8)).

[106]Neil MacCormick, 'The Rational Discipline of Law', *Juridical Review* (1981), 146-60; W M Gordon, 'Stair, Grotius and the Sources of Stair's Institutions', in *Satura Roberto Feenstra sexagesimum quintum annum aetatis complenti ab alumnis collegis amicis oblata*, ed. J A Ankum, J E Spruit and F B J Wubbe (Fribourg, 1985), 571-83.

[107]Sir Walter Scott, *The Heart of Midlothian*, ed. Andrew Lang (2 vols, London, 1893), i, 62.

scribed in *Guy Mannering* as having in his study and consulting room 'the best editions of the best authors, and in particular an admirable collection of classics'. The advocate explains: '"These", said Pleydell, "are my tools of trade. A lawyer without history or literature is a mechanic, a mere working mason; if he possesses some knowledge of these, he may venture to call himself an architect"'.[108] This echoes the views of Spotswood on the types of education distinguishing writers - masons - from advocates - architects: in part, it was their experience of legal education in the Netherlands that helped the advocates to see how they could become architects rather than masons, with important consequences for the history of Scots law and Scottish legal education in the era of the Enlightenment.

---

[108]Sir Walter Scott, *Guy Mannering, or the Astrologer*, ed. Andrew Lang (2 vols, London, 1892), ii, 89.

11

CROSS CURRENTS IN EUROPEAN ART AND DESIGN: PARALLELS BETWEEN BELGIAN ART NOUVEAU AND THE GLASGOW STYLE, c. 1890-1905

Juliet Simpson

For many years, the historical reputation of Charles Rennie Mackintosh has been founded on his perceived strengths as an architect. These have earned him a justly prominent place in the ranks of the early European Modernists.[1] Recent appraisals, however, take a wider view. They now situate this aspect of Mackintosh's work in the context of a distinctive 'Glasgow Style': a collective enterprise involving Mackintosh and his contemporaries which laid an equal emphasis on fine art and design as well as architecture.[2] Yet such reassessments have only shown the need to look further at the relation between the Glasgow Style and the broader artistic and cultural trends with which it shares important affinities: namely the European Symbolist movement and the emergence of Art Nouveau. In the following discussion I shall examine one key aspect of this inadequately studied area: the marked parallels which exist between the evolution of the Glasgow Style in terms of style and ideas, and developments in Belgian Art Nouveau. Not only do these parallels suggest that Belgian Art Nouveau was an important stimulus for the emergence of a new design style in Glasgow, they also indicate that even at its most radical the Glasgow Style can be linked to the currency of Symbolist ideas which were instrumental in the rise of decorative art to prominence in late nineteenth-century Europe.

I

In fact, it is the Symbolist context which forms the unifying theme in this investigation. Art Nouveau emerged in Belgium from a fusion of Symbolist and decorative tendencies which developed within the Brussels society known as *Les XX*

NOTE: I would like to thank Pamela Henderson at Glasgow University, Vivien Hamilton at the Burrell Collection, Peter Trowells, Taffner Curator at Glasgow School of Art, and Frances Fowl, for their helpful advice and assistance.

[1] On this, see especially Thomas Howarth, *Mackintosh and the Modern Movement* (London, 1952, revised 1977) (hereafter Howarth, *Mackintosh*).

[2] For examples, see R Billcliffe, *Mackintosh Watercolours* (London, 1979) (hereafter Billcliffe, *Watercolours*), and Billcliffe, 'How many swallows make a summer? Art and Design in Glasgow in 1900' in *Scotland Creates: 5000 Years of Art and Design*, ed. W Kaplan (Glasgow, 1990), 136-48 (hereafter Billcliffe, 'How many swallows').

('The Twenty'). Their activities provide an important introduction to the development of the discussion.

On 28 October 1883, twenty artists rejected by the Brussels Salon met to draw up plans for the formation of a new exhibiting body, marking the first major secessionist activity of its kind in the history of modern art.[3] Supported by Octave Maus, the progressive art critic of the journal *L'Art Moderne*, the society's guiding principles stressed democracy and above all each artist's right to freedom of aesthetic expression. Ten annual exhibitions were held from 1884 to 1893, after which the society voluntarily disbanded itself and was replaced by a new body, 'La Libre Esthétique', which ran from 1894 to 1914.[4]

The Society's overall purpose was to provide an open forum for young artists and in doing so *Les XX* distinguished itself in four very specific areas. These have a direct bearing on the second part of this paper. First, the democratic constitution allowed for twenty 'invités', chosen for their avant-gardism, to exhibit alongside regular members.[5] This in turn created a more international and progressive forum for art than any parallel body in France of the period. Secondly, although diverse, the artists of *Les XX* were united by their shared concern to create a new pictorial reality based on non-naturalistic and expressive criteria. Thirdly, by 1891, there was a marked emphasis on exposure of the decorative arts as well as the fine arts (which pre-empted similar co-existences in France and Scotland); and, by 1893, commitment to the decorative arts was total. Finally, this desire to promote an equality of the arts (whose parallel can be seen in a concentrated form in the work of the Glasgow 'Four', discussed below) echoes the Wagnerian notion of 'Gesamtkunstwerk'.[6] Indeed, this idea was enshrined in *Les XX*'s initial declaration of aims, and has a direct source in Symbolist literary ideas of the period. Such pervasive development of 'Wagnerist' goals can also be traced in Mackintosh's work, with important implications for his designs.

By 1887, the artistic styles of the artist members of *Les XX* divided broadly into Neo-Impressionism (following the impact of Seurat at *Les XX* in 1887) and Symbolism (in the work of Fernand Khnopff, Georges Minne, Jan Toorop and the

---

[3]For details on this group see Octave Maus, *Trente années de lutte pour l'art, 1884-1914* (Brussels, 1926), F C Legrand, *Le Groupe de XX et son temps* (Brussels, 1962) (hereafter Legrand, *Le Groupe*), Jane Block, *Les XX and Belgian Avant-Gardism* (Ann Arbor, 1984) (hereafter Block, *Les XX*), and Mary Anne Stevens, 'Belgian Art: Les XX and the "Libre Esthétique"', in *Post-Impressionism* (London, 1979), 252-4.

[4]The principal goal of this organization was to concentrate on the applied arts in order to show all art as interconnected; see 'Manifeste de la Libre Esthétique', *L'Art Moderne*, October 1893. For a general survey of its activities, see R L Develoy, *Symbolists and Symbolism* (London, 1982), 145-51.

[5]The largest group of 'invités' came from France, England and Holland. On the British connection, see Bruce Laughton, 'The British and American contributions to "Les XX", 1884-93', *Apollo*, xcvi (1967), 372-9 (hereafter Laughton, 'British and American contributions').

[6]The theory was initially promoted extensively in Paris during the 1880s, largely by the critic Téodor de Wyzéwa and in the *Revue Wagnérienne* which ran from 1885 to 1886.

'invité' Mellery).[7] However, the broadly decorative-based movement known as Art Nouveau - which was to have such important consequences in the field of applied arts and design during the 1890s - emerged from a fusion of interests common to both groups. This encompassed a revolutionary approach to image-making and a shared commitment to the potential of decorative art.

It is in the work of artists of Symbolist persuasion within *Les XX*, concerned with producing an 'art of dream and evocation',[8] that the tendencies which united both movements by 1890 can be most clearly identified. The most salient of these was a desire to dispense with the world of phenomena and create instead a pictorial form which would suggest, or correspond to, the invisible world of the spirit or to a private emotional experience. Often, however, as in Fernand Khnopff's *I Lock My Door Upon Myself*, 1891 (plate 1), which derives from Pre-Raphaelite sources,[9] the artist relies on conventional allegorical attributes to evoke a Symbolist mood of otherworldliness. Yet Khnopff's painting, with its blend of melancholic image and controlled linear design, suggests the concern to create a synthesis of expressive form and image: one which developed more radically after 1890 in the turn to decorative art within the ranks of *Les XX*.

The key inspiration for this desire to achieve a suggestive visual synthesis is to be found in the wide variants on Wagnerist theories. These featured in avant-garde reviews during the 1880s such as *L'Art Moderne*, and *La Wallonie*, and in the lectures[10] organized by the Brussels lawyer Edmond Picard to coincide with Vingtist Salons.[11] Galvanized by Wagner's theory of 'Gesamtkunstwerk', the Wagnerists of the 1880s promoted the ideal of 'total art': a synthesis of music, poetry and painting capable of expressing a complete unity of aesthetic experience. The members of *Les XX*, however, were not interested in Wagnerian aesthetics alone. Guided by its strongly democratic principles, the Society actively developed the ideal of 'Gesamtkunstwerk' in two very important respects: first in the combination of artistic, literary and musical events which actually constituted the Salons of *Les XX*; and secondly in an emphasis on equality of artistic disciplines which was a motivating factor in the bias towards decorative art.

---

[7]On the various groupings, see Block, *Les XX*, and Legrand, *Le Groupe*.

[8]A definition given by the Belgian Symbolist writer, Emile Verhaeren, see Block, *Les XX*, 69. On the Belgian Symbolist movement in general see J Paque, *Le Symbolisme Belge* (Brussels, 1989).

[9]In particular Edward Burne-Jones's work, which was known in Brussels at this time; see Laughton, 'British and American contributions', 377-9.

[10]The French poet Catulle Mendès was invited to lecture on Wagner at *Les XX*'s opening exhibition in 1883. Such writers as Rodenbach and Picard regularly lectured on Wagner. In 1889 Henry Van de Velde and the poet Charles Van Lerberghe attended Villiers de l'Isle-Adam's famous lecture on Wagner in Paris. There were also lectures at *Les XX* by such Wagnerists as Mallarmé (1890) and Gustave Kahn (1891).

[11]Picard held regular literary salons in Brussels throughout the 1880s and from spring 1885 published a series of articles in *L'Art Moderne* on the emergence of literary Symbolism in Paris; for further details see A J Mathews, *La Wallonie, 1886-92* (New York, 1947), 16-18.

Coinciding with the influx of non-naturalistic art from Paris into Brussels from 1889 (represented chiefly by Gauguin, Van Gogh and Toulouse-Lautrec),[12] the Wagnerist tendency in *Les XX* found a vigorous new outlet in a renewal of interest in decorative art forms. Indeed, by merging fine and applied arts, the Belgian avant-garde aimed to develop the Symbolists' primarily esoteric preoccupation with the expressive significance of colour and line in a more public and social context.[13]

The Vingtist Salon of 1891 was the first to show a major selection of decorative works including examples by Jules Chéret, Walter Crane and Paul Gauguin. Georges Lemmen's catalogue cover (plate 2) for the Salon, with its bold and dramatic stylization of a sun inset with the Vingtist emblem rising over a tumultuous sea, symbolizes the expressive potential that the group now identified in the applied arts. This concern with synthesizing form and correspondent symbol by means of decorative design, with a vocabulary of distorted, simplified shapes inspired by an interest in primitive art forms,[14] is demonstrated clearly in the work of Jan Toorop, Johan Thorn-Prikker and Henry Van de Velde. It was from such concerns, moreover, that the characteristic features of and early formulation of Art Nouveau emerged.

Jan Toorop, who has come to be regarded as the foremost Dutch Symbolist, was invited to join *Les XX* in 1888.[15] Many of his works of the early 1890s are influenced by the Wagnerian principle of 'Gesamtkunstwerk'; but their thematic and formal expressiveness is also controlled by tightly-conceived design. This is strikingly exhibited in Toorop's arguably most significant Symbolist work, *The Three Brides* of 1893 (plate 3), where line is paramount. It serves not only to delineate the curious figures with the expressive freedom and complexity reminiscent of Aubrey Beardsley's illustrations, it also denotes the more abstract element of sound.

Toorop gave a full explanation of the word's complex symbolic content at the time of its creation.[16] Essentially a mystic contrast between good and evil, the fairy-tale and fantastic elements inspired by literary sources and Toorop's childhood in Java comprise a very eclectic Symbolist iconography, deriving from no single origin. Even so, Toorop's intention was clearly to find formal analogies for

---

[12]There were 12 works by Gauguin at the 1889 Vingtist Salon including *Vision after the Sermon*. Van Gogh was represented in 1890, and Lautrec in 1891.

[13]This was especially so in the avant-grade groups formed outside Brussels, such as 'L'Association pour l'Art' and the 'Pour l'Art' founded in Antwerp in 1891 by Van de Velde, and the Hague 'Kunstkring' in which Toorop was active - all of which encouraged the renewal of applied arts. For details, see Susan M Canning, *Henry Van de Velde, 1863-1967* (Antwerp, 1988) (hereafter Canning, *Van de Velde*).

[14]The main stimulant for this was provided by a large exhibition of Japanese art organized by Siegfried Bing in Brussels in 1889.

[15]For biographical details on Toorop and particularly on his involvement with the Symbolist movement in Belgium, see V Hefting, *Jan Toorop, 1858-1928* (The Hague, 1989).

[16]Toorop sent an unusually full explanation of the work to the painter Antoon Markus in 1892-3. See ibid., 22-4, for further details on this subject.

this complexity. He writes, for example, of the 'stylized, tender virginal shapes' whose 'flowing undulating movement of hair'[17] gives greater expressivity to the work's theme through the abstract potential of sound. But if Toorop's intention in *The Three Brides* was to produce a suggestive Symbolist work, the effect is also highly decorative. The symmetrical composition, severe linearity, all-over pattern, non-naturalistic forms and groupings of figures corresponded not only with the appearance of Art Nouveau elements in the fine arts, but also with features shown in the posters, illustrations, and ceramics exhibited in the final Salons of *Les XX*.

In Johan Thorn-Prikker's painting *The Bride*, 1892 (plate 4), the sacrifice of Symbolist content to the demands of harmonious design is even more marked than in Toorop's work. The linear arabesques energize the symbolic contents rather than describe natural forms. Decorative pattern threatens to overwhelm content; whilst the colours, soft violets, greys, greens, emphasize harmony of surface elements. It comes as no surprise to find that from 1893 onwards Thorn-Prikker was working out design ideas in his paintings (and drawings for the periodical *Van Nu en straks*)[18] before transferring these to the applied arts.

All these tendencies are most forcefully shown in works by Van de Velde, who from 1891 was also the Belgian avant-garde's most prominent theorist.[19] Van de Velde's own interest in the decorative arts was stimulated by his awareness of the English Arts and Crafts movement in the mid-1880s. After 1889, this was greatly encouraged by the range of decorative art on display in Brussels,[20] the stimulus of non-naturalistic art from Paris, and Van de Velde's focus on the expressive role of line and inherently decorative arrangement of form in Seurat's Neo-Impressionist works such as *Le Chahut* (1890). Indeed, in a discussion of *Le Chahut* in April 1890, Van de Velde prophetically asserts that 'the significance of line will soon be revealed to us'.[21] Such interests are manifest in Van de Velde's graphic work of the period: his illustrations and his numerous studies of organic growth, such as *Abstract Composition: Plants*, 1893 (plate 5). Here, the free rhythms of line and shape which Van de Velde found in Seurat's and Van Gogh's art are pushed to a decorative extreme.[22] They no longer refer to observed reality, but combine in a synthetic, almost abstract, form to symbolize the idea of growth and renewal.

---

[17]Letter to Antoon Markus, 1892-3, quoted ibid., 22-3.

[18]Translated as 'Today and the Day After', founded 1892 by August Vermeylen, a young Flemish writer who enlisted Dutch and Flemish artists of Symbolist tendency to illustrate the review, including Henry Van de Velde and other members of *Les XX*.

[19]For a full acocunt of Van de Velde's career as artist and Art Nouveau theorist, see Canning, *Van de Velde*, and A M Hammacher, *Le Monde de Henry Van de Velde* (Paris, 1967).

[20]For a discussion of Van de Velde's relation to other emergent Art Nouveau developments of the period, see P Selz and M Constantine, eds, *Art Nouveau - Art and Design at the Turn of the Century* (New York, 1959).

[21]"Car, la signification des lignes nous sera révélée bientôt', Henry Van de Velde, 'Notes sur l'art' - "Chahut"', *La Wallonie*, v (1890), 122-5.

[22]The large Van Gogh retrospective shown at *Les XX* in 1891 was also a likely source for Van de Velde's interest in expressive line.

Between 1891 and 1894, running parallel to these experiments, Van de Velde published a series of essays which were, in fact, the first contemporary formulations of a design aesthetic.[23] Their importance for this discussion rests not so much in their socialist overtones, but in the fact that they bring together two distinct sets of ideas: those of Morris and his circle, and Symbolist art theory, notably the Wagnerian idea of 'Gesamtkunst'. Van de Velde historically situates the new tendencies in decorative art as a fusion of the expressive, non-naturalistic art of Paris and the work of the English Arts and Crafts movement. In *Déblaiement d'art* (1894),[24] he envisages a new synthesis of fine and applied arts (in a re-invigorated decorative style) which will both restore the lost unity of art, and unite the expressive will of the individual with the community.

By making Symbolist art theory and practice the vital component in his design aesthetic, Van de Velde effectively defined the terms of 'l'art nouveau'. It was thus the Belgian example which provided decorative art movements across Europe with a formal and theoretical basis for new development. One of the most innovative responses to the Belgian impetus emerged in Glasgow in the work of 'The Four'. This displays a unity and consistency of style and direction matched by no other European group at this period.

II

There are a number of broad historical parallels between artistic developments in Glasgow and those in Brussels, which created a climate receptive to the development of an avant-garde movement in design. As in Brussels, the 1880s in Glasgow witnessed the emergence of a small but active group, devoted to making Glasgow an international artistic centre in which decorative art would soon play an prominent role. This group, known as the 'Glasgow Boys',[25] did not, in contrast with *Les XX*, espouse a radical secessionist ideology. But their activities were strongly supported by a circle of enlightened dealers and collectors: wealthy industrialists who, keen to expand Glasgow's cultural base, performed a role parallel to that of the founders of *L'Art Moderne* and *La Wallonie* in encouraging new developments in the arts.[26] They included Alexander Reid and Craibe Angus, both of whom had direct access to continental dealers, particularly in Amsterdam, The

---

[23]This was developed in a series of three articles entitled 'Première prédication d'art', published in *L'Art Moderne*, xiii-xiv (1893-4), 420-1, 20-1, 27.

[24]First given as a lecture entitled 'L'Art futur', on 6 March 1894 at the opening Salon of *La Libre Esthétique*, and later published as 'Déblaiement d'art', *Société Nouvelle*, x (April 1894), 444-56, it is the most moralistic of Van de Velde's early texts, preaching a theory of ornament which would join the expressive will of the individual to the social needs of the community.

[25]On this group, see Robert Billcliffe, *The Glasgow Boys* (London, 1980).

[26]See Elizabeth Bird, 'International Glasgow', *Connoisseur*, 183 (1973), 280-8, for an account of some of these activities. A more detailed survey of collecting activity has appeared in Frances Fowl, 'Alexander Reid: Collecting and Dealing during the late 19th and early 20th centuries' (unpublished Ph D thesis, University of Edinburgh, 1993).

Hague and Paris.[27] The results of these contacts were reflected in a taste for continental art, notably Hague School and Barbizon, which pervaded Glasgow's progressive artistic coterie during the 1880s. Reid's taste, however, ranged further
afield, shown in his active promotion of Japanese art through the large exhibition
held at his gallery in 1889.

Encouraged by these collecting activities, and by first-hand experience,[28] the
young Glasgow school of artists turned to avant-garde developments in Europe for
inspiration: this initially embraced Naturalism, but soon extended to include
newer tendencies. This cosmopolitan outlook, contrasting sharply with the Royal
Scottish Academy's more parochial inclination, was clearly demonstrated in the
contents of a new magazine: the *Scottish Art Review*, which ran initially from
June 1888 to December 1889. Its philosophy, although biased towards French
Naturalism, shows the extent to which developments in art in Glasgow were now
informed by a wider range of ideas current in European avant-garde circles.
Along with a regular report on the Paris Salon and the larger independent exhibi-
tions, for example, were articles on such subjects as: the Wagner Festival at
Bayreuth, Wagnerism, the ideas of the 'l'art pour l'art' movement, Japonisme and
Baudelaire's poetry.[29]

In fact, this diversity of theme, which notably embraced the poetic and the fantastic, can be seen in many respects to signal a move away from the hegemony of
Naturalist taste in the work of the Boys. Coinciding with a renewal of interest in
Celtic art and literature,[30] the late 1880s in Glasgow saw (paralleling the tendencies of *Les XX*) a shift towards a more suggestive, symbolic and non-naturalist art:
one of primarily decorative intention.

This tendency is markedly evident in the work of the younger members of the
Glasgow School. Chief amongst this group was Edward Atkinson Hornel who oc-
cupies a key place in the transition towards a decorative-based art within the Glasgow group. In Hornel's later paintings such as *Summer* of 1891 (plate 6), a rural
Galloway landscape (where Hornel worked with fellow artist George Henry) has
been transformed. The Japanese motifs (such as the cowherd's costume), flattened
and distorted perspective, the fragmented surface with its emphasis on two-dimen-

---

[27]Angus in particular had strong links, via Daniel Cottier in London, with the Amsterdam
dealer E J Van Wisselingh who was noted for his interest in progressive art; see Bird, 'International Glasgow', 250-1. For further details on Van Wisselingh, see Joop Joostens,
'Painting in Holland', in *Post-Impressionism* (London, 1979), 255-9.

[28]Most of the 'Boys' trained abroad between 1877 and 1884-5.

[29]The 'Paris Causerie', which included reports from the Salon and appeared in almost
every issue. In August 1889 there was additionally a review of the 'Monet-Rodin' exhibition at Georges Petit's gallery. William Renton's article on Baudelaire featured in September 1889 and articles on Wagner, September-October 1889.

[30]The so-called 'Celtic Twilight' or Celtic renaissance developed more prominently in
Edinburgh, influenced by the ideas of the visionary social reformer Patrick Geddes who
founded *The Evergreen*. On this subject see Lindsay Errington's essay 'Celtic elements in
Scottish art at the turn of the century' in *The Last Romantics*, ed. John Christian (London,
1989), 46-53.

sional pattern and brilliant colour, owe a clear debt to French non-naturalistic styles.[31] Hornel's example indeed is particularly relevant to this discussion because of his close links during the 1880s with Belgian avant-garde art.

From 1883 to 1885, Hornel studied at Antwerp Academy under Charles Verlat, where it is likely that he met James Ensor - one of the founder-members of *Les XX*[32] - and Henry Van de Velde. This period seems to have been a fruitful one for Hornel's career in general. Hornel was the only Scottish artist to be invited to exhibit at the last Salon of *Les XX* in 1893.[33] Four works were shown, including *The Goatherd* of 1889. With its strangely unreal subject-matter drawn from Celtic lore and folk-tales, and its expressive, non-naturalistic technique, the painting was quite in keeping with the mystic and fantastic Symbolist works which featured at *Les XX*.

Such contact with the Belgian avant-garde at the genesis of its development may well have been a catalyst for Hornel's own art. Directly or indirectly, it is also possible that Hornel brought a younger group of artists who knew his work at first hand[34] into touch with Belgian Symbolist art and theory. These included the circle around Charles Rennie Mackintosh (1868-1928) - James Herbert MacNair (1868-1955), and the Macdonald sisters, Margaret (1865-1933) and Frances (1874-1921)[35] - known as 'The Four' who, from 1889 to 1893, were completing their training at Glasgow School of Art under the enlightened patronage of Francis Newbery.[36] 'The Four' shared with those artists who exhibited at *Les XX* between 1889 ad 1893 a common interests in creating a non-naturalistic art in which decorative and Symbolist elements co-exist in an aesthetic unity of design. It was, moreover, in the field of design that Mackintosh and his circle fully developed these ideas in a more radical way than any of their Scottish contemporaries. There are a number of factors which seem to have been of major significance in shaping

---

[31]On the artistic influences on Hornel's work, see W R Hardie, 'E A Hornel reconsidered', *Scottish Art Review*, xi, 3/4 (1968), 19-26.

[32]Hardie, ibid., suggests that certain of Hornel's works of the 1890s such as *The Dance of Spring* and *The Brownie of Blednoch* suggest Ensor's influence quite strongly.

[33]See Hardie, ibid., and Laughton, 'British and American contributions', 376.

[34]Hornel's work was well known amongst the younger Glasgow artists at this period, largely as a result of Reid's promotion; see Hardie, 'Hornel reconsidered', 19-21. R Billcliffe records that Herbert MacNair bought one of Hornel's Japanese-style paintings, *The Brook*: Billcliffe, 'How many swallows', 141.

[35]For biographical details on each artist, see Howarth, *Mackintosh*, Robert MacLeod, *Charles Rennie Mackintosh* (2nd edn, London, 1983), and R Billcliffe, *Charles Rennie Mackintosh: the Complete Furniture, Furniture Drawings and Interior Designs* (London, 1978) (hereafter Billcliffe, *Interiors*). Mackintosh and MacNair met in 1889 during their apprenticeship with Honeyman and Keppie. According to Billcliffe, *Watercolours*, 9-11, it was the Glasgow School of Art Club Show in autumn 1893 which first brought the four together as a group.

[36]On Newbery's role as promoter of the Glasgow style, see Isobel Spencer, 'Frances Newbery and the Glasgow School', *Apollo*, xcviii (1973), 286-93.

this evolution. These all relate to the direct influences on 'The Four' in the formative stages of their careers.

As outlined above, the general artistic climate in Glasgow throughout the 1880s (as in Brussels) was increasingly receptive to the decorative arts. This was encouraged by influences both from abroad and, notably, from within Glasgow institutions themselves. Following Francis Newbery's appointment to Glasgow School of Art in 1885, the balance of the School shifted from an emphasis on fine to applied arts. Newbery, however, was quick to affirm that whilst the applied arts might usefully reach a wider audience, aesthetic considerations remained of paramount concern in their creation.[37]

It is not surprising, therefore, that the appearance in 1893 of *The Studio*, the first magazine in Britain to be devoted substantially to decorative art, was received with great interests by the Glasgow School of Art group, particularly since one of its leading writers, W Shaw Sparrow, had also been a regular contributor to the *Scottish Art Review* between 1888 and 1889. In the September issue, Shaw Sparrow published the first of two short pieces on Belgian Symbolist art: on Toorop's *The Three Brides*, praising 'the fantastic spirit of the design' alongside a reproduction of the work.[38] The second, on Khnopff, appeared in March 1894, and was accompanied by several examples of the artist's radically stylized book-plate designs (see plate 8).[39]

It seems quite certain that 'The Four' knew these articles. Certainly, Jessie Newbery records that Toorop's painting was one of several key influences which 'gave impetus and direction' to their work.[40] Leaving aside the illustrations, perhaps the most significant aspect of these articles for 'The Four' lay in their broader implications: the association of the Belgian artists' expressive individualism with a new spirit in decorative design. Newbery's teaching had already encouraged the pursuit of individuality of style. Exposure to the work of the Belgian Symbolists seems both to have encouraged this approach and given 'The Four' a new stylistic and iconographical vocabulary with which to experiment. This direction is clearly shown in a series of watercolours produced by 'The Four' between 1893 and 1897.

---

[37]Newbery broadly supported the doctrine of 'Art for Art's sake' - as he wrote of the 'Boys': 'they yet have one thing [in common] which is that it is quite different for Art to be Art and to be the most beautiful thing that the hand of man is capable of making her.' See ibid., 290.

[38]W Shaw Sparrow, 'Toorop's "The Three Brides"', *The Studio*, i (1893), 247. Of note is the reproduction, courtesy E J Van Wisselingh, Amsterdam, the family of dealers who were in contact with Glasgow collectors, see note 27 above.

[39]W Shaw Sparrow, 'English Art and Fernand Khnopff', *The Studio*, i (1894), 202-7. Biographical information on Khnopff's membership of *Les XX* suggests a reasonable knowledge of Belgian avant-garde activity at this period.

[40]Jessie Newbery, 'A Memory of Mackintosh' in *Charles Rennie Mackintosh, Margaret Macdonald. The 1933 Memorial Exhibition: A Reconstruction* (Glasgow, 1983), iv.

Here, the affinities with Dutch and Belgian counterparts in terms of style and content seem more than coincidental.[41]

Apart from seeing the *Studio* articles, Mackintosh may have had some direct contact with the Belgian avant-garde during his travelling scholarship tour of Italy, France and Belgium in 1891.[42] His earliest watercolours such as *Harvest Moon*, 1892 (plate 7) and *Fragment of an Indian carpet* (1889-91)[43] show him exploring the decorative and expressive potential of non-naturalistic styles of the past in the search for novel, but symbolically suggestive, forms.[44] This interest embraced so-called primitive art (such as Japanese and Celtic art) and closely parallels avant-garde experiments with expressive form in France and Belgium at this period.

After 1893, and the publication of the *Studio* articles, the four artists' work displays a greater degree of stylization. There is a marked tendency for dramatic linear simplification which parallels Khnopff's book-plate designs (see plate 8). The evocation of Symbolist themes through the expressive arrangement of shape bears a close similarity to Toorop's and Thorn-Prikker's work, as too the imagery of virginal types and hypertrophied nature which occurs repeatedly in the Macdonald sisters' designs. Margaret and Frances Macdonald's early watercolours, in fact, display a striking attempt to fuse symbolic and formal elements in an overall unity of design. Yet, as with the Belgian Symbolists' work, the result is governed by the dictates of an expressive individualism. Frances Macdonald's *A Pond*, 1894 (plate 9),[45] for example, combines in an elongated format a symmetrical arrangement of curious bulbous-topped plants with attenuated emaciated nudes whose hair (and bodies), as in Toorop's *The Three Brides*, flows into the decorative forms. In a slightly later work, *The Sleeping Princess* of 1895-6,[46] the image and the frame form a decorative unit. Like Toorop's work, it is repetition of elements, such as the

---

[41]A number of these watercolours of the 1892-6 period and some small designs were originally pasted into *The Magazine* - a scrapbook produced by Glasgow School of Art from April 1894. See A McLaren Young, 'The Glasgow Style and its Origins' in *Charles Rennie Mackintosh 1868-1928* (Edinburgh, 1968), 19-29 (hereafter *Mackintosh*) and Billcliffe, *Watercolours*, for details and provenance of individual works.

[42]This took place during Mackintosh's apprenticeship with the Glasgow firm of architects, Honeyman and Keppie. Mackintosh kept a diary of the Italian travels (now in the collection of Glasgow University). On 7 July he records: 'We returned to Milan and came home by Paris, Brussels, Antwerp and London'. See A McLaren Young in F Alison, *Charles Rennie Mackintosh as a Designer of Chairs* (Glasgow, 1973), 8 (hereafter Alison, *Chairs*).

[43]See *Mackintosh*, no. 22.

[44]*Cabbages in an Orchard*, first shown and defended by Mackintosh in the March 1894 issue of *The Magazine*, is perhaps one of the most striking of these early works. Both work and text are reproduced in *Scottish Art Review*, xi, 4 (1968) (special issue devoted to Mackintosh).

[45]Featured in *The Magazine*, November 1894; see also Howarth, *Mackintosh*, 26, and *Mackintosh*, no. 65.

[46]See *Mackintosh*, no. 75.

hair, the abstracted plant forms in linear arabesques, which creates a single unify-ing rhythm, merging surface and depth, fine and applied art elements.

The greatest degree of formal stylization at this period, however, is exhibited by Mackintosh's watercolours such as *The Tree of Personal Effort* and particularly *The Tree of Influence* (plate 10), both of 1895.[47] As has been pointed out, the symbolism of these works is extremely obscure.[48] Yet, the expressive and distorted forms, suggestive of bud, plant and tree motifs, can be seen as a logical de-velopment of the experimentation in earlier works. There is also a striking paral-lel in theme with Van de Velde's evocation of organic growth in his almost ab-stract drawings and plant studies c.1893 (see plate 5).[49] In both examples, the symbolism of renewal would seem to be an important early manifestation of the search for a new formula in design: one which would synthesize radical simplicity of form and the evocative complexity of Symbolist-inspired decoration.

The early watercolours by 'The Four' can as readily be seen as 'designs' as paintings, for in fact it was these very works which provided the experimental basis for the applied arts and (to an extent) the architecture which followed. In-deed, it is in their desire to give all aspects and elements of the designed work equal aesthetic importance that the aims of 'The Four' most broadly approximate to those of Belgian Art Nouveau. In the several poster designs executed between 1895 and 1897, such as Mackintosh's large advertisement for the *Scottish Music Review* of 1896 (see plates 11, 12),[50] any tension between Symbolist theme and decorative form has been resolved in favour of clarity of visual design. As in Toorop's or more forcefully Van de Velde's case, the Glasgow artists have im-ported from more artistically complex works (the watercolours) the essentials of linear rhythm, decorative shape and harmonious pattern. It is their combination of formal abstraction and simplicity of detail which, in contrast with graphic designs inspired by the Arts and Crafts movement, makes these posters so decoratively inventive.

Some knowledge of these innovations may well have reached Europe at an early date. In March 1895, Newbery received an invitation from the secretary of 'L'Oeuvre artistique' in Liège to show examples of his students' work at the forth-coming Liège Arts and Crafts exhibition.[51] Several early works by 'The Four' must

---

[47]Featured in the Spring 1896 issue of *The Magazine*, see Billcliffe, *Watercolours*, nos 43, 44.

[48]See Billcliffe's remarks in *Watercolours*, 11-12.

[49]For illustrated examples, see Canning, *Van de Velde*, nos 66-82.

[50]See *Mackintosh*, nos 76, 77, 80. Many examples of posters including these were illus-trated in Gleeson White, 'Some Glasgow designers and their work', *The Studio*, xi (1897), 86-97 (hereafter Gleeson White, 'Glasgow designers').

[51]At the 'Exposition d'Art Appliqué', Casino Grétre in Liège, Spring 1895. The reasons for the invitation to Glasgow are still not known precisely. The 'Annual School Report - Ses-sion 1894-95' (*Mackintosh Archive*, Glasgow School of Art) records that Newbery re-ceived 'an invitation in March last to send an exhibit to an Arts and Crafts Exhibition or-ganized by the city of Liège'; this invitation in the one to which Howarth refers, 35-6.

almost certainly have been included in the consignment of 110 works sent, although precise details of the contents are not actually known. The favourable response to the exhibition, however, indicates that in Belgium at least there was clear support for the Glasgow School's emergent precedence in design.[52] Furthermore, the appearance later in 1895 of posters by Mackintosh and MacNair in the Paris-based magazine *La Plume* suggests that the work of the Glasgow artists was already prompting comparison with the latest trends in European decorative art.[53]

Such parallels can be noted in two extensive articles by Gleeson White which appeared in *The Studio* in 1897.[54] The articles marked the first substantial publicity for 'The Four' in Britain and were richly illustrated with the latest examples of their work in graphic and domestic design. Indeed, it is in these areas that the most significant innovations of the style are emphasized. They were also distinguished quite clearly from Arts and Crafts tendencies:[55] 'There is a distinct effort to decorate objects with certain harmonious lines and strive for certain jewelled effects of colour which may quite possibly evolve a style of its own, owing scarce anything to precedent.'[56]

This aesthetic inventiveness, also a characteristic feature of early Belgian Art Nouveau, is defined as the hallmark of the distinctive new style. Mackintosh's set of mural designs for Miss Cranston's Buchanan Street tea-rooms, 1896-8 (plate 13), for example, display 'the first examples of a permanent mural decoration evolved through the poster'.[57] 'The richly swelling surfaces'[58] of the various metalwork pieces by the Macdonald sisters - candlesticks, clocks and sconces (see plate 14) - bring to mind the expressive arabesques of Art Nouveau. Certainly the most inventive example of this transference of decorative design principles from two to three dimensions is illustrated in Herbert MacNair's *Smoker's Cabinet*,

---

[52]For the letter of response from the Exhibition organizers of 10 May 1895, see Howarth, *Mackintosh*, 35-6. The *Annual Report* mentions 'favourable press comments' whilst a comment in 'Studio Talk', *The Studio*, vi (1896), 245, notes 'some warm encomiums ... passed upon an exhibit of the Glasgow students' work which was sent to the Exposition d'Art Appliqué held at Liège lately'.

[53]In 'Les Affiches Etrangères', *La Plume*, 155 (1895), 411-40. These were Mackintosh's large poster for *The Scottish Musical Review* (plate 11) and MacNair and the Macdonalds' *Glasgow Institute for the Fine Arts* poster (plate 12), whose appearance here indicates that it must have been completed in 1895 and not in 1896 as is commonly supposed (see for example *Mackintosh*, no. 80). Of this it is noted: 'Les demoiselles MacDonald [sic] en on fait deux affiches pour L'Exposition des Beaux-Arts à Glasgow qui rappelent un peu trop Schwabe', *La Plume*, 430.

[54]Gleeson White, 'Glasgow designers', 86-97, 226-36.

[55]Works by 'The Four' shown at the annual Arts and Crafts' Society exhibition in London in 1896 had received a very poor press. Thereafter, they were not invited to exhibit again.

[56]Gleeson White, 'Glasgow designers', 88.

[57]Ibid., 97.

[58]Ibid., 92.

c.1896 (plate 15).[59] With its curvilinear forms and apparent lack of reference to any utilitarian function, the piece is clearly the realization of an aesthetic idea - an art object which translates the abstract shapes and rhythms of Art Nouveau ornament into three-dimensional form.

For all its aestheticism, however, White notes 'how admirably the work of the Glasgow school adapts itself to domestic surroundings'.[60] In fact, the projects for totally designed environments developed and realized from 1896 to 1902 represent the Glasgow artists' most dramatic exploration and transformation of Art Nouveau elements present in their earlier projects.[61] It is here also that their work comes closest to the 'Gesamtkunstwerk' principles which were a guiding force in the Belgian avant-garde. The clearest illustration of this idea is shown by Mackintosh's work, which will be the focus of discussion in the concluding section of this paper.

III

Mackintosh's belief in a fundamental equality of the arts was clearly articulated in his lecture 'Seemliness' given at the Glasgow School of Art in 1905: 'The architect must become an art worker ... the art worker must become an architect ... the draughtsman of the future must be an artist.'[62] Newbery's teachings undoubtedly provided the basis for these ideas. But their correspondence with the Belgian avant-garde notion that artistic reform could be achieved only by a complete synthesis of fine and applied art is striking. This desire to bring art out of the museum and into life applies from the earliest stage in Mackintosh's career as a designer. The designs for tea-rooms of 1896-8, and particularly the interiors for *Windyhill* of 1899[63] for William Davidson of Gladsmuir, and *120 Mains Street*, 1900-2,[64] show Mackintosh's concern to exert aesthetic control over all the individual elements from furnishings and decor to the details of fireplaces and light-fittings.[65] Decorative and fine arts are combined to produce a unified aesthetic whole in which every designed element carries equal status.

---

[59]Ibid., 228-9.

[60]Ibid., 92.

[61]This was an idea stressed by Herman Muthesius in his review of the four artists' work exhibited at the 'International Exhibition of Decorative Art', Turin 1902: 'All the artists mentioned share a fundamental aim: the room as an artefact, organically complete in a unity of colour, outline and mood. Starting from this concept, they develop not only the room but ultimately the whole house'. Text reproduced in *Scottish Art Review*, ix (1968), 12-19, 30 (trans. Eithne O'Neill).

[62]Quoted in Billcliffe, *Watercolours*, 13.

[63]See Billcliffe, *Interiors*, 105-13.

[64]For detailed discussion see Howarth, *Mackintosh*, 43-4, 51-5, and Billcliffe, *Interiors*, 70-82, and accompanying plates.

[65]On examples of Mackintosh's concern with the intricacies of aesthetic detail see Mary Sturrock, 'Remembering Charles Rennie Mackintosh', *Connoisseur*, 183 (1973), 280-8.

Mackintosh's designs for murals and light-fittings for Miss Cranston's Buchanan Street tea-rooms mark the first stage in this evolution.[66] The stencilled murals, based on a watercolour design, feature elongated women entwined in roses and other plant forms (see plate 13) and exploit the attenuated rhythms which characterize the earlier work of 'The Four'. But Mackintosh now responds to the specific demands of the architectural setting and to the design possibilities of mural art.

The rhythmic repetition of identical figures across the wall at regular intervals in a repeat-pattern unifies the surface area. Yet this is carefully balances by large portions of blank wall which serve to create a free flow of space and animate the various elements of the design. This dynamic interaction between negative and positive shape recalls the inventiveness of Belgian early Art Nouveau graphic works such as Lemmen's catalogue cover (plate 2) or Van de Velde's illustrations for *Van Nu en straks*. It emphasizes, along with the delicate colour-scheme (adapted from the watercolours), that Mackintosh in no way wished to make the artistic component of designs subservient to craft.

In the interiors designed for *Windyhill* and *120 Mains Street*[67] individual furnishings, chairs, cabinets, fittings, become almost abstract elements in a totally decorative composition. Such enterprises parallel in spirit, although not in style, the activities of Belgian designers at this period, such as Victor Horta whose furnishings and fittings for the *Hôtel Solvay*, begun in 1898,[68] are almost an outgrowth of the abstract interior decoration. In the variety of chairs designed for these interiors between 1899 and 1902, Mackintosh envisages the human figure subordinated to the dictates of linear pattern. Forsaking craftsmanship for aesthetic appearance, the Mackintosh 'Chair' departs from historical example and figures instead as a compositional unit.[69] It is both an aesthetic totality, signified by the organically-based decoration which appears on its surfaces, as well as being a design component in each of Mackintosh's interiors from *Windyhill* onwards.

Nowhere is this more consummately shown than in the so-called 'white' interiors of 1898-1902, such as *120 Mains Street*, Glasgow. Mains Street was the flat which Mackintosh turned to furnishing and decorating in anticipation of his marriage to Margaret Macdonald in 1900. It was also one of two productive collaborations, the other being *14 Kingsborough Gardens*, 1901-2, for Jessie Rowat, between Mackintosh and Macdonald.[70]

---

[66]See Gleeson White, 'Glasgow designers', 92-7, and Billcliffe, *Interiors*, 11-15, 39-41.

[67]A photograph of the original drawing room *in situ* can be found in Howarth, *Mackintosh*, plate 12a.

[68]For details and illustrations see T Madsen, *The Sources of Art Nouveau* (Oslo, 1956), and P Selz and M Constantine, *Art Nouveau: Art and Design at the Turn of the Century* (New York, 1959).

[69]In the 'Introduction' to Alison, *Chairs*, 14, A McLaren Young writes: 'Of the furniture, the chair (particularly when high backed), perceived in its iconographic and almost fetishistic quality, was the object which he felt best delineated space'.

[70]See Billcliffe, *Interiors*, 114-18, and Howarth, *Mackintosh*, 48-9.

Overall, the effect is one of grace, harmony and carefully contrived unity of design. In the drawing-room, each wall had some major focal point, such as a wide fireplace and double bookshelf, functioning as visual counterpoints in the room's total decorative scheme. The *Bedroom* (plate 16)[71] with its four-poster bed and huge double wardrobe, featured organic decoration on all separate furnishings. This, combined with the first appearance of the white-painted chair (see plate 17),[72] cabinets, tables and mirror-frames, reinforced the concept of the unified interior. So as to harmonize completely with their surroundings, these furnishings were aesthetically transformed by a thick layer of white enamel paint and inlays of coloured glass which concealed and denied the construction of the pieces themselves.

The delicate and almost feminine effect which Mackintosh contrived to produce in this interior was matched at *14 Kingsborough Gardens*. This project also shows a close unity of purpose in Mackintosh and Macdonald's aims at this period. Macdonald's stencilled murals and gesso panels for Kingsborough Gardens[73] reveal her preoccupation with the mystic and fairy-tale themes in the Belgian Symbolist writer Maeterlinck's stories and plays. The elaborate stencil designs and hangings for the drawing-room and bedroom with their other-worldly subject-matter can be seen as Macdonald's attempt to create, in the manner of a Symbolist painting, an evocative setting or mood for Mackintosh's more austere furniture. This suggestiveness was perhaps conveyed more abstractly in Mackintosh's turn to white: a potent symbol of artistic purification and renewal, a 'déblaiement' (clearing) of all previous aesthetic conventions.

In their stress on total stylistic and aesthetic unity, these interiors and designs represent the most sophisticated transformation of the Art Nouveau and Symbolist tendencies present in the earlier work of 'The Four'. After 1904 and the designs for *Hous'hill*, Mackintosh moved away from specifically Art Nouveau influences to develop the spare and rectilinear vocabulary typical of his later work. Even so, the aesthetic inventiveness which characterizes these early interiors remains a consistent and unifying feature of the mature designs.

In this discussion, I have shown that the movement which emerged during the 1890s in Belgium as Art Nouveau has a wider application to the work of Mackintosh and his group than just that of stylistic influence. Indeed, one of the most striking parallels between the Belgian avant-garde and 'The Four' was their evolution of a general design aesthetic, based not on revivalism, but on the radical formal and theoretical innovations of non-naturalist painting. There are important differences between the two groups; notably, 'The Four' did not share the Belgian

---

[71]See Billcliffe, *Interiors*, 80-1, and, for a photograph of the original room, Howarth, *Mackintosh*, plate 16a.

[72]For examples, see Billcliffe, *Interiors*, plate 77, Howarth, *Mackintosh*, plates 12a, 13, and Alison, *Chairs*, 40-1.

[73]For examples of these see Billcliffe, *Interiors*, 117. Hangings and stencils also featured in the *Rose Boudoir* created for the 1902 Turin exhibition.

avant-garde's concern to justify their activities in terms of socialist or utopian ideals. Even so, there is a manifest similarity of intention between the 'Gesamtkunst' principles of Belgian Art Nouveau and the emergent characteristics of the Glasgow Style. In fact, the most innovative aspect of the work of 'The Four' in the sphere of design derives from its extension of such 'Gesamtkunst' possibilities. Mackintosh and his group sought to revitalize not just the practical, but above all the aesthetic, dimension in design, to imbue it with the expressive and symbolic potential more usually associated with fine art.

1   Fernand Khnopff, *I Lock my Door upon Myself*, 1891. Oil on canvas. 72 x 140 cm. Munich, Neue Pinakothek. (Reproduced by kind permission of the Neue Pinakothek)

2   Georges Lemmen, Catalogue Cover for 1891 Salon of *Les XX*. Brussels, Institut Royal du Patrimoine Artistique. (Reproduced by kind permission of the Institut Royal du Patrimoine Artistique)

3 Jan Toorop, *The Three Brides*, 1893. Black chalk and pastel. 78 x 98 cm. Otterlo, Rijkmuseum Kröller-Müller. (Reproduced by kind permission of the Rijkmuseum Kröller-Müller)

4   Johan Thorn-Prikker, *The Bride*, 1892. Oil on canvas. 146 x 88 cm. Otterlo, Rijkmuseum Kröller-Müller. (Reproduced by kind permission of the Rijkmuseum Kröller-Müller)

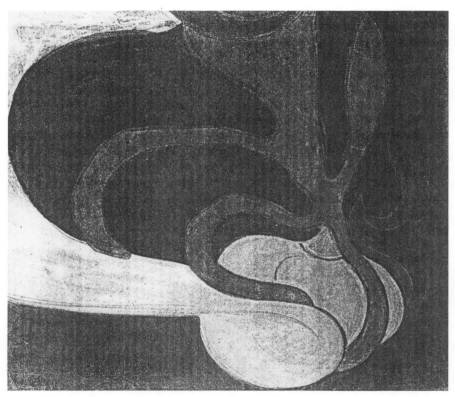

5   Henry Van de Velde, *Abstract Composition: Plants*, 1893. Oil pastel. 47.5 x 51 cm. Otterlo, Rijkmuseum Kröller-Müller. (Reproduced by kind permission of the Rijkmuseum Kröller-Müller)

6   Edward Atkinson Hornel, *Summer*, 1891. Oil on canvas. 127 x 101.5 cm. Liverpool, Walker Art Gallery. (Reproduced by kind permission of The Board of Trustees of the National Museums and Galleries on Merseyside (Walker Art Gallery))

7   Charles Rennie Mackintosh, *The Harvest Moon*, 1892. Watercolour and ink. 35.2 x 27.7 cm. Glasgow, Glasgow School of Art, Mackintosh Collection. (Reproduced by kind permission of Glasgow School of Art)

8   **Fernand Khnopff,** *Book plate - 'Ex Libris'*, 1892. Brussels, Bibliothèque **Royale,** **Cabinet des Estampes.** Reproduced, *The Studio*, March 1894.

9   **Frances Macdonald,** *A Pond*, 1894. Pencil and watercolour on grey paper. 32 x 25.8 cm. **Glasgow, Glasgow School of Art, Mackintosh Collection. (Reproduced by kind permission of Glasgow School of Art)**

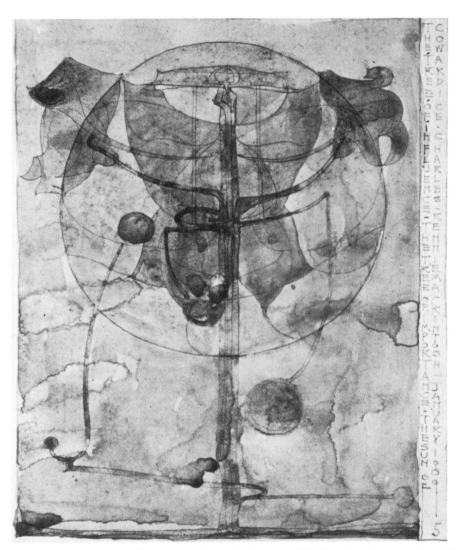

10   Charles Rennie Mackintosh, *The Tree of Influence*, 1895. Pencil and watercolour. 32
x 25 cm. Glasgow, Glasgow School of Art, Mackintosh Collection. (Reproduced by kind
permission of Glasgow School of Art)

11   Charles Rennie Mackintosh, *Large Poster Design for the Scottish Musical Review*, 1896. Pencil and watercolour on tracing paper. 37.3 x 17.1 cm. Glasgow, University of Glasgow, Hunterian Art Gallery. (Reproduced by kind permission of the Hunterian Art Gallery)

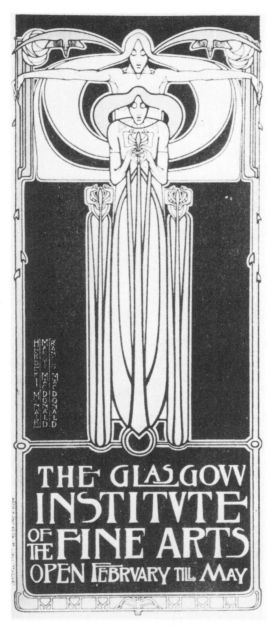

12   Herbert MacNair, Frances Macdonald and Margaret Macdonald, *Poster for the Glasgow Institute of the Fine Arts*, c. 1896. Colour lithograph. 236 x 102 cm. Glasgow, University of Glasgow, Hunterian Art Gallery. (Reproduced by kind permission of the Hunterian Art Gallery)

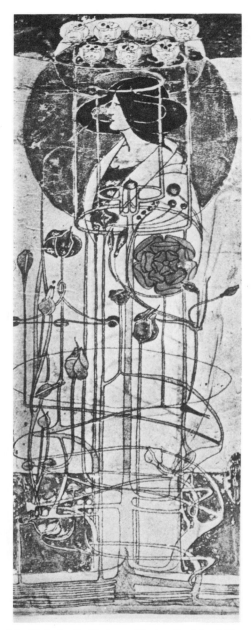

13   Charles Rennie Mackintosh, *Preliminary Design for Mural Decoration of the First Floor Room of Miss Cranston's Buchanan Street Tea-Rooms*, 1897. Pencil and watercolour on tracing paper. 36.2 x 74.7 cm. Glasgow, University of Glasgow, Hunterian Art Gallery. (Reproduced by kind permission of the Hunterian Art Gallery)

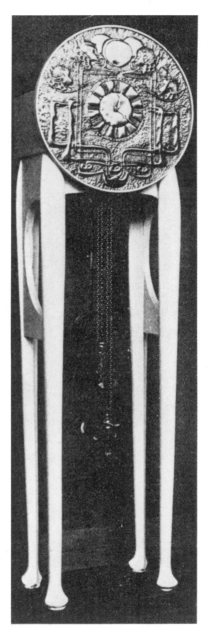

14   Margaret and Frances Macdonald, *Clock in brass and ivory*, c. 1896. Reproduced, *The Studio*, July 1897.

15   Herbert MacNair, *Smoker's Cabinet*, c. 1896. Reproduced, *The Studio*, September 1897.

16   Charles Rennie Mackintosh, *Four Poster Bed and Double Wardrobe for 120 Mains Street Bedroom.* Bed, oak, painted white with pink glass panels. 205.8 x 180.3 x 202.2 cm. Wardrobe, oak, painted white. 206.1 x 271.8 x 49 cm. Glasgow, University of Glasgow, Hunterian Art Gallery. (Reproduced by kind permission of the Hunterian Art Gallery)

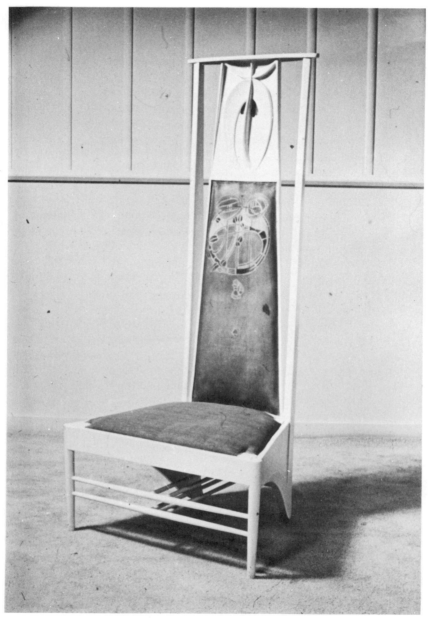

17   Charles Rennie Mackintosh, *Chair*, 1901-2. Oak, painted white with stencilled canvas back. 113.6 x 70.2 x 57 cm. Glasgow, University of Glasgow, Hunterian Art Gallery. (Reproduced by kind permission of the Hunterian Art Gallery)

12

TWENTIETH-CENTURY SOCIAL HOUSING IN SCOTLAND, BELGIUM AND THE NETHERLANDS

Miles Glendinning

INTRODUCTION

Although the main purpose of this monograph is to identify contacts and links between the above three countries, that is, unfortunately, a difficult task in the present instance, for the simple reason that in the field of 'social' housing, or low-income or working-class housing, there are almost no direct cause-and-effect links to be traced. Most direct connections are at 'small print' level. But not only are there few specific bonds: there are also very significant differences.

Initially, this might seem rather strange. After all, we are at first glance dealing with rather similar countries: urbanised, north-west European countries with long-standing industrial economies. But this is really the interest of the subject: differences alongside similarities, comparison and contrast. For that reason there will be few 'big themes' in this paper - or, at any rate, big themes that are not in some way qualified by significant counter-tendencies. I should stress that my subject is the provision of housing: its planning and building. There is no space to deal with the related, but separate, matter of how dwellings fared after they were built: how they were looked after, how they were experienced by their occupants.

Within this overall heading of housing provision, I shall be dealing with two areas in particular: firstly, housing policy, mainly at the political and organisational level; and secondly, the physical form, especially the architecture, of housing. I shall be pursuing these in parallel within a roughly chronological framework. One main 'story' will run through this framework: the establishment of large-scale building of 'social housing' in all three countries, a story whose culmination in the 1960s coincided with the ascendancy of Modern architecture, and was then followed by a reaction in favour of supposedly 'traditional' forms and a move towards improvement rather than new building. There are various paradoxes and partial overlaps. For instance, by the 1960s Scots and Belgian social housing policy had diverged as far as could be imagined: in the one case, a near-State monopoly with enormous developments of big Modern blocks of flats, in the other a virtual private monopoly with very few, scattered, multi-storey developments; yet the architectural style of the relatively few large schemes of high blocks built in Belgium, and that of the most influential of the many schemes in Scotland, was unusually close. So we have to note in advance that there is no simple, single pattern to emerge from this comparison, and no easy way to summarize it.

I: THE BEGINNINGS OF 'SOCIAL HOUSING'

Nor is there any obvious starting point from which to trace the beginning of 'social housing' across Europe. Lacking any such obvious origin, we can only fall back on this century's most dramatic landmark in housing policy: the First World War. Before that, in most developed countries, rented housing was largely the norm for the working class and for most better-off people too. This rented housing, since the Industrial Revolution, had been provided by a dense, unco-ordinated but increasingly regulated patchwork of market forces, including speculative builders, investors, landlords, factors and tenants. The stresses and strains of this system were largely contained within the economic cycle of boom and 'bust'.

Of course, there were considerable variations. For instance, in Belgium, one of the most entrenchedly capitalist economies, the individualism prevalent in the nineteenth century had led to a tradition of people building their own houses, although there were very early examples of collective housing built by industrialists, notably the group at Le Grand Hornu. In Scotland - where of course the tenements of New Lanark had been the earliest planned industrial settlement in Europe - speculative building for rent was by far the general rule, although the equilibrium of this system had, before the war, become threatened by an unusual (in the European context) degree of landlord-tenant antagonism, and by the political weakness of landlords: one possible alternative was pointed to by the scattered initiatives of municipal bodies, beginning with the Glasgow City Improvement Act of 1866. But the first national State intervention in housing in Europe was not here but in Belgium, where the Beernaert Law of 1889 set guidelines for the State's role in social housing. This was to be almost purely financial, confined to issuing subsidies to private local initiatives: a task co-ordinated from 1911 by a new National Housing Association. But it was only the Netherlands' 1901 Woningwet, or Housing Law, which pioneered the idea of comprehensive national planning of a housing programme, financed by government loans to building agencies including both co-operatives and municipalities: a national measure bolstered by the powerful social-democratic work of the Amsterdam municipality in setting up a Housing Department four years later. This law was so successful that it lasted until 1963; during the first 47 years of its operation there were, however, no cheap loans to private builders as in Belgium.

The disruption of World War I soon created scarcity rents and discontent among workforces which were vitally involved in the 'war efforts' of the belligerent countries: such discontent was usually alleviated by rent controls and other emergency measures. In most places these were strictly temporary, and the market was restored to some extent after the war, with the state subsidising low-rent construction to 'fill in' any gaps in market provision. For instance, in Belgium the pre-war policy was restored rapidly, and was expanded by loans to a proliferation of local building societies and co-operatives. Now the scope of the Beernaert Law was extended to middle-income people: schemes were built to rent, or (especially after 1923, when there was an anti-socialist reaction) to buy. The government did not regulate this expanded system directly, but in 1919 set up a separate trust to do so: the National Association for Cheap Housing. But this social-housing pro-vision was increasingly pushed from centre stage by a new policy: cheap loans for individuals building their own houses. This was co-ordinated, from 1935, by a new body, the National Society for Small Properties.

In towns in Scotland (as, to a lesser extent, elsewhere in Britain), the violence of the wartime rent controversies, and the political weakness of landlords, meant that wartime rent control was extended by the government into the dismantling of the entire private rented market in 1919, and, as municipalities were the only al-ternative bodies which had even dabbled in this field, they were handed, almost overnight, responsibility for working-class housing as a whole. After that turning point, common to all parts of the United Kingdom, there was a continuous diver-gence: the two polarities of this process were the inter-war policy of Northern Ireland, which, like Belgium, was chiefly concerned to subsidise private builders, and at the other extreme the policy in Scotland, where, with the long-established power and prestige of burgh government, the municipalities were rapidly elevated into an almost monopoly position of housing provision for lower and middle incomes (the only major exception being Edinburgh Corporation).

During the 1930s, this trend was paralleled by, and in its turn reinforced, the rise of the Labour Party to municipal power in the cities and large burghs. And the result was the strongest possible contrast with the pre-war position. In place of high rents and uncertain tenure, there were low rents and security of tenure. In place of fragmented building, management and occupancy, there were large co-ordinated programmes, often by municipal direct labour - a further vital instru-ment of municipal patronage. Between the wars, this municipal building was occasionally paralleled elsewhere in Europe, but was only outdone by the massive flat-building campaign of the Socialist municipality of Vienna.

In the neutral Netherlands, by contrast, the war was of less importance. Here the 1901 Housing Law had not only provided for the finance and organization of housing production, but also laid out a town-planning framework in each munici-pality, under the control of that municipality. Thus, where the state in Belgium was a mere moneybox, and in Scotland it increasingly both built and owned the houses, in the Netherlands its involvement, and especially that of the municipali-ties, was focused on co-ordination. However, there was an appreciable degree of direct municipal building and letting, and some very innovative policies were introduced: such as, in management, the so-called 'controle-woningen' in Den Haag, Amsterdam and Utrecht, estates where, between 1924 and 1940, 'anti-so-cial' tenants were kept together in enclosed courtyard developments. But the key co-ordination by each Dutch municipality was that of planning: planning of the physical layout and 'urban design' of what was to be built. In a country some of whose regions were entirely man-made, this was hardly surprising. But this also brings us to our other main theme: the architecture of housing.

Here, in relating Scotland to the other two countries, we first have to discuss a fundamental anomaly in their relationship: an anomaly in which physical form, architecture and tenure interact in a complex way. The norm of urban, and much suburban housing throughout Europe by the early twentieth century (including Scotland, by then the continent's most urbanised country), was that of massive blocks of apartments. However, one region of the north-west of Europe, for a variety of reasons, diverged from this norm: its urban dwellings were not stacked vertically, in monumental rendered or stone-faced blocks, but horizontally in rows, and built of brick. As we shall see, both Belgium and the Netherlands were a part of this region. But so also was England, the culturally dominant element in the centralised United Kingdom state. This was to create a somewhat topsy-turvy situation, where something quite normal in the wider perspective was labelled abnormal in the narrower. For there were very few fundamental differences between tenements in Scotland and those elsewhere. Those differences that there were - the absence of cellars and attics (which gives Scots tenements, to continental eyes, a curiously 'shaved off' roofline), the aversion to building 'Mietskaserne'-style deep-plan blocks with internal courtyards, or the practice of putting drainage pipes outside the building - all may have been influenced by 'British' norms. But in all key respects, the residential areas of cities here are quite similar to their equivalents in, say, France, Germany, Poland, or (perhaps most comparable) Sweden.

In the Low Countries, on the other hand, just as in England, traditional urban housing follows the 'row-house' pattern, with its curiously restless mixture (to Scots eyes) of low horizontal rows chopped up into vertical slices. Anti-monumentality and miniaturisation seem to be the governing aesthetic: only by building hugely long rows can it be avoided. Of course this is an immense over-simplification - some middle-class terrace houses were after all built in Scotland, as were many tenement 'woonkasernes' in Amsterdam. But perhaps the main exception to this rule was evident in Brussels. During the nineteenth century, the influence of France was very strong in the architecture of the Low Countries. In Brussels, as a capital city governed by a francophone elite, there was an attempt, as in French provincial centres such as Lille, to remodel a basically brick-built terraced city into a Haussmannesque capital of *grands boulevards*, lined with dense rendered or smooth-fronted apartment blocks, and vast public buildings - culminating on Poulaert's Palais de Justice. But at the end of the nineteenth century, there was a strong nationalistic movement in the Low Countries against this international monumentality: this resulted in the brick rationalism of Berlage and Horta. But, in general, both Brussels, and Scotland as a whole, were outposts of mainstream nineteenth-century European urbanism, stranded in a culturally anti-urbanistic context. We shall see later that both these cases would have interesting repercussions.

Between the wars, there were two conflicting tendencies in the architecture and planning of working-class housing in all three countries. The dominant tendency seemed to be anti-monumental, anti-urbanistic, and the main sources of this were the Garden Suburb and cottage/villa-building traditions emanating from England and the United States. From the turn of the century, garden suburbs proliferated in all 'tenemental' European countries. In Scotland, for instance, J A W

Grant and F Unwin designed Westerton, near Glasgow (from 1913): at the same time, the politically motivated imposition of rent controls (from 1915) began to drive many of the existing, nineteenth-century tenements into an increasingly dilapidated condition. During the same period, garden suburbs also spread in Belgium, under the auspices of the National Society for Cheap Housing (plate 1), while the influential Delft School of architects, also committed to 'primitive vernacular' domestic architecture, arose in the Netherlands. But this activity lacked the cultural edge of the onslaught against the tenement in countries such as Scotland or Germany.

During these years, there were also counter-tendencies. In a time of great pressure for new housing, many saw garden suburbs as an extravagance of land; so flats continued to be built, and often appeared where there had been few or none before. For instance, dense five-storey tenement groups appeared in Flemish cities, and two-storey 'four in a block' flats in the remotest towns of Scotland, such as Stornoway. In Scotland, the building of new tenements, between the wars, was at first confined to utilitarian blocks for displaced slum dwellers, but flat-building was powerfully reinvigorated in the 1930s, and was given an explicitly nationalistic twist by architects such as Edinburgh's City Architect, Ebenezer Macrae, and by the government-sponsored 'Highton Report', which advocated a revival in tenement building, based both on national traditions and on continental Modern architecture, including the Modern of the Netherlands. Here we encounter one of the relatively few direct Scoto-Netherlandish housing links of major significance. Modern architecture, or at any rate its mainstream, laid great stress on social building, and on housing in particular - and the Netherlands was one of the hotbeds of architectural innovation during this formative period of Modern architecture, and a place where the lack of a pre-existing flat tradition made possible more free-ranging solutions.

The first of these was the evolution of Berlage's brick Modern style into an often extravagant Expressionism, at the hands of the Amsterdam School of architects (one of whose influences, it should be pointed out here, was Charles Rennie Mackintosh). Long blocks of Housing Law flats, entire ranges laid out on Berlage's Amsterdam-South extension plan of 1915, were given unified but most unclassical facades. The Amsterdam School's influence was at first dominant in the Netherlands, but it also flowed into Belgium. Then, following the Amsterdam school, there appeared successively more rectilinear variants of Modern, whose housing manifestations included Oud's terraces but also high flats: Staal's Victorieplein twelve-storey tower of 1930, and an International Modern nine-storey slab, the Bergpolderflat in Rotterdam, by van Tijen, Brinkman and van der Vlugt. It may sound perverse to the point of absurdity to say this, but Bergpolder, with its access balconies, once again reminds us, in Modern form, of the unusual regional housing pattern - that of the terrace-house - which the Low Countries shared with England (and with Wales, Ireland, north-east France and north-west Germany). A much more direct manifestation of this was the building of Modern terraced houses, such as Oud's two schemes in Hoek van Holland and Rotterdam. But flats were more central to Modern architecture, and, in both the Low Countries and England, there were the most persistent attempts to reproduce the horizontal rows of terrace houses in one way or another. Most inter-war flats in the Netherlands were accessed by the normal European method of an internal common staircase, but there were distinct efforts to devise alternatives. One method in all three countries, in two-storey blocks, was to have access to the upper and lower floors by separate staircases from separate external entrances. More important for the future was the idea of access by external balconies.

Up to World War I, balcony access was quite common in Belgium and England, but in utilitarian blocks. It was unknown in the Netherlands, and in Scotland was only found as a local tradition, in Dundee. But Michiel Brinkman's Spangen project in Rotterdam, in 1919-22, introduced it into the realm of avant-garde housing architecture (plate 2). Spangen, a municipal housing project of 273 flats in flat-roofed four-storey blocks, was one of the first big avowedly collective housing schemes in the Netherlands, with such features as communal bathhouse and central heating. It was of immense significance at a national level, as, after a long process of germination via the revised International Modern form of Bergpolder, 'galerijbouw' was to become, after World War II, the overwhelmingly dominant type of Dutch high flats.

Parallel changes were taking place in the use of materials. Dutch architects remained generally faithful to brick, used by the Amsterdam School with Arts and Crafts attention to irregularity of detail - although some very significant schemes were built in mass concrete, such as the 900-dwelling Betondorp development in Amsterdam, built in the 1920s. In Belgium, a kind of schizophrenia developed between brick and concrete. Private houses were generally built in a simplified Amsterdam School manner, although the brick was treated in a harder, somewhat French-Rationalist way. But flat building, and that of some co-operative garden suburbs, became more thoroughly French-influenced, with more and more concrete construction. Now brick was often logically treated merely as cladding or frame infill (with an appropriately machine-like finish); an alternative was rendered brick or concrete treated in a cubistic manner. In Scotland, the masonry building tradition had become too expensive, and brick, owing to its cheapness, was used; but, as the popular perception had grown up in the nineteenth century that brick was an alien and cheap material, it was used rendered. But the most logical development from load-bearing ashlar walls seemed to be load-bearing pre-cast or blockwork concrete - and it was forcefully developed. Just as France evolved a new tradition of reinforced concrete frame construction out of her long-standing tradition of trabeated (that is, beam-supported) construction, figures such as Glasgow Corporation's Housing Director Fyfe evolved advanced casting methods, and put them into practice on a grand scale. For instance, many thousands of dwellings, tenements and cottages were built of blockwork as part of Glasgow's own drive. And Fyfestone, of course, has a particular significance in Aberdeen, as, in its more colourful post-1945 variants, it formed one of the bases for almost a regional north-eastern style of Modern housing. In a direct link between the

Netherlands and Edinburgh, 208 'Korelbeton' dwellings in 2-storey flats were built in 1925-6 in Restalrig, as part of a programme of experimental concrete building in the capital, masterminded by Burgh Engineer A H Campbell.

II: POST-1945: HEYDAY OF MODERN HOUSING

The period after World War II, in the cases of Scotland and Belgium, led to a further divergence in tenure and production. In Scotland there was a massive bolstering of the new structure of municipal housing, to a near monopoly status. This was achieved in the 1940s by Labour Minister George Buchanan's ruthless use of building licensing to squash any private housing revival. From that point on, the municipal building empires entered the height of their power and vigour. And, as a result, United Nations statistics show that, by the mid-1960s, we were building by far the highest annual percentage of public housing, as a percentage of total output, of any European country: 72 per cent. The runner-up was the USSR, at a mere 66 per cent. And in Glasgow, the figure was a staggering 96 per cent.

But which was the European country with the smallest percentage of public housing in those same years? It was Belgium, with just 0.3 per cent - two hundred times less public housing than Scotland - which built 85 per cent of its housing through private builders. It is unsurprising that this was closely bound up with political policy: where George Buchanan sought to bolster Labour's ascendancy, Belgium's Christian Democratic leaders sought to 'deproletarianize' their country. This they pursued chiefly through the De Taeye Law of 1948, a measure which massively reinforced the subsidies to private builders, by creating the concept of the 'Volkswoning'. Whereas the British government's 'People's House' of the 1950s was a public authority dwelling, Belgium's were privately built with subsidies from the Algemene Kas - although half of all private dwellings were in fact unsubsidised altogether. Thus even the one key role of the Belgian State in housing, that of subsidy distribution, which it did through 'quango' organisations such as the National Society for Cheap Housing, applied to a much more limited proportion of housing than the corresponding aspect of State activity here: the 100,000th house subsidised by the National Society was only completed in 1954, whereas between 1945 and 1954 alone, Scots local authorities had built 250,000 dwellings, all subsidised. However, these organizations were given an increasingly influential new role, after a law of 1953, in co-ordinating slum redevelopment (including purchase and clearance). It is not too surprising that Belgium's overall per capita rate of production by all tenures in the 1960s was only half that of Scotland and the Netherlands.

In the latter case, co-ordination was also prominent - but here it meant something slightly different. The Netherlands was one of the relatively few, generally better-off, European countries (others were, for instance, West Germany and France), which attempted to devise a comprehensive national housing strategy, by setting overall target figures, splitting these down into different agencies - private, public and co-operative - and then strictly enforcing these proportions. In both Scotland and Belgium, where the entire programme was effectively given over to one agency, this would have been unnecessary! But in the Netherlands, where it was feared, until the 1970s, that the country's population was facing a massive increase, a far more complex national programme was pursued methodically through the post-war years. Principal weapons in the government's armoury were stringent building licensing, which took in any building work over £500 (allowing quotas to be set and enforced in each municipality), and town planning controls over building land and building plans, latterly through a Reconstruction Law of 1950.

The results of this in terms of tenure were about half-way between Belgium and Scotland. In the mid-1960s, 55 per cent of Dutch national housing output was private (of which some 75 per cent was State-aided), 24 per cent was co-operatively built, and 21 per cent was built under the terms of the Housing Law (mostly by municipalities). As in Scotland, the mid/late 1960s saw coincident maxima in the building both of all dwellings, and of Housing Law dwellings (that is, social housing); both figures then fell back, but a subsequent burst of private output revived the national total for a while before it seemed to subside for good in the mid-1970s. We have noted that the Dutch national housing programme was supported by comprehensive provisions of town planning - a State-sponsored urbanism, originating in the 1901 Act, which in some ways matched that of France. The cornerstone of the post-war planning system was a pre-war plan which, as one might expect, concerned Amsterdam: the AUP, or Amsterdam General Extension Plan, published in 1934 largely under the direction of van Eesteren, which laid down guidelines for development of areas to the south and west of the city. After the war, there was also much planning activity in Rotterdam: substantial land annexations, and plans for the reconstruction of the bombed centre, including some flats; and plans proliferated for other towns, large and small. Public controversy only began in the mid-1960s when the large-scale further extension of Amsterdam to the south-west on the van Eesteren principles was authorised - this was the renowned, later notorious Bijlmermeer - and numerous fantastic projects in an Archigramesque vein were published, such as a proposal of 1964 by van den Broek and Bakema for a linear 'spine' extension, City on Pampus, to be built across the Ijmeer.

In this prolonged process of plan-making for housing, over decades, the inevitable happened, in the form of clashes between planning and housing groupings, which were concerned respectively with 'design' and 'quantity'. In Amsterdam, the first 1950s developments on the western extension - areas such as Osdorp, Geuzenveld and Slotervaart - were the focus of clashes within the municipality, between the Town Planning Section, or Stadsontwikkeling, still up to 1959 headed by van Eesteren, and the longer-established Municipal Housing Department, which controlled all Housing Act building in the city. Essentially, the Housing Department thought that Stadsontwikkeling were being too elaborate and aesthetic in their urban design, and that this would obstruct production.

But if 'design versus production' or 'planners versus housers' caused a stir in the Netherlands, in Scotland it caused open warfare. This controversy was partly focused on building type - a continuation of the 'tenement versus cottage' debate of the first quarter of the century - but also now concerned broader questions of urban politics and design. The municipalities, whose new housing programmes the housing reformers had expected to be an ideal vehicle for propagating the values of garden-suburb 'domestic architecture', had instead, in the 1930s and 1940s, started having ideas of their own, and had become increasingly interested in flat-building. The reformers were incensed, and a new and different grouping emerged - namely, town and country planners.

The planners were concerned not with 'nitpicking' questions of what type of dwellings should be built, but with a broad strategy of curbing municipal power over housing as a whole, and especially at its heart, in Glasgow. Here all were agreed that there must be large-scale slum-clearance, but the planners argued that those displaced should not be rehoused within the city, but 'overspilled' away from it to planned New Towns. This amounted to a direct political challenge to Glasgow's power in housing., and it was met by a determined counter-strategy, aiming to build as many dwellings within the city as possible. We shall see that the results of this counter-attack by Glasgow's municipal housing machine were some of the largest social housing projects in Europe.

In Belgium, by contrast, all such controversy was quite beside the point. The dominance of private building gave housing a nineteenth-century-like atomised character, and the comparatively few big housing-association developments, such as the grouped development of the Linkeroever, Antwerp, were planted like islands of CIAM (mainstream 1930s Modern Architecture) monumentalism in a sea of de Taeye Law 'huisje met een tuintje' (little house and little garden) suburbia. By the 1960s, 60 per cent of all new dwellings in Belgium were detached houses.

Yet, although there was relatively little Modern housing in Belgium, while in Scotland there was so much, the two resembled each other quite strongly in architectural style. Both used multi-storey blocks of an intensely and uncompromisingly monumental character - something which in both cases perhaps had its roots in the past, whether in Scots tenements or in the Beaux-Arts francophile strain in Belgian architecture. Whereas Dutch avant-garde post-war architects such as Aldo van Eyck, along with their English counterparts such as the Smithsons, were trying to repudiate strict Modern rectilinearity and geometry in favour of more broken-down 'cluster' patterns, Belgium and Scotland saw nothing fundamentally the matter with mainstream CIAM. Both countries evolved, for housing use, a kind of Modern Functionalism very similar to that of France, where the Beaux-Arts tradition was partly preserved in the work of Perret and in the post-war work of various institutes (and a Ministry) of urbanism.

In Belgium, this Modern Functionalist style of housing concentrated on long slab blocks, whose construction might either be exposed reinforced concrete frame or engineering-brick cladding. The first big Belgian post-war development set the tone: Professor Hugo van Kuyck's Luchtbal project for a housing society in Antwerp, 'Onze Woning'. Built in 1950, this comprised four immensely long, brick-clad nine-storey blocks laid out rigorously in parallel. But the key figure in the evolution of a Belgian Modern Functionalism was the Flemish architect Renaat Braem. He had been an avant-garde socialist and International Modern propagandist between the wars, and from 1951 had several big commissions from housing societies, which allowed him to realise his ideas. These were on a scale unprecedented for Belgium, and the first of them, the Wooneinheid Zaanstraat (or Kiel), Antwerp, built for the society 'Huisvesting Antwerpen' in 1951-8, caused a major public controversy, with its spiny rationalistic slabs raised on columns, and its gleaming engineering - brick cladding and boldly expressed services (plate 3). This manner was inflated further in scale at the Cité Modèle, Heysel, Brussels, in 1956-69, with slabs of 18 and 23 storeys; but perhaps the climax of Braem's work was the somewhat eccentric St Maartensdal redevelopment in Leuven, built in 1957-66 for the Maatschappij voor de Huisvesting Leuven: a tremendous, rigidly axial layout of serrated slabs and squat, polygonal towers. The tallest, central tower of 22 storeys has a television mast forming a kind of spire. Imitations of this axial, post-Beaux Arts manner went up to even greater height elsewhere: for instance the Europark development on the Linker Scheldeoever, Antwerp, including an immense 27-storey slab, almost square on section, surrounded symmetrically by lower slabs and towers. This 3000-dwelling development, designed by a consortium of four architect-planners following a 1961 competition win, was built jointly by two local housing societies.

In Scotland, too, despite the constant pressure of British professional media which were imbued with a wholly different architectural world-view - the anti-urban, anti-monumental English Picturesque - an equivalent Modern Functionalist style gradually emerged, and established dominance within the housing field. Here one prime mover was the architect Sam Bunton. He was a wholly inimitable mixture of designer, urbanist, engineer, building contractor, political and professional lobbyist, and one-man research institute. However, we can identify two main strands in his work. The first was that of architect-planner. Here he trenchantly rejected the planners' strategy of overspilling population away from Glasgow, and advocated redevelopment at high densities, using massive multistorey blocks, as a way of blocking this. These ideas were promoted though often fantastic propaganda projects. The second main theme in Bunton's work was that of architect-engineer. He was fascinated by experimental building, and in this field established a prodigious record of personal invention, especially in the development of this country's mainstream constructional tradition, whose focus, as we noted, had by now moved from masonry to blockwork or pre-cast concrete construction. His aim was to adapt pre-cast construction for use in large blocks of flats.

Where Braem's scope was necessarily limited by the relative paucity of large developments of flats in Belgium, Bunton's urbanist utopia became an inspiration for the most dramatic 1960s housing drive in Europe, in Glasgow. This was because, around 1960, a forceful municipal housing 'crusader', David Gibson, came to power in Glasgow Corporation's Housing Committee, determined to rehouse the city's slum-dwellers without 'overspilling' them. Emboldened chiefly by Bunton's 1950s propaganda schemes, Gibson became determined to carry out his strategy by building multi-storey blocks on a scale unprecedented anywhere in Europe. Many of these blocks were isolated towers planted on small gap sites. However, where land was available, the pattern in Glasgow was very similar to those in Belgium or France: rectilinear patterns of massive slab blocks laid out in typical CIAM 'Zeilenbau' (that is, in parallel lines), but - because of the violent political and architectural pressures at work - much higher and more abrupt than the continental norms, and set on open sites lacking the lush greenery customary on the continent. The culmination of this national variant of Modern Functionalism was, appropriately, Bunton's own final major project, at Red Road, Glasgow (1962-9), with its 31-storey blocks as the highest housing scheme at that date in Europe (plate 4). But there were other major realisations of this style: the schemes of Sighthill in Glasgow, and Ardler in Dundee designed by the staff of the building firm Crudens; or in Aberdeen, where rubble-faced slab blocks were set against lavish landscaping, of a Scandinavianising character.

But, ironically, the CIAM pattern of parallel 'Zeilenbau' was of most influence, within our trio of countries, in the supposedly 'anti-monumental' Netherlands: where 'Zeilenbau' was called 'strokenbouw'. It shows the complexity and paradoxes of the Modern period (often parodied by its detractors for its 'sameness') that this influence in the Netherlands existed for exactly the opposite reason to that in Scotland: the strength, rather than the weakness, of town planning. For, ever since Berlage's plan for Amsterdam-Zuid and van Eesteren's AUP in 1934, municipal designers had been able and accustomed to specify in outline not only the layouts but even also the elevations of blocks to be built on city extensions, by whatever agency: public, co-operative or private. In Scotland, the only bodies with this power and attitude were the government-controlled New Town Development Corporations, which were scattered and of lesser influence on overall output.

In the Netherlands, the result was a tremendous formal homogeneity in the large urban extensions of the period - just as in the case of France, and, later, Eastern Europe. Early on, for instance in the 1950s development of Amsterdam West or Rotterdam extensions such as Kleinpolder, or even in the extensions of lesser municipalities such as the Malberg extension to Maastricht, a relentless 'Zeilenbau' rectilinearity prevailed. Later, however, in the big developments of the late 1960s and early 1970s, above all Amsterdam's Bijlmermeer but also Ommoord in Rotterdam, blocks were grouped into geometrical patterns, offset with taller punctuation blocks. These may be compared, in Scotland, with Dundee's Whitfield, built from 1967, and with much later developments of the 1980s in Eastern Europe.

New Dutch dwellings themselves were increasingly contained in large blocks of flats: the proportion of total national output contained in multi-storey blocks rose to a maximum of 45 per cent in 1967. Construction was mostly now reinforced concrete, sometimes steel-framing, but brick was used for cladding and sometimes for load-bearing construction: relatively little use was made of heavy concrete prefabrication and most 'systems' were for rationalised traditional construction. 'Galerijbouw', in the Modern form pioneered at the Bergpolderflat, now became the norm for flats of all heights, spreading at first hesitantly (with the first gallery block in Den Haag, for instance, built 1952), then very rapidly; and it also spread to Belgium (where it was, for instance, used at both Zaanstraat and Heysel). Concerning 'galerijbouw', we must once again draw attention to the continuing interaction between the Netherlands and that other traditional 'terrace house' country, England, where 'galerijbouw' was developed by avant-garde architects such as the Smithsons into the 'deck access' pattern, with blocks linked by bridges; and this in turn fed back into late 1960s Dutch schemes such as Bijlmermeer (plate 5).

In both the Netherlands and England, post-war 'galerijbouw' was often used in combination with the maisonette, a two-storey flat with internal staircase. Although this had been mainly invented by Le Corbusier, in Dutch and English hands this seemed largely to be used as a way of trying to reproduce terrace houses, along with their narrow, intricate plans, up in the sky: this was explicitly stated, for instance, in an elaborate 1958 survey of Pendrecht, one of the first big 'galerijbouw' schemes in Rotterdam. Another traditional Dutch feature which adapted well to 'galerijbouw' was the openness of the dwelling, with large areas of fenestration not curtained at night. It need hardly be stated that this 'flatted terrace' ideal had little appeal in Scotland, where the brick terrace house has been generally viewed, even in the nineteenth century, as an alien and somewhat utilitarian type: only relatively few deck-access schemes were built. For Dutch cottage housing, terraces were still the norm, although - in a further link with English patterns - some single-storey and two-storey 'patio dwellings' were also built.

III: The reaction against Modern Housing: 1970s to 1980s

The final part of this survey is a very brief summary of the period from around 1970, when a reaction swept across Western Europe away from large-scale building of Modern blocks, and in favour of conservation. In Belgium, with its fragmented housebuilding structure, and smaller proportion of mass housing, this movement was relatively unemphatic. In the United Kingdom, official attitudes were traditionally dictated by the highly polarised, fluctuating view of architecture and building in England. Within that framework, the underlying cause of the change of fashion away from Modern housing - namely, the success of that movement, in its own terms, in abolishing the vast slums and remedying the worst shortages - was concealed beneath a trenchant rhetoric which instead denounced it as a total failure, and the swing away from Modern flats happened in a sudden and theatrical fashion: the partial collapse of a high block in London in 1968 was followed by a virtual government ban on the building of high flats in England. In Scotland, however, as elsewhere in Europe, the decline in the proportion of high building was gradual, spread over five to ten years - in the Netherlands, for instance, from 45 per cent in 1967 to 21 per cent in 1973 - and the building of multi-storey blocks still continued even after that. In Aberdeen, for instance, the popularity of the municipality's soundly managed high blocks led the Housing

Committee, under Councillor Robert Robertson, to embark on a major programme of building 11-storey towers for elderly people during the late 1970s and early 1980s, while the years around 1990 saw several private high blocks built in Glasgow. In the Netherlands, while some Modern housing experiencing management problems was being demolished (for instance, late 1940s flats at Linnaeusstraat, Leeuwarden, demolished in 1977), the late 1980s saw a revival in the selective building of tall blocks, including a circular 25-storey block of Housing Act flats at Den Haag Bezuidenhout-West (1985-7), and, exceeding 30 storeys for the first time, Henk Klunder's privately-built Weena tower at Rotterdam, completed in 1992.

But throughout Western Europe the dominant trend in housing provision was nevertheless a swing away from Modern blocks, and towards rehabilitation of older housing and the self-conscious revival of 'traditional' housing patterns. In Belgium, several major area rehabilitation projects were undertaken during the 1970s, notably in Bruges. In the Netherlands and in Scotland, the mushrooming of housing improvement during the 1970s was much associated with 'user-participatory' co-operative agencies, often with younger architects and other professionals working informally in a so-called 'enabling' role. In the Netherlands, these were often spawned by post-1968 protest groups, which then developed into neighbourhood associations. In Rotterdam, by 1978, there were 11 such local groups, while Amsterdam saw such pioneering examples of 'participation' as the Dapperbuurt scheme, involving the architect Hans Borkent. In Scotland, a vigorous programme of improvement of nineteenth-century tenements, like the Modern housing drive before it, was overwhelmingly focused on Glasgow, and on numbers and basic standards: much of this, as in Belgium, was achieved by individual grants to landlords or owners, but, after the 1974 Housing Act, housing associations began to play a prominent role - a tendency powerfully promoted by the prototype schemes of the Glasgow architectural co-operative ASSIST, led by Raymond Young. There is not space here to discuss more recent policies, which are attempting to break up the big municipal empires by such mechanisms as council house sales or transfers to co-operatives.

But, in the field of architecture, equally important was the revival of supposedly 'traditional' patterns in new building, whether of tenements in Scotland - although a recent, contradictory tendency has been to build such blocks in brick - or the burghers' houses and brick terraces of the Netherlands (plate 6). Another kind of Dutch 'revival', in the 1980s, was the architect Piet Blom's return to a kind of bizarre, de Klerkian expressionism, seen in projects at Helmond and Rotterdam-Blaak.

CONCLUSION

To sum up: is there anything we can say to draw together this complex and disparate picture? I think the answer is: comparatively little. Obviously, we can pick out big themes, but these are constantly undermined by contradictory sub-themes: for instance, the post-war drive for Modern flats across Western Europe is qualified by its patchy distribution and by anti-monumental elements such as 'galerij-bouw'; and the great building-up of the public or municipal housing 'empires' is balanced by the fact that this was found only in some countries but hardly at all in others. All we can say in the end is that housing, in the twentieth century, has been elevated into such an enormously complicated and wide-ranging subject, involving so many different groups and interests, that, even in superficially similar countries, very wide divergences were inevitable in both policies and in the resulting physical patterns. And, of course, it is precisely this complexity, this lack of uniformity, which makes it now such a richly rewarding subject for the historian.

Bibliographical note

The nature of the subject would have made it very complex to provide detailed footnote references in the above; but the following select bibliography should be of assistance.

BELGIUM
L'Architecture d'Aujourd'hui, 57 (1954), 66; and 120 (1965), 28-9 (on Zaanstraat and St Maartensdal)
Bekaert, G, Strauven, F, *La Construction en Belgique, 1945-71* (Brussels, 1971)
Eyckerman, T, *Gids voor Antwerpen, Moderne Architektuur* (Antwerp, c.1990)
Jacobs, H B, 'Wonen in België', *Bouw*, 1969
Stynen, H, *Urbanisme et Société* (Brussels, 1978)

NETHERLANDS
Bouw, 1952, 730 ('Vijftig jaren Woningwet'); 1955, 768 ('galerijbouw' study); 1965, 946 (Bijlmermeer); 25 April 1970, 765
Grinberg, D I, *Housing in the Netherlands* (Delft, 1987)
Groenendijk, P, *Guide to Modern Architecture in the Netherlands* (Rotterdam, 1967)
Jensen, R, *Journal of the Royal Institute of British Architects*, September 1956, 454-6
Journal of the Royal Town Planning Institute, July 1971, 313 (Bijlmermeer)
Ministry of Housing and Physical Planning, *Some data of housebuilding in the Netherlands* (Den Haag, 1974)
Rijksdienst voor de Monumentenzorg, *Architektuur en Stedebouw in Amsterdam 1850-1940* (Zwolle, 1993)
Rosner, R, 'Housing and Planning in Holland', *The Builder*, 18, February 1966, 339

SCOTLAND
Adams, Ian H, *The Making of Urban Scotland* (London, 1978)
Bowley, M, *Housing and the State* (London, 1945)
Chapman, S A, ed., *The History of Working Class Housing* (London, 1971) (ch. by Butt)
Corporation of Glasgow Housing Department, *Review of Operations 1919-47* (1947)
Daunton, M J, *House and Home in the Victorian City* (London, 1983)
Frew, J, 'Concrete, cosmopolitanism and low-cost house design: the short architectural career of A H Campbell, 1923-6', *Architectural Heritage*, v (1995), 29-38
Gibb, A, *Glasgow, the Making of a City* (Glasgow, 1983)
Horsey, Miles, *Tenements and Towers* (Edinburgh, 1990)
Smout, T C, *A Century of the Scottish People, 1850-1930* (London, 1986)
Worsdall, Frank, *The Tenement* (Edinburgh, 1979)

1   Cité-Jardin Floreal, near Brussels: garden city built just before World War I (architects: Eggericx and others). (Copyright author)

2   Spangen housing, Rotterdam (by M Brinkman, 1919): the first example of 'galerijbouw' in the Netherlands. (Copyright author)

3   Renaat Braem's Zaanstraat housing scheme, Antwerp (1951-8): Modern
Functionalism in Belgium. (Copyright author)

4   The official opening of Red Road Housing Scheme, Glasgow, in October 1966.
Standing in front of the 31-storey Block 1 are: (left-right) George Campbell, Direct Labour
manager; Sam Bunton, architect; William Ross, Secretary of State for Scotland.
(Copyright *Glasgow Herald*, Caledonian Newspapers, Glasgow)

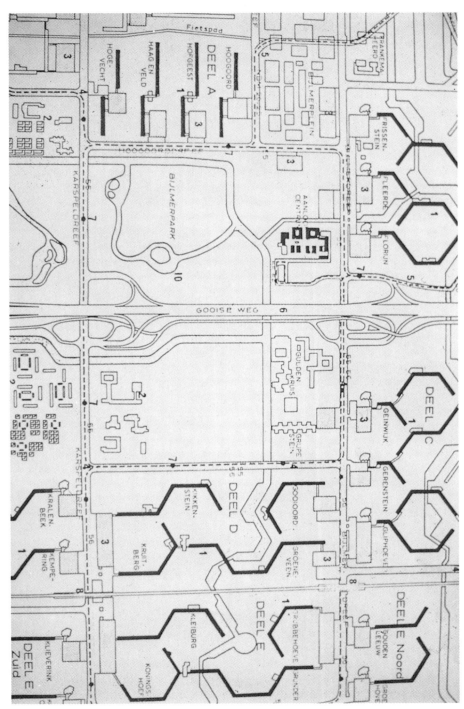

5   Plan for Amsterdam's late 1960s Bijlmermeer development, showing linear blocks and grade-separated layout. (Copyright author)

6   Aldo van Eyck's Zwolle housing project, 1975: return to 'traditional' housing patterns
in the Netherlands. (Copyright author)

13

THE IMPACT OF NORTH SEA OIL AND GAS ON THE ECONOMIC BASES OF SCOTLAND AND THE NETHERLANDS: A COMPARISON

William J Pike

I: THE DEVELOPMENT OF THE OIL AND GAS INDUSTRIES OF SCOTLAND AND THE NETHERLANDS

Both Scotland and the Netherlands have a history of hydrocarbon exploration and exploitation that pre-dates their North Sea activities. The oil industry in Scotland developed in the mid-nineteenth century when the oil shales of the Lothians began to be mined, crushed and distilled to produce oil. By the turn of the century, Scotland was second only to Russia as a European oil producer. However, the expensive distillation process and the increasing availability of cheap imported oil led to the virtual demise of the Scottish shale oil industry by the late 1920s.[1]

Although the Dutch experience with hydrocarbon production, mainly in the form of gas, does not stretch so far into the past, it pre-dates North Sea oil and gas development by at least 25 years and was the catalyst for North Sea development. Prior to World War II the Dutch had made discoveries of natural gas in the northern regions of the Netherlands. At the advent of the war, Dutch discoveries, such as the pre-war Schoonebeck gas formation, were paralyzed, and at times sabotaged, to prevent them falling into German hands.[2] Despite this, the Germans were very successful during the war in developing the North German Basin, thus ensuring some form of continuity in the exploration for oil and gas in Northern Europe. The pre-war and wartime exploration and development that was carried out in Northern Europe, and particularly in the Netherlands, was picked up after the war by the major international oil companies.

One joint venture formed after the war to explore for hydrocarbons in the Netherlands is of particular significance to the discovery of North Sea oil and gas.

---

[1] Although in 1913 Winston Churchill, concerned with fuel oil for the Royal Navy, believed that the Scottish shale oil industry could produce 400,000 to 500,000 tons of oil per year for the next 150 years, the industry was doomed by the end of the nineteenth century when drilled wells could produce substantial amounts of liquid oil without the necessity of distillation. See R G Carruthers, *The Oil-Shales of the Lothians* (Edinburgh, 1927), and John Butt, 'James Young, Edinburgh Industrialist and Philanthropist' (unpublished Ph D thesis, University of Glasgow, 1964).

[2] Professor Arthur J Whiteman maintains that the Dutch had had a very successful programme at Schoonebeck prior to the war and had falsified the electric logs to keep the knowledge from the Germans during the occupation. (Interview, Professor Arthur J Whiteman, Department of Geology, University of Aberdeen, 27 August 1989.)

In 1947 a new company, NAM (Nederlands Aadrolie Maatschappij) was formed with Esso and Shell as equal partners, and Shell as operator.[3]

For ten years, the company enjoyed only minor successes and none of them was commercial. In 1958, however, the decision was made to drill a deep well at Slochteren in the Groningen area of the Netherlands. So unsuccessful had Dutch exploration been that the programme would probably have discontinued had the crucial Slochteren No. 1 well not been

> spectacularly successful in finding gas in an ideal reservoir rock which allowed the gas to be produced freely. The significance of the find was obvious. Appraisal took place over the next couple of years, with reserves being upgraded in leaps and bounds as the extent of the field was established. As well as searching onshore, NAM extended the search to the Friesian Islands, found gas on Ameland and drilled the first exploration well in the North Sea in 1961.[4]

Not only did the Dutch discovery at Groningen result in the first North Sea well, it can also be identified as the catalyst that initiated exploration in the UK sector. The Groningen field is at the rim of a deep sedimentary basin that underlies the surface strata of the North Sea. As sedimentary formations are the normal depositories of hydrocarbons, extrapolation led geologists to the realisation that the entire basin and its rims might be excellent candidates for oil and gas development.

Almost immediately after the magnitude of the Groningen discovery became known, the major oil and gas companies began to seek concessions from all countries surrounding the North Sea, but most particularly from Britain whose southern North Sea waters were adjacent to those offsetting the Groningen discovery. However, the early demands for concessions were denied until an equitable division of the North Sea waters could be reached.

Due to American demands for extended territorial waters rights in the mid-1950s, 'the Geneva Convention on the Law of the Sea, which resulted from the first UN Law of the Sea Conference in 1958, established the sovereign rights of the States bordering the Continental Shelf as "the ... seabed and the subsoil of the marine area adjacent to the coast to a depth of 200 metres or beyond that limit to where the depth of the superadjacent waters admits the exploration of the natural resources"'.[5] To become a binding statute, the Continental Shelf Convention required the signatures of 22 member nations; in early 1964 there were 21. With a balance of payments and monetary crisis causing immense concern in Britain, and with the major oil and gas companies clamouring for concessions, Britain became the twenty-second signatory in early 1964.

---

[3]Francis Goodall, unpublished manuscript written for Shell UK Exploration and Production Ltd, detailing Shell Expro's 25-year history in the North Sea, p. 1.5.

[4]Ian R Manners, *Planning for North Sea Oil: The UK Experience*, Policy Study no. 6 (Austin, Center for Energy Studies, The University of Texas at Austin, 1978), 21.

[5]British Petroleum Ltd, *Our Industry: Petroleum* (London, British Petroleum Ltd, 1970), 151.

It was agreed that the North Sea should be divided according to the stipulations of the newly ratified Continental Shelf Convention. Each country's coastal boundary was extended to a median line drawn between landfalls on a North-South axis. By this division, Britain obtained the lion's share of the North Sea for petroleum development, some 95,300 square miles. This area was further divided at 55° 50" north latitude into a Scottish sector of 62,500 square miles and an English sector of 32,800 square miles.[6] By contrast, the Dutch sector contained approximately 20,000 square miles. Scotland obtained more than three times as much North Sea acreage as the Netherlands. The Netherlands' share of the North Sea amounted to about 10 per cent of the total; the British sector totalled about 46 per cent, while the Scottish sector comprised approximately 31 per cent.[7] Thus, Scotland was granted the largest share of the North Sea, and, as it turned out, probably the richest.

Exploration began in southern British waters while it continued in Dutch waters. Initial British discoveries occurred in 1965; by 1967, the first gas was coming ashore in the southern English sector. However, by 1967 the monopoly buying power granted to the British Gas Council, and the low prices they offered, began to make the economics of large scale gas development in the southern sector questionable, especially to the oil companies. Considerable seismic activity had occurred since 1965 in Scottish waters, often with promising results, and it was to this region that the major oil and gas companies turned in 1967. After two disappointing years, the first real success came in December of 1969. This was followed by the discovery of the massive Forties field, by British Petroleum, in 1970. Through 1973, discoveries such as the Brent and Ninian fields made the Scottish sector one of the most over-heated oil development provinces in the world.

Meanwhile, steady, though not spectacular, progress was being made in the development of the Dutch Continental Shelf, which, it was discovered, contained mainly gas deposits. After the initial discoveries, development continued at a fairly stable pace in the Netherlands, due primarily to the less buoyant market for gas in Europe, and worldwide.

By 1989, in spite of the collapse of high oil prices in 1986, the oil and gas provinces of both Scotland and the Netherlands had matured, and in the process had generated vast revenues for industry and treasuries (see graphs 1-4). In the Netherlands, the potential for growth of the economic base due to North Sea development was very good. In Scotland, it should have been outstanding, given the size of the area that was awarded and the richness of the finds that were made. However, it was the Dutch economic base that benefited most from offshore development, not the Scottish economic base. To understand this seemingly contra-

---

[6]Guy Arnold, *Britain's Oil* (London, 1978), 34.

[7]The Norwegian sector accounts for a further 27 per cent, with Denmark controlling 9 per cent and Germany 7 per cent. The remaining 1 per cent is divided equally between Belgium and France. Keith Chapman, *North Sea Oil and Gas: Geographical Perspective* (Newton Abbot, 1976), 41.

dictory outcome, one must turn to an examination of the economic bases of both countries.

II: A SHORT HISTORY OF ECONOMIC BASES

By the turn of the century, both countries possessed a strong industrial base. Scotland's economy was supported by three basic industries: coal mining, iron and steel making, and heavy construction, especially in the shipbuilding industry. These industries were centred in a band between Dundee and Edinburgh in the east and Ayr and Greenock in the west.

> The region's economy was so successful ... because its industries supported each other. Coal supplied the power and fed the iron and steel plants. Iron and steel supported a complex array of shipbuilding and engineering industries which in turn were linked to the needs of maritime and land transport. The prosperity rested heavily on the single group of metal and engineering industries, and the whole structure was geared to supply of capital goods to developing nations. The world needed ships, rails, bridges, locomotives, coal and machinery, and Glasgow and the west of Scotland were well placed to meet the demands.[8]

So industrialised and productive was the region that, in the last five years before 1914, 'the Clyde launched 36 per cent of British tonnage and 21 per cent of world output'.[9]

However, in the two world wars following the turn of the century, the yards of Scotland, and particularly the Clyde area, expanded tremendously to meet wartime demands, with the consequence that, after both wars, much excess capacity existed. Generally, this capacity was well utilized for a short period to replace tonnage lost in the wars. Eventually, though, the excess capacity took its toll as shipping tonnage normalized and demand dropped. This, coupled with the increasing competitiveness of foreign yards (many subsidized), abnormally high inflation and excessive wage demands, led to the demise or amalgamation of many of Scotland's famous shipbuilders in the 1960s and 1970s (see graph 2).[10]

The decline of the shipbuilding industry, as well as other heavy construction industries such as locomotive engineering which declined with the introduction of

---

[8]Anthony Slaven, *The Development of the West of Scotland, 1750-1960* (London, 1975), 11.

[9]Ibid.

[10]'In 1967 Scotts and Lithgows on the lower Clyde merged; in 1968, Upper Clyde Shipbuilders - an amalgamation of Fairfield's, John Brown's, Charles Connell's, Yarrow's and Stephens' - came into being. On the east coast, Robb Caledon was formed by the joining together of Henry Robb of Leith, the Caledonian Shipbuilding Co. of Dundee and the Burntisland Shipbuilding Co. Government funds poured into the industry not, as was intended, to build up capital equipment and eliminate technical weaknesses, but overwhelmingly to meet contract losses occasioned by uneconomic tendering exacerbated by inflationary pressures and excessive wage demands' (Frank Broadway, *Upper Clyde Shipbuilders*, London, Centre for Policy Studies, 1976, 19).

diesel electric traction engines, had serious impacts on the iron, steel, and coal industries. Although the iron and steel industry did not contract as significantly during the period, it suffered from rationalization, government intervention in market management and a generally disoriented view of current and future conditions. For example, according to Peter Payne, after intense pressure, especially from the government, Colvilles was 'persuaded' to build a strip mill at Ravenscraig, despite formidable arguments raised by Colvilles' chairman, Sir Andrew McCance. 'Commissioned in 1962, the mill at Ravenscraig, unanimously agreed to be a technical masterpiece, was a financial disaster.'[11] Its products lacked demand. Ravenscraig characterized the condition of the Scottish steel industry in the period immediately prior to the discovery of North Sea oil and gas. Scottish steel, while continuing to increase output, was not healthy; it was unsure in outlook and not attuned to the market.

The Scottish coal industry was in much worse shape. Production had been steadily declining since 1913. The slide reflected a falling demand for Scottish coal, for a number of reasons.

> Among them may be mentioned the check to aggregate demand by economies in the use of coal by the iron and steel producers; the growing substitution for coal of gas, electricity and oil in home and industry; the erosion of export markets by severe competition, and the failure of the Scottish iron and steel, shipbuilding and engineering industries.[12]

By the advent of North Sea oil and gas, the Scottish coal industry, and indeed all three of the traditional Scottish heavy industries, had deteriorated to a point from which recovery was highly doubtful, if not impossible.

By the 1930s, the collapsing position of traditional Scottish heavy industry was understood and plans were advanced to deal with declining industrialism in Britain as a whole. Many groups, including the Scottish Development Council, the Scottish Economic Committee, the Scottish Office and the Special Areas Committee focused their attention on a new, planned and diversified structure. Their focus was correct, but success was lacking due mainly to events beyond their control. The Second World War dramatically, but temporarily, created great demand for the traditional industries. After the war, the move of much of British industry into light industries did not take place to any significant extent in Scotland. Despite all plans, and 'the expenditure of some £350 million each year [in the 1960s] by successive United Kingdom governments on regional assistance' to disadvantaged areas or regions such as Scotland, no new industrial growth arose to offset the

---

[11]Peter Payne, *Colvilles and the Scottish Steel Industry* (Oxford, 1979), cited in Neil K Buxton, *The Economic Development of the British Coal Industry: From Industrial Revolution to the Present Day* (London, 1978), 94.

[12]Peter Payne, 'The decline of the Scottish heavy industries, 1945-83', in Richard Saville, ed., *The Economic Development of Modern Scotland, 1950-80* (Edinburgh, 1985), 83.

decline in the Scottish heavy industries.[13] Ominously, there was no corresponding, dramatic rise in the service sector, to replace the declining industries.

During the same period, the industrial base of the Netherlands managed spectacular growth (see graph 6). Johan de Vries explains the growth of the Dutch economy in general on four points, two of which are vital to the understanding of growth in the industrial sector. The first point is that the Netherlands industries have traditionally been involved with the larger world economy in a diversified manner. As de Vries notes,

> It is immediately apparent that since the Second World War, and especially during the 'Fifties, imports of raw materials and semi-manufactures, together with those of capital goods, have risen more steeply than imports of consumer goods. Here lies the link with the continuing process of industrialization, a link which can also be demonstrated in the area of exports.
>
> The process of industrialization is unmistakably reflected in the composition of pre-war Dutch exports; however, it has been even more evident in the post-war years and has also displayed an acceleration. It is thus not surprising to find that between 1955 and 1965 the share of agricultural exports fell from 11% to 8.8% and that of the food industry from 19% to 15.3%, while exports of chemicals products rose from 7.8 to 12.5% and those of the electrical engineering industry from 9.3 to 12.9%.[14]

These figures clearly illustrate not only the growth of industrialization, but a trend toward a growth in light manufacturing, which indicates an ability to adapt to changing markets that was lacking in the Scottish industrial base.

De Vries's fourth point is also important to the understanding of the characteristics of the Dutch industrial base: the size of the undertakings in various industrial sectors was generally very large. In 1963, small companies made up only 16.6 per cent of the industrial base, while medium-size companies represented 23.9 per cent and large companies 59.5 per cent.

In the service sector, important and impressive growth was also taking place. One indication of this growth was employment within the sector, which rose from approximately 1.6 million in 1947 to over 2.5 million in 1970 (see graph 7). Growth in the marine transport and services industry was especially important. The rise in importance of the Rotterdam shipping infrastructure, with its marine construction and repair capabilities, its service and transport fleet and its international orientation, cannot be dismissed; its capabilities proved vital in increasing the Dutch share of North Sea oil and gas involvement (see graph 8). As in the industrial sector, in the services sector, and especially in the maritime service sector, size of undertakings would be important.

---

[13]J R Firn, 'External control and regional development: the case of Scotland', *Environment and Planning*, 7 (1975), 393.

[14]Johan de Vries, *The Netherlands Economy in the Twentieth Century* (Assen, 1978), 3-4.

A similar preponderance of medium-sized and large undertakings also existed in the transport and communications sector - which embraces shipping and aviation - in 1963, with 21.3% for small enterprises, 18.8% for the medium-sized and 59.9% for the large, making a total of 78.8% for the last two.[15]

The combination of a diversified industrial base experiencing exceptional growth, an international orientation, and industrial companies of large size and, therefore, generally increased capabilities in terms of capital investment and production, especially in the area of maritime transport and construction and repair, meant that the Netherlands' industrial base was well placed to take advantage of North Sea oil and gas development.

In contrast, because Scottish traditional industry was in decline and light industry was not developed, in addition to the slow, and sometimes non-existent development of a large, viable service sector, Scottish industry was poorly placed to take advantage of the opportunities offered by North Sea oil and gas development.

III: CONCLUSIONS

The result has been a great variance between the proportional benefits that have accrued to the economic bases of both countries due to North Sea oil and gas development. Scottish industrial content in the development of its own North Sea oil and gas province has been much lower than the Dutch content in the Dutch continental shelf. Over the period of North Sea development, Scottish industrial content in the development of its own oil and gas province amounts to less than 30 per cent. More importantly, little of this content has been in areas of higher or high technology which would provide a point for further industrial development; most Scottish content has been in areas variously labelled 'rope, soap and dope' or 'heat and beat'. Scottish content represents, for the most part, labour. Very little has been in light or heavy industries.

In the service sector, Scottish content has been even lower; it is estimated to be below 22 per cent. This is due to the lack of a developed service sector which could be readily utilized, or adapted for utilization, by the oil and gas industry.[16]

By contrast, certain Dutch industries have done well indeed from North Sea oil and gas development. Dutch industrial content in the development of its own offshore oil and gas resources has been high. Industrial content is estimated at over 55 per cent though 1989. Service content for the same period is estimated at 83-85 per cent. More importantly, Dutch content in the development of the non-Dutch sectors in the North Sea is particularly high in some industrial and service sectors.

---

[15]Ibid., 10. Company size ranges are categorized as: small - 1 to 10; medium - 11 to 49; large - 50 and above.

[16]William J Pike, 'The Development of the North Sea Oil Industry to 1989, with special reference to Scotland's contribution' (unpublished Ph D thesis, University of Aberdeen, 1991, passim).

Perhaps the most notable Dutch economic achievements in the development of the North Sea occur in the maritime services sector. With well developed maritime interests, large companies and an international orientation, all developed prior to North Sea oil and gas development, the Dutch marine construction and transport sectors have managed to secure large markets for their goods and services. The Dutch, for example, control about 12 per cent of the supply boat hire market (see graph 9). In heavy transport and towing, Dutch companies have managed to claim 52 per cent of the market for the entire North Sea (see graph 10). Their construction and heavy lift vessels control 43 per cent of the whole North Sea market for such vessels (see graph 11). Dutch pipelaying vessels control 27 per cent of the total pipelaying market in the North Sea (see graph 12).[17] Perhaps more significantly, the Dutch have been able to develop strong markets in the oil and gas maritime transport and construction sectors outside the North Sea. This has been possible because the Dutch had a strong and expanding economic base upon which to build a substantial offshore industry. Nowhere has this performance been matched by any indigenous Scottish industrial or service sector.

As a result, the Dutch, while having been apportioned a much smaller area of the North Sea than Scotland, have been able to secure much larger benefits to their economic base. However, those benefits may now be in some jeopardy. Oil and gas production in the Dutch offshore sector has matured. Activity in the sector began to wane in 1992, primarily due to decreases in economy of scale, declining prospects and environmental restrictions. By 1994, when Mobil Oil Co. announced that it was, for the most part, withdrawing from activities in the Dutch sector, a substantial lobbying effort was attempting to alter government policy with regard to oil and gas development.[18] It has been partially successful. Although indigenous offshore oil and gas activity has played a less important part in the development of the Dutch service and supply industry, its existence as a healthy base from which to launch operations farther afield is essential.

---

[17]These percentages are the author's estimates based on figures in Smith Rea Energy Analysts, *Offshore Logistics: Boats, Bases and Aviation* (SREA: Canterbury, 1992), 26, and figures and information published in *FT North Sea Letter, Ocean Industry, Offshore: Including the Oilman*, and *Offshore Engineer*, various issues.

[18]The effort was mounted on two fronts: the service and supply industry lobbied through their representative body, IRO, while the oil and gas producers brought pressure to bear through a similar organization, NOGEPA.

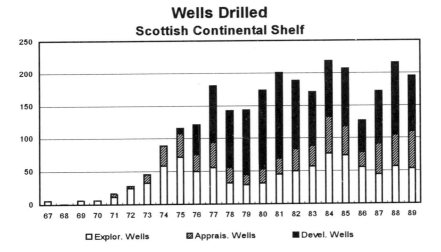

Graph 1 Source: United Kingdom Department of Energy, Development of the Oil and Gas Resources of the United Kingdom, various issues

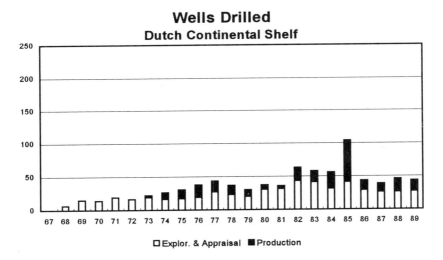

Graph 2 Source: Ministerie van Economische Zaken, Olie en gas in Nederland opeporing en winning 1991, 's Gravenhage, April 1992, pp. 15-21.

Drilling Activity, Scotland and the Netherlands

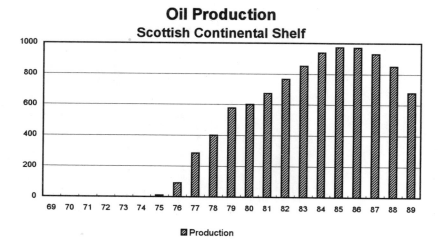

Graph 3 Source: County NatWest WoodMac Oil and Gas Conference Paper
Offshore-Northern Seas Conference, Stavanger, 30 August 1990

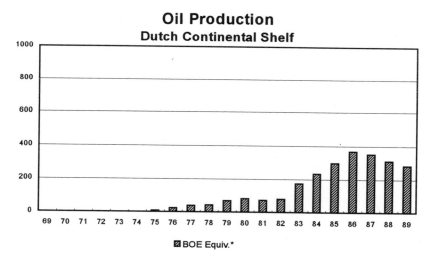

Graph 4

Oil Production, Scotland and the Netherlands
N.B. To compare production figures, gas production was converted to barrels of oil equivalent production.

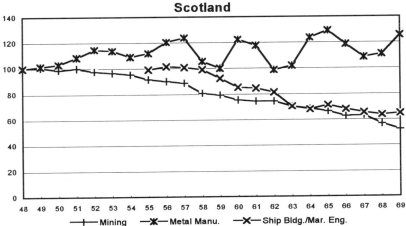

Graph 5 Source: Digest of Scottish Statistics, various issues
NB. Prior to 1956, the category for shipbuilding included non-marine engineering
and does not accurately reflect marine construction and engineering.

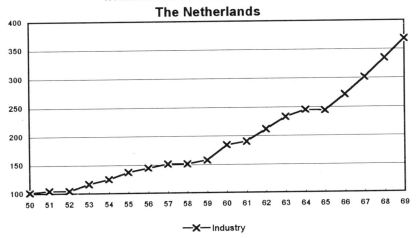

Graph 6 Source: Johan de Vries, The Netherlands Economy in the
Twentieth Century, Van Gorcum & Co: Assen, 1978, p. 66

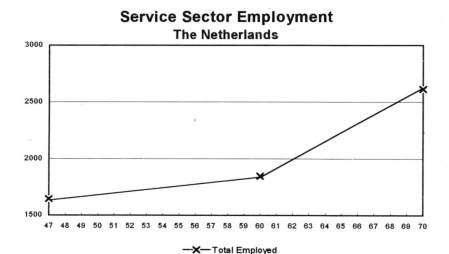

Graph 7 Source: Johan de Vries, The Netherlands Economy in the Twentieth Century, Van Gorcum & Co: Assen, 1978, p. 66

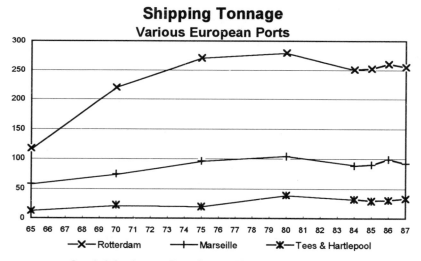

Graph 8 Conference Européen des Ministres des Transports, Annales Statistiques de Transport, 1965-1987, CEMT, Paris, p. 171.

Supply Vessels
Percentage Market Share
North West European Continental Shelf

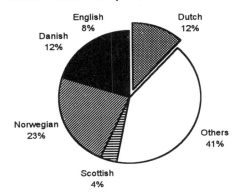

Graph 9 Source: Author's estimates based on figures in Smith Rea Energy Analysts, Offshore
Business: Offshore Logistics, Bases,
Boats and Aviation, SREA, Canterbury, 1992, p.26.

Heavy Transport and Towing
Percentage Market Share
North West European Continental Shelf

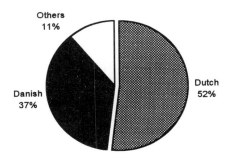

Graph 10 Source: Author's estimates based on figures and information
published in FT North Sea Letter, Ocean Industry, Offshore:
Incorporating the Oilman, and Offshore Engineer, various editions.

Const. and Heavy Lift Vessels
Percentage Market Share
North West European Continental Shelf

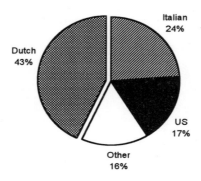

Graph 11 Source: Author's estimates based on figures and information published in FT North Sea Letter, Ocean Industry, Offshore: Incorporating the Oilman, and Offshore Engineer, various editions.

Pipelaying Vessels
Percentage Market Share
North West European Continental Shelf

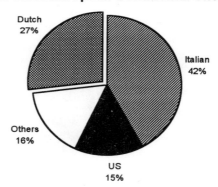

Graph 12 Source: Author's estimates based on figures and information published in FT North Sea Letter, Ocean Industry, Offshore: Incorporating the Oilman, and Offshore Engineer, various editions.

Index

This index is selective rather than exhaustive. It concentrates almost entirely on persons and places, since main subjects can be followed by use of the Contents Table. Places are usually located by country, but where no country is stated it is to be understood that the place is situated in Scotland.